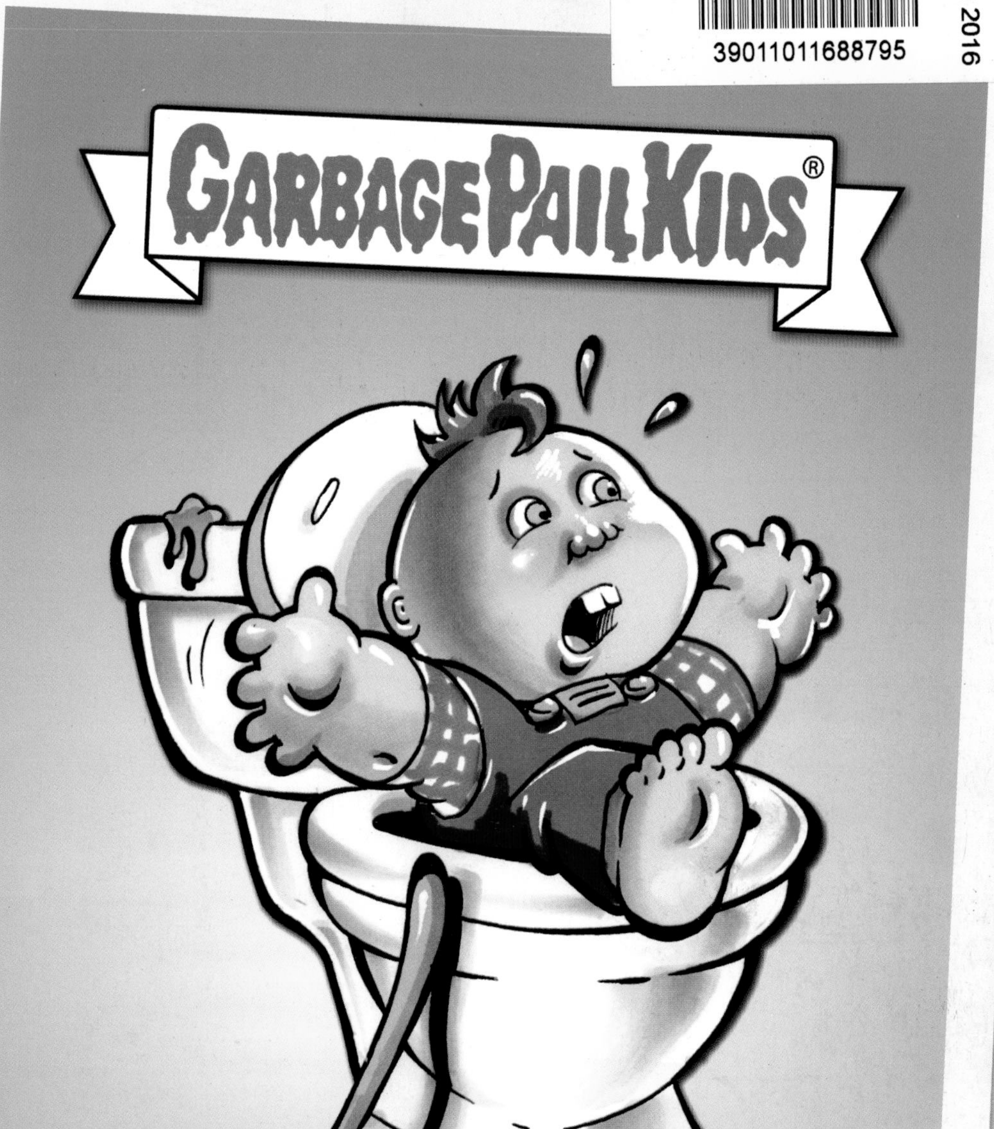
GARBAGE PAIL KIDS®
BEANS
POTTY SCOTTY

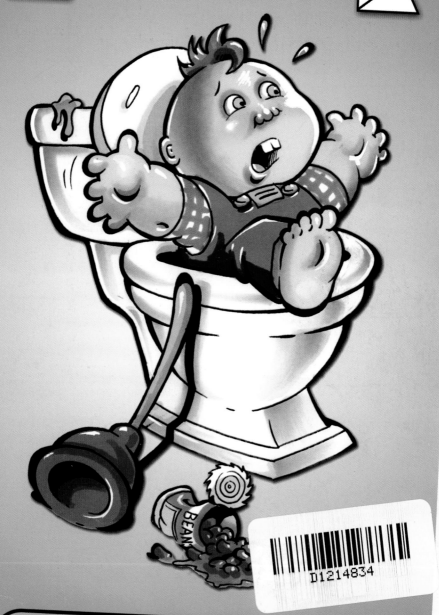

IDW **topps**

Become our fan on Facebook **facebook.com/idwpublishing**
Follow us on Twitter **@idwpublishing**
Subscribe to us on YouTube **youtube.com/idwpublishing**
See what's new on Tumblr **tumblr.idwpublishing.com**
Check us out on Instagram **instagram.com/idwpublishing**

978-1-63140-510-5   19 18 17 16   1 2 3 4

COVER BY MARK PINGITORE

Special thanks to Ira Friedman of Topps for his invaluable assistance.

Originally published as GARBAGE PAIL KIDS: COMIC-BOOK PUKE-TACULAR, GARBAGE PAIL KIDS: LOVE STINKS, GARBAGE PAIL KIDS: FABLES, FANTASIES, AND FARTS, GARBAGE PAIL KIDS: GROSS ENCOUNTERS OF THE TURD KIND, and GARBAGE PAIL KIDS: GO HOLLYWOOD.

Ted Adams, CEO & Publisher
Greg Goldstein, President & COO
Robbie Robbins, EVP/Sr. Graphic Artist
Chris Ryall, Chief Creative Officer/Editor-in-Chief
Matthew Ruzicka, CPA, Chief Financial Officer
Dirk Wood, VP of Marketing
Lorelei Bunjes, VP of Digital Services
Jeff Webber, VP of Licensing, Digital and Subsidiary Rights
Jerry Bennington, VP of New Product Development

For international rights,
please contact licensing@idwpublishing.com

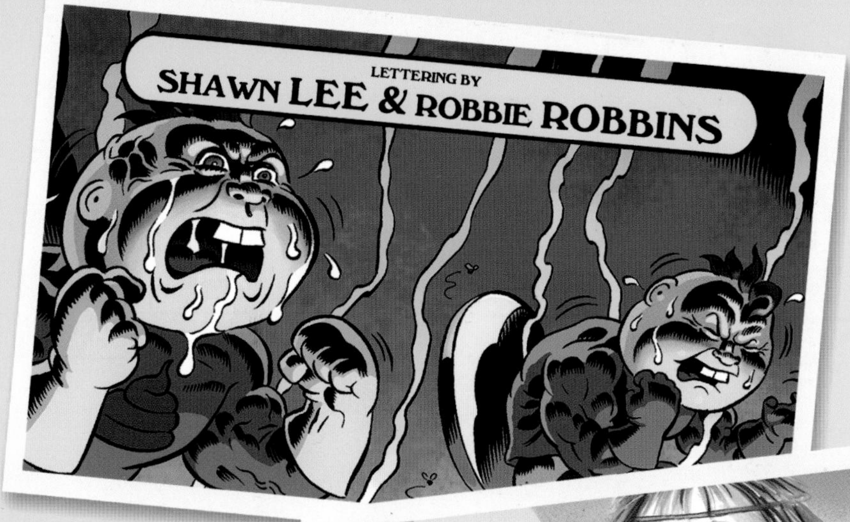
LETTERING BY
SHAWN LEE & ROBBIE ROBBINS

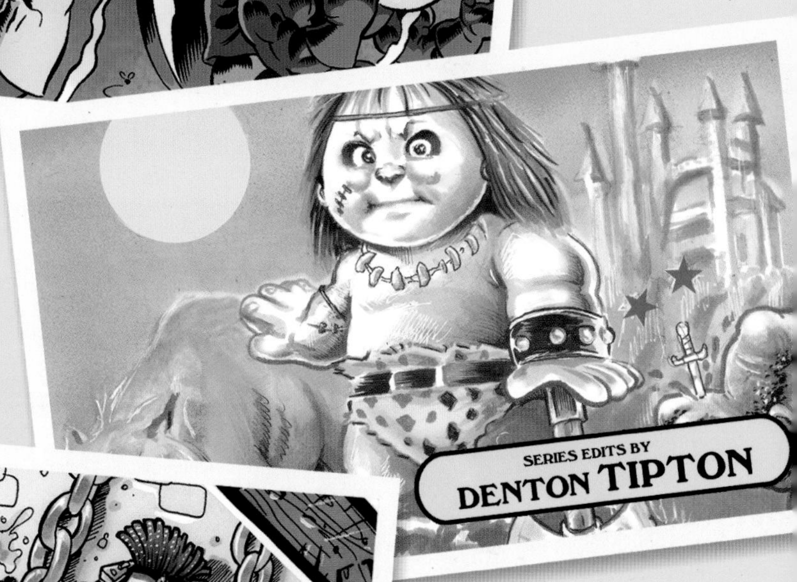
SERIES EDITS BY
DENTON TIPTON

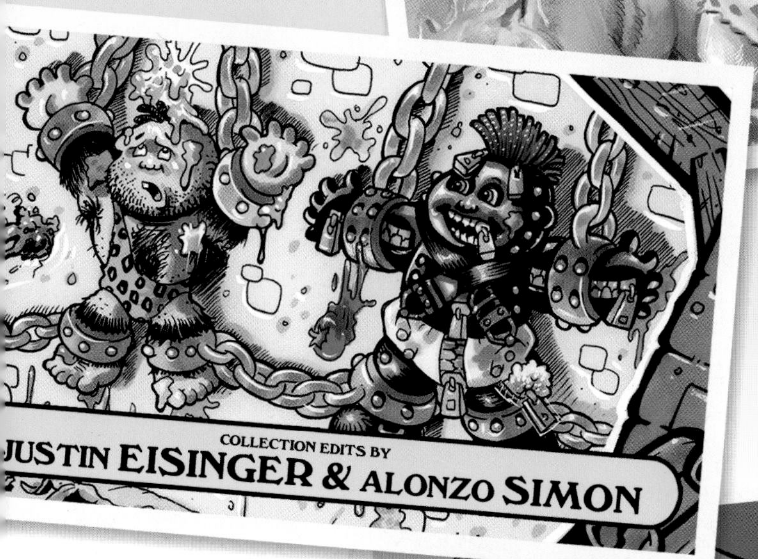
COLLECTION EDITS BY
JUSTIN EISINGER & ALONZO SIMON

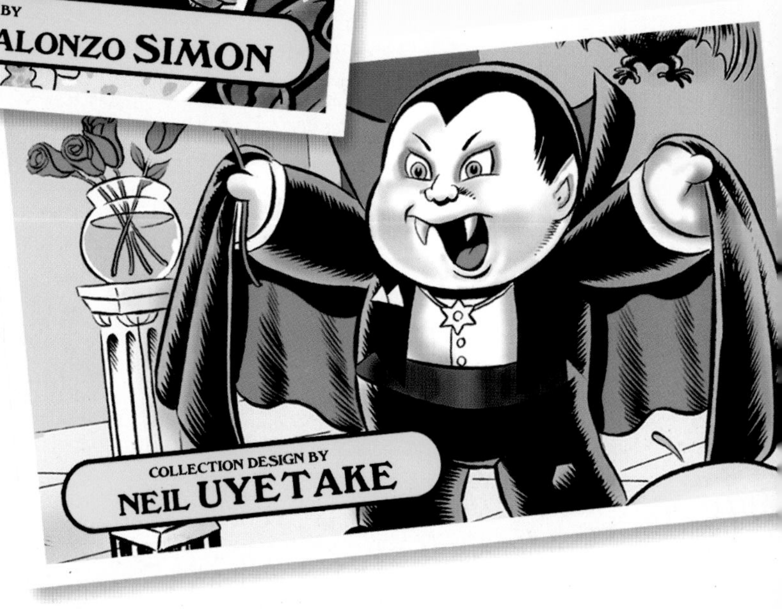
COLLECTION DESIGN BY
NEIL UYETAKE

CHAPTER 01

GARBAGE PAIL KIDS®

PUKE-TACULAR

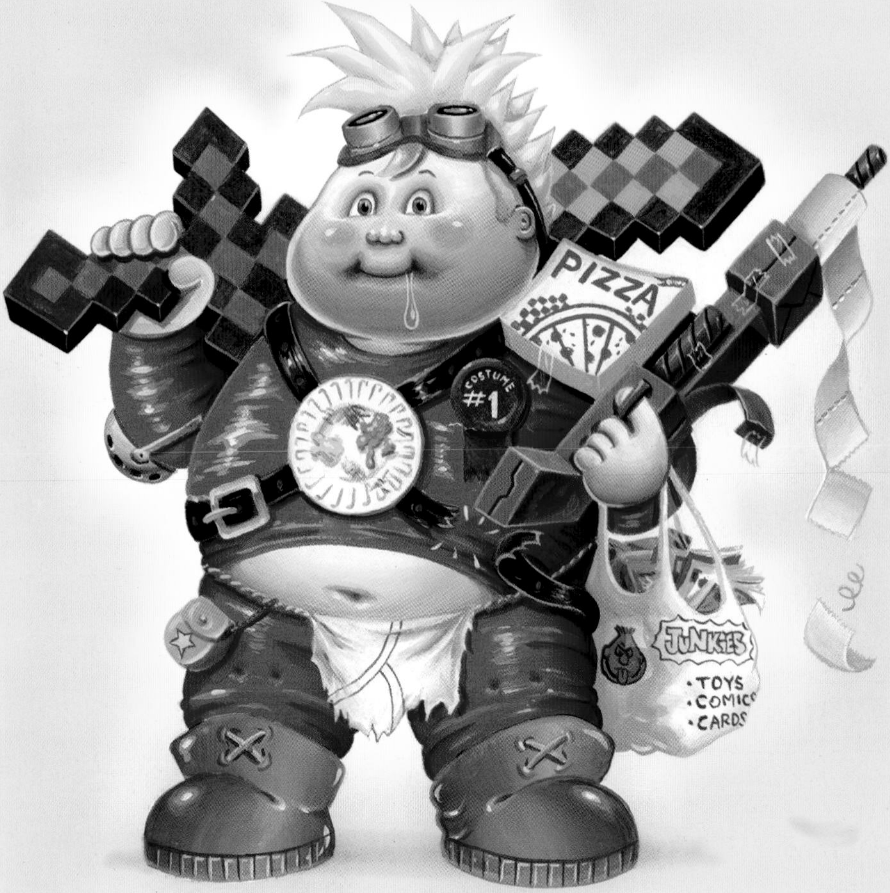
PIZZA
COSTUME #1
JUNKIES
•TOYS
•COMIC
•CARDS

art by
JOE SIMKO

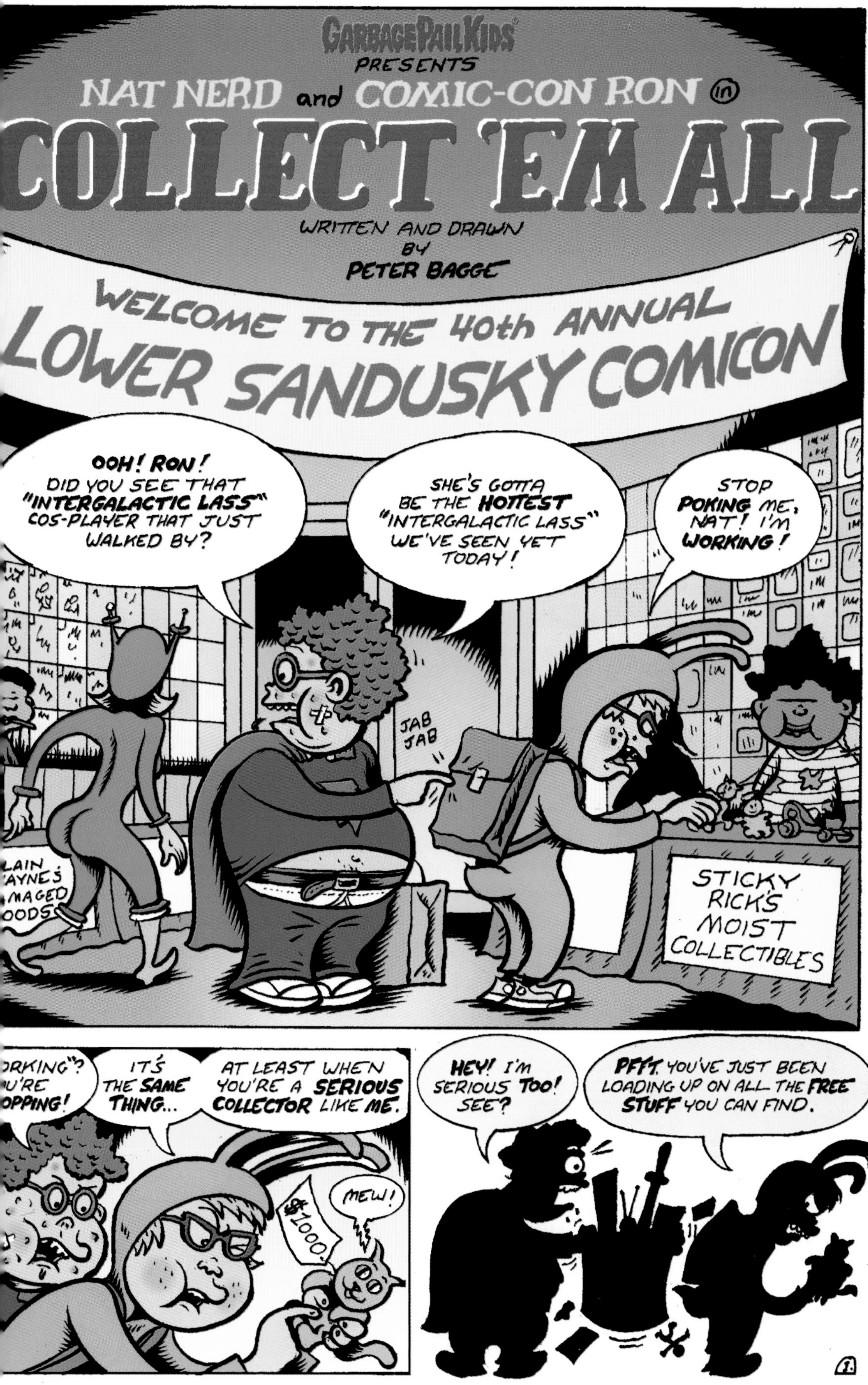
GARBAGE PAIL KIDS PRESENTS
NAT NERD and COMIC-CON RON in
COLLECT 'EM ALL
WRITTEN AND DRAWN BY PETER BAGGE
WELCOME TO THE 40th ANNUAL LOWER SANDUSKY COMICON
OOH! RON! DID YOU SEE THAT "INTERGALACTIC LASS" COS-PLAYER THAT JUST WALKED BY?
SHE'S GOTTA BE THE HOTTEST "INTERGALACTIC LASS" WE'VE SEEN YET TODAY!
STOP POKING ME, NAT! I'M WORKING!
JAB JAB
STICKY RICK'S MOIST COLLECTIBLES
ORKING"? U'RE OPPING!
IT'S THE SAME THING...
AT LEAST WHEN YOU'RE A SERIOUS COLLECTOR LIKE ME.
$1000.
MEW!
HEY! I'M SERIOUS TOO! SEE?
PFFT. YOU'VE JUST BEEN LOADING UP ON ALL THE FREE STUFF YOU CAN FIND.
1.

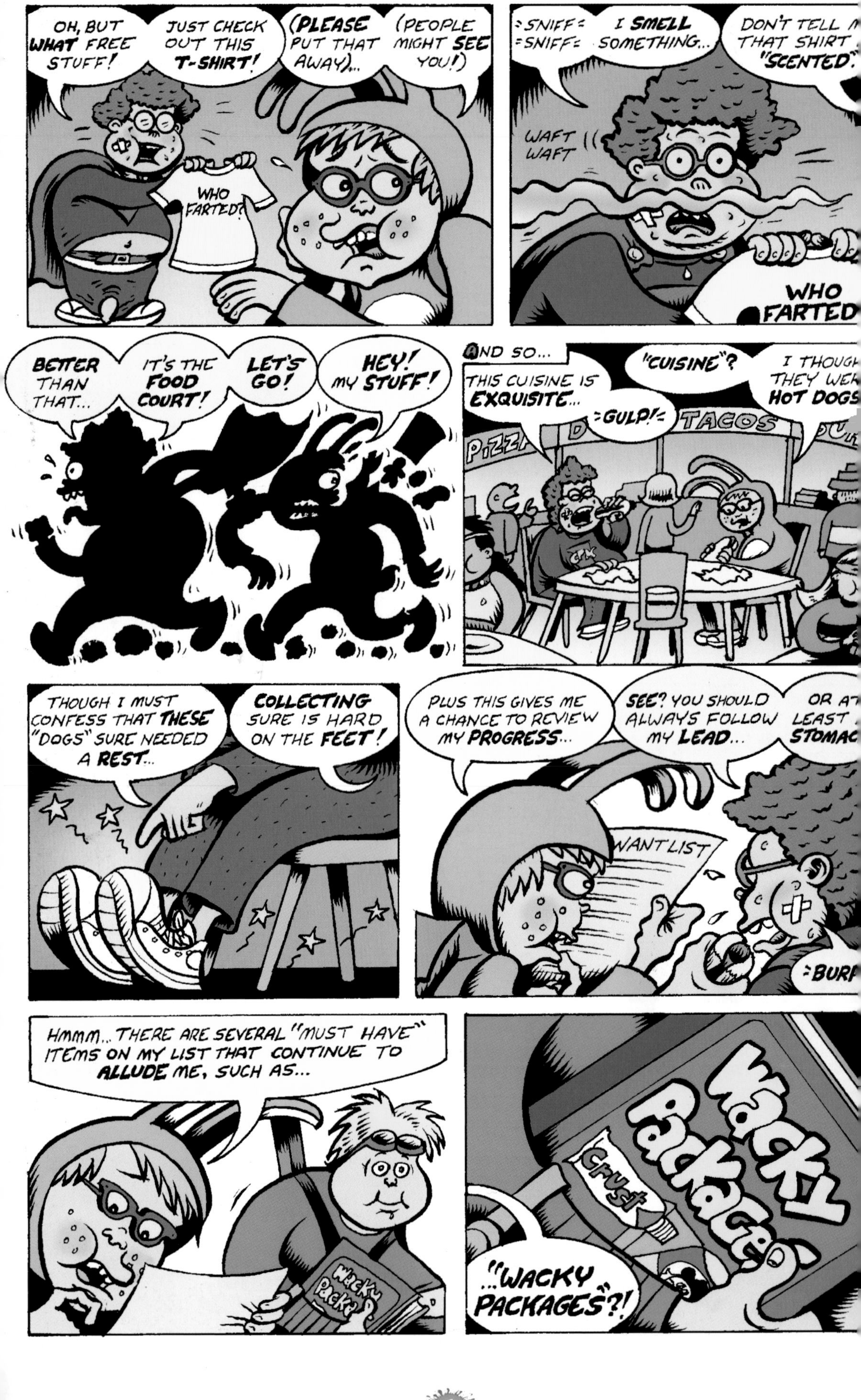

OH, BUT WHAT FREE STUFF!
JUST CHECK OUT THIS T-SHIRT!
(PLEASE PUT THAT AWAY)...
(PEOPLE MIGHT SEE YOU!)
WHO FARTED?
=SNIFF= =SNIFF=
I SMELL SOMETHING...
DON'T TELL M THAT SHIRT "SCENTED"
WAFT WAFT
WHO FARTED
BETTER THAN THAT...
IT'S THE FOOD COURT!
LET'S GO!
HEY! MY STUFF!
AND SO...
THIS CUISINE IS EXQUISITE...
=GULP!=
"CUISINE"?
I THOUGH THEY WER HOT DOGS
PIZZA
TACOS
THOUGH I MUST CONFESS THAT THESE "DOGS" SURE NEEDED A REST...
COLLECTING SURE IS HARD ON THE FEET!
PLUS THIS GIVES ME A CHANCE TO REVIEW MY PROGRESS...
SEE? YOU SHOULD ALWAYS FOLLOW MY LEAD...
OR AT LEAST STOMAC
WANT LIST
=BURP
HMMM... THERE ARE SEVERAL "MUST HAVE" ITEMS ON MY LIST THAT CONTINUE TO ALLUDE ME, SUCH AS...
Wacky Packages
Crust
..."WACKY PACKAGES"?!

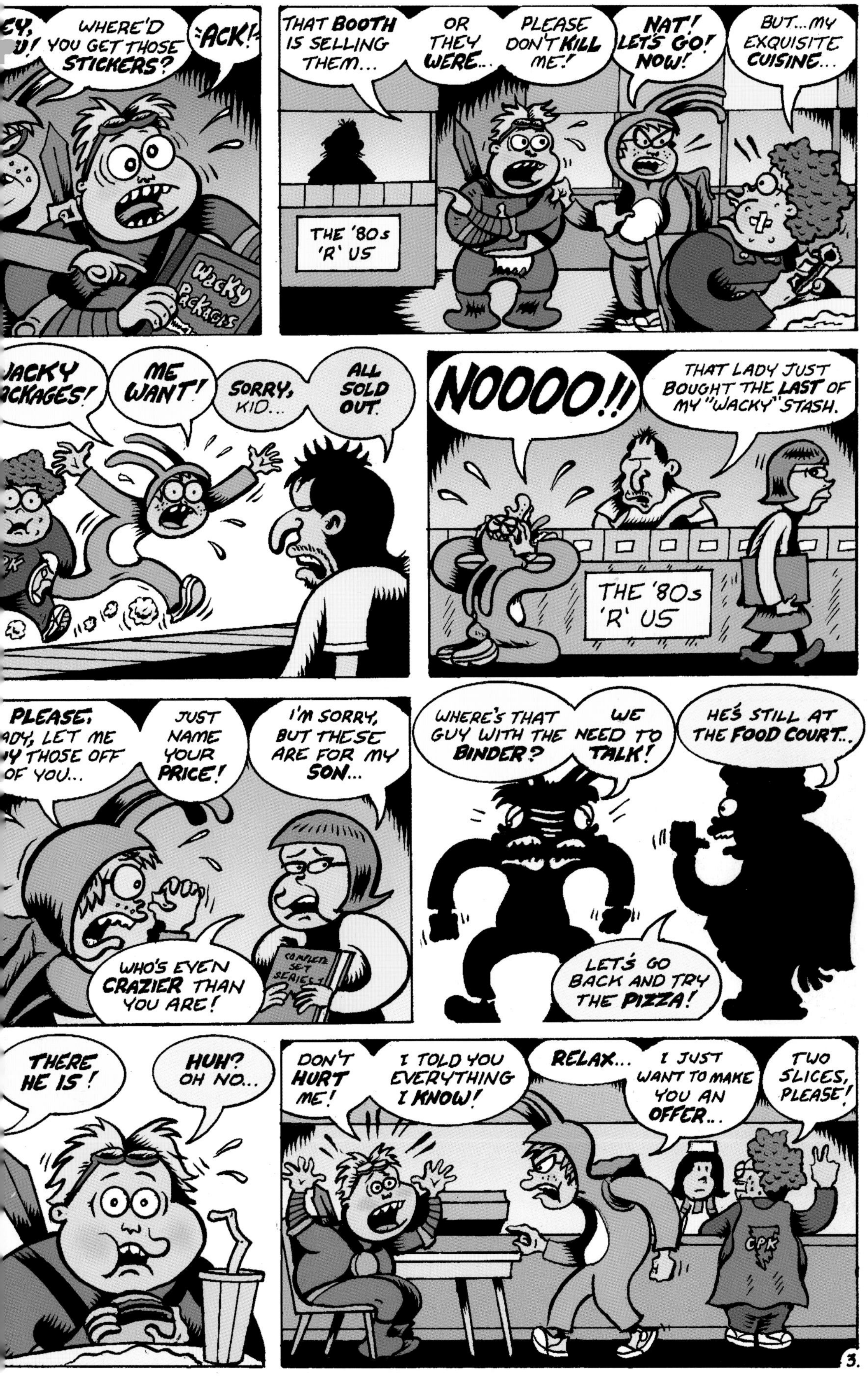
EY, U!
WHERE'D YOU GET THOSE STICKERS?
ACK!
THAT BOOTH IS SELLING THEM...
OR THEY WERE...
PLEASE DON'T KILL ME!
NAT! LET'S GO! NOW!
BUT... MY EXQUISITE CUISINE...
THE '80s 'R' US
WACKY PACKAGES
Wacky Packages
ACKY CKAGES!
ME WANT!
SORRY, KID...
ALL SOLD OUT.
NOOOO!!
THAT LADY JUST BOUGHT THE LAST OF MY "WACKY" STASH.
THE '80s 'R' US
PLEASE, ADY, LET ME Y THOSE OFF OF YOU...
JUST NAME YOUR PRICE!
I'M SORRY, BUT THESE ARE FOR MY SON...
WHO'S EVEN CRAZIER THAN YOU ARE!
COMPLETE SET SERIES 1
WHERE'S THAT GUY WITH THE BINDER?
WE NEED TO TALK!
HE'S STILL AT THE FOOD COURT...
LET'S GO BACK AND TRY THE PIZZA!
THERE HE IS!
HUH? OH NO...
DON'T HURT ME!
I TOLD YOU EVERYTHING I KNOW!
RELAX...
I JUST WANT TO MAKE YOU AN OFFER...
TWO SLICES, PLEASE!
CPK
3.

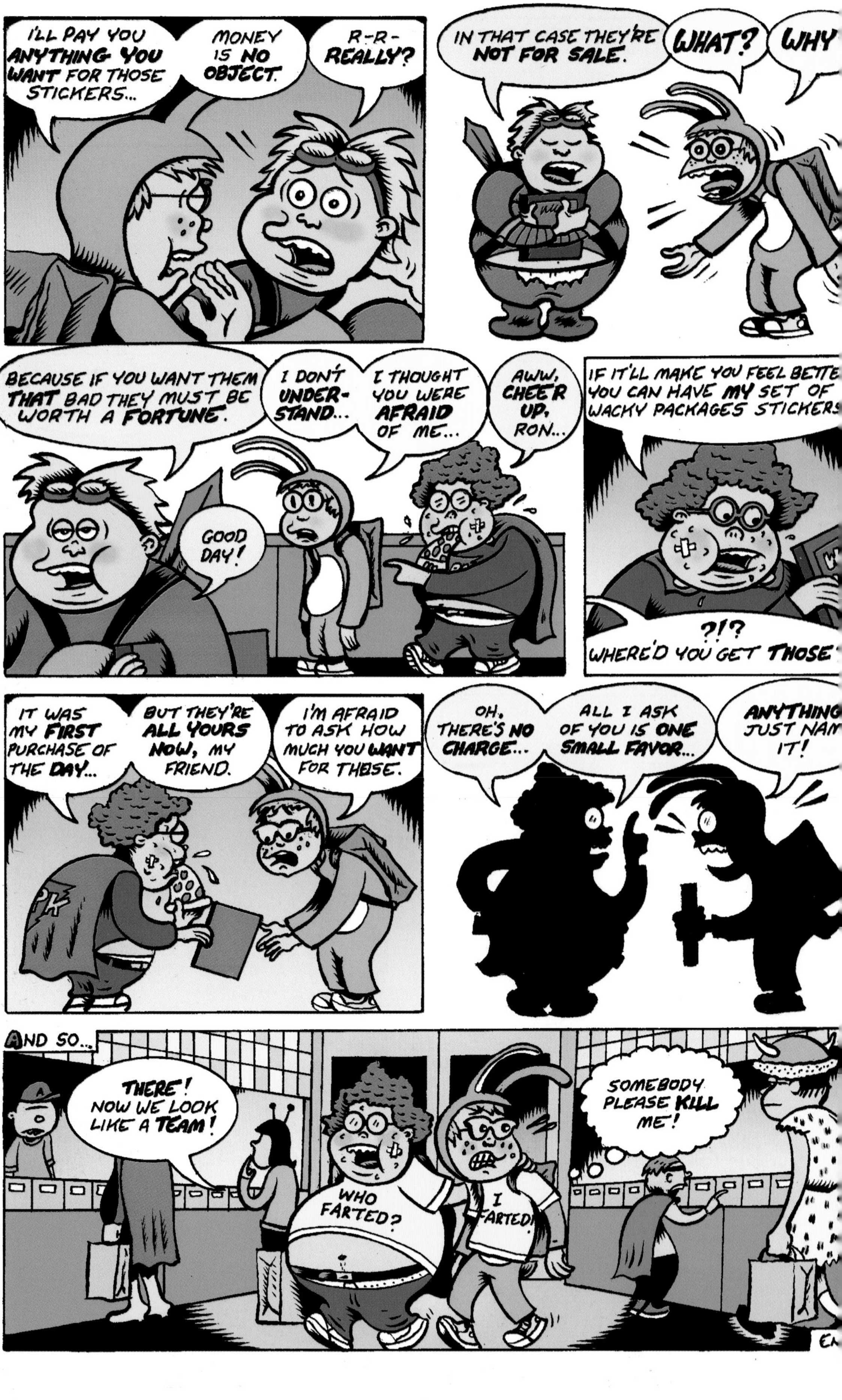
I'LL PAY YOU ANYTHING YOU WANT FOR THOSE STICKERS...
MONEY IS NO OBJECT.
R-R-REALLY?
IN THAT CASE THEY'RE NOT FOR SALE.
WHAT?
WHY
BECAUSE IF YOU WANT THEM THAT BAD THEY MUST BE WORTH A FORTUNE.
GOOD DAY!
I DON'T UNDER-STAND...
I THOUGHT YOU WERE AFRAID OF ME...
AWW, CHEER UP, RON...
IF IT'LL MAKE YOU FEEL BETTE
YOU CAN HAVE MY SET OF
WACKY PACKAGES STICKERS
?!?
WHERE'D YOU GET THOSE
IT WAS MY FIRST PURCHASE OF THE DAY...
BUT THEY'RE ALL YOURS NOW, MY FRIEND.
I'M AFRAID TO ASK HOW MUCH YOU WANT FOR THESE.
OH, THERE'S NO CHARGE...
ALL I ASK OF YOU IS ONE SMALL FAVOR...
ANYTHING
JUST NAM
IT!
AND SO...
THERE! NOW WE LOOK LIKE A TEAM!
SOMEBODY PLEASE KILL ME!
WHO FARTED?
I FARTED!

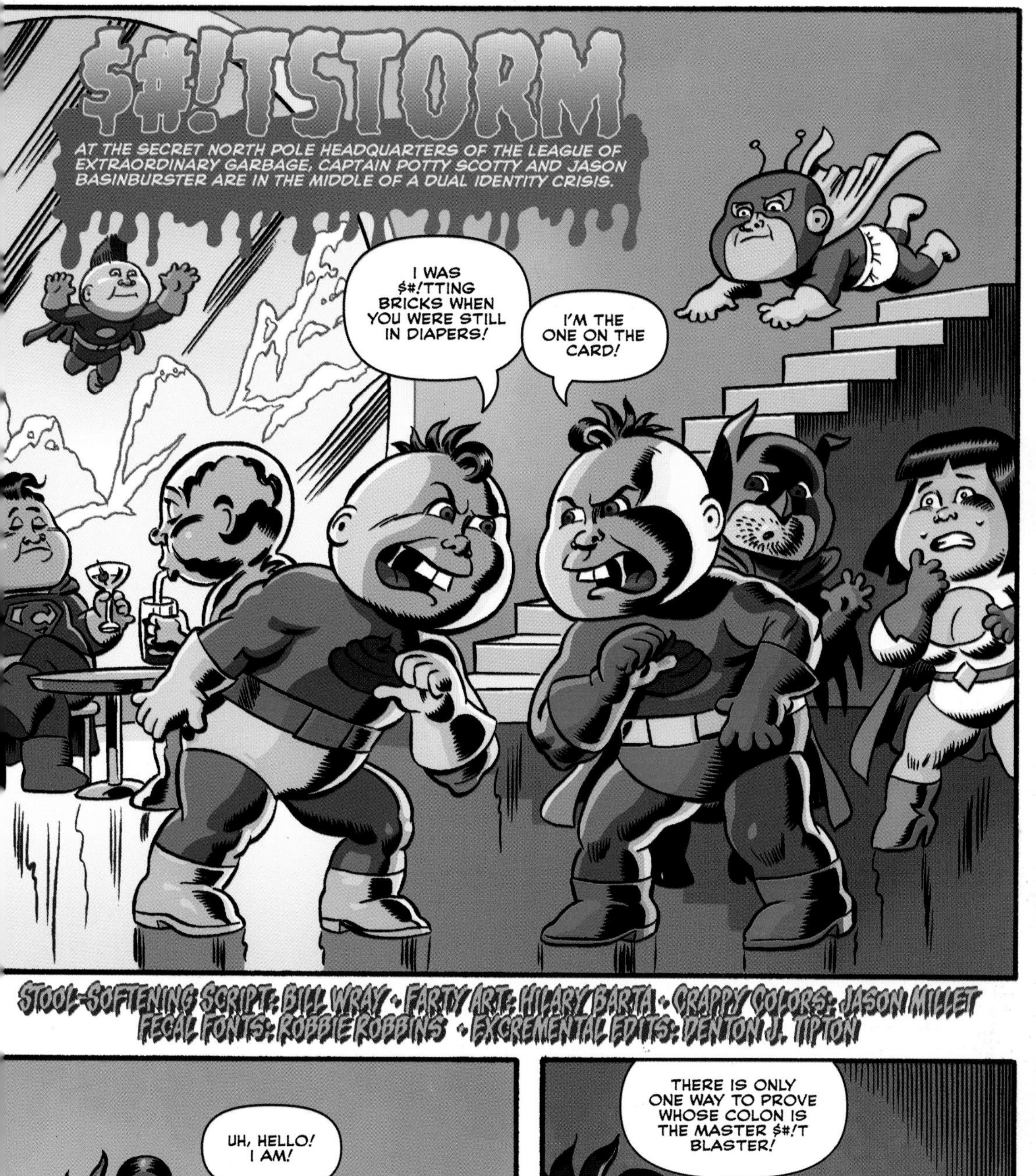
$#!TSTORM
AT THE SECRET NORTH POLE HEADQUARTERS OF THE LEAGUE OF EXTRAORDINARY GARBAGE, CAPTAIN POTTY SCOTTY AND JASON BASINBURSTER ARE IN THE MIDDLE OF A DUAL IDENTITY CRISIS.
I WAS $#!TTING BRICKS WHEN YOU WERE STILL IN DIAPERS!
I'M THE ONE ON THE CARD!

STOOL-SOFTENING SCRIPT: BILL WRAY • FARTY ART: HILARY BARTA • CRAPPY COLORS: JASON MILLET
FECAL FONTS: ROBBIE ROBBINS • EXCREMENTAL EDITS: DENTON J. TIPTON

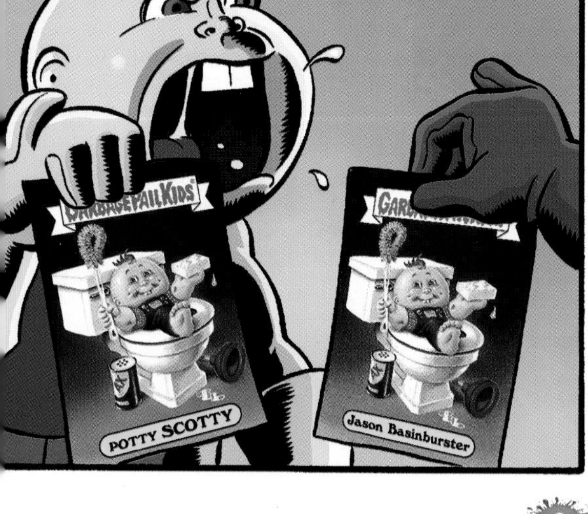
UH, HELLO! I AM!
GARBAGE PAIL KIDS
POTTY SCOTTY
Jason Basinburster

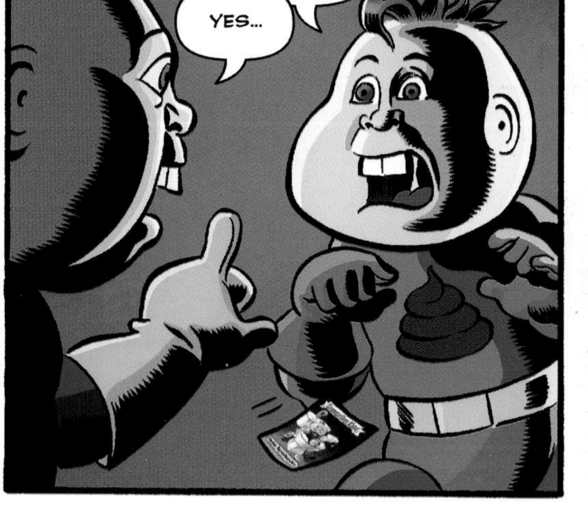
THERE IS ONLY ONE WAY TO PROVE WHOSE COLON IS THE MASTER $#!T BLASTER!
YOU MEAN...?
YES...

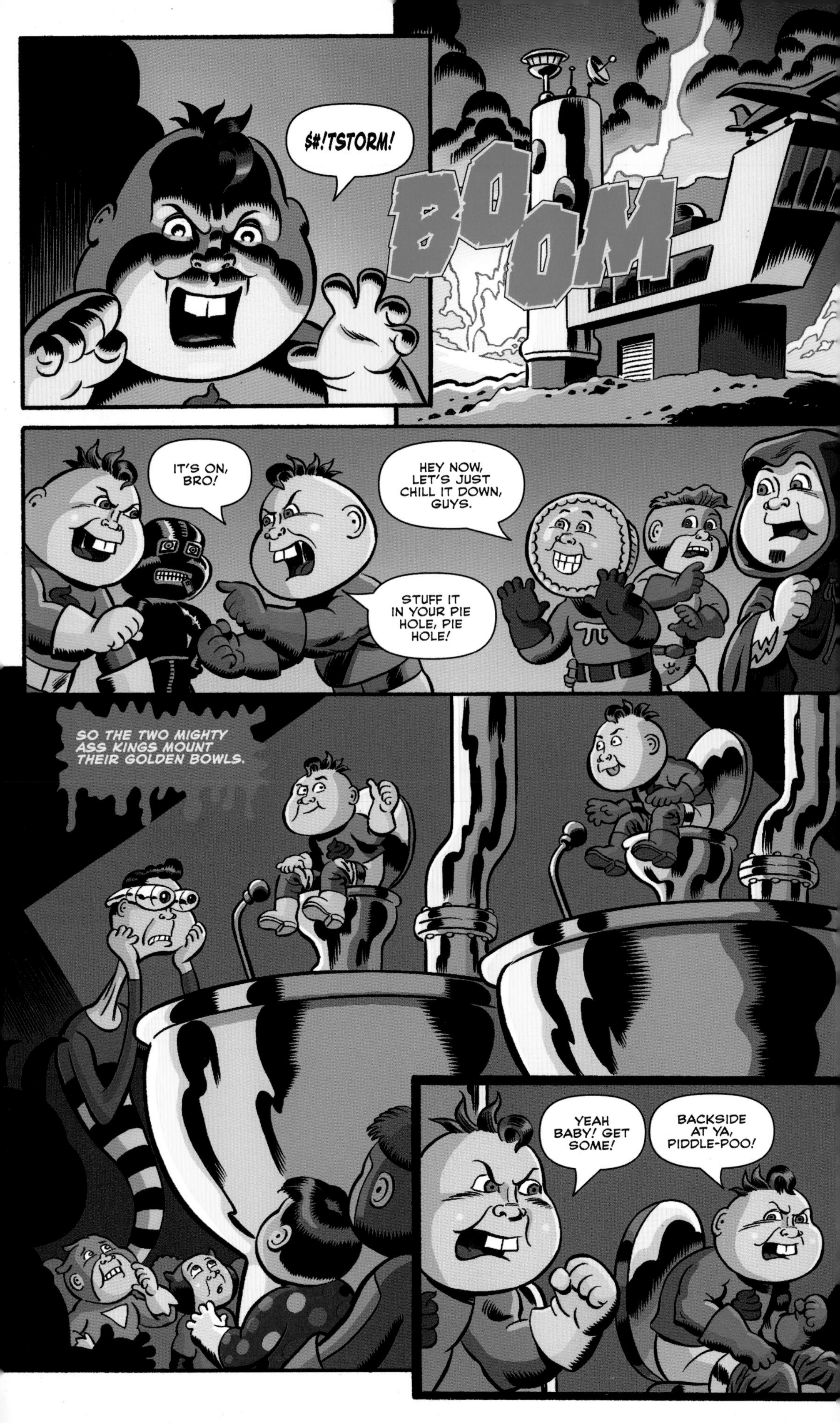
$#!TSTORM!
BOOM
IT'S ON, BRO!
HEY NOW, LET'S JUST CHILL IT DOWN, GUYS.
STUFF IT IN YOUR PIE HOLE, PIE HOLE!
SO THE TWO MIGHTY ASS KINGS MOUNT THEIR GOLDEN BOWLS.
YEAH BABY! GET SOME!
BACKSIDE AT YA, PIDDLE-POO!

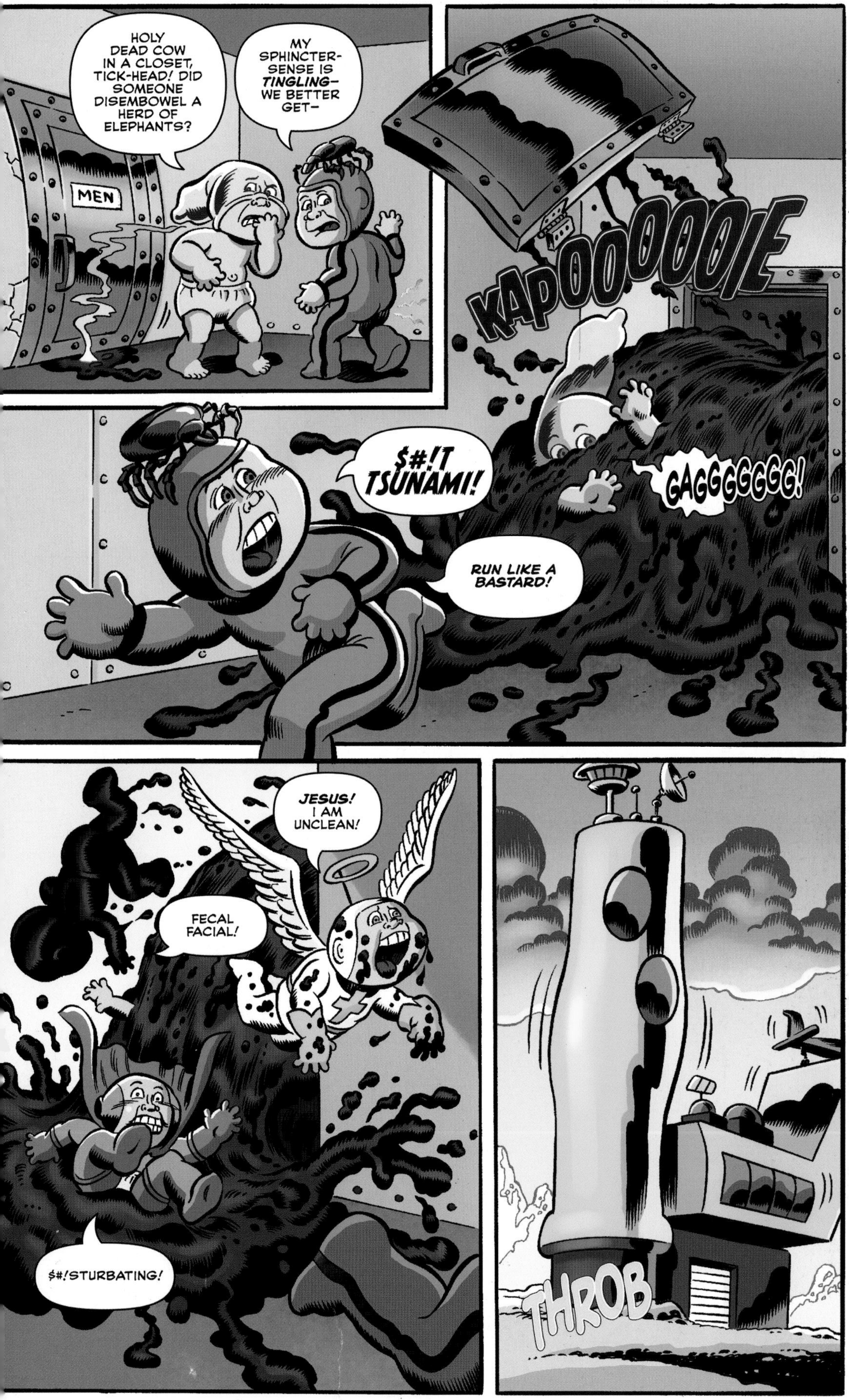
HOLY DEAD COW IN A CLOSET, TICK-HEAD! DID SOMEONE DISEMBOWEL A HERD OF ELEPHANTS?
MY SPHINCTER-SENSE IS TINGLING— WE BETTER GET—
MEN
KAPOOOOOOIE
$#!T TSUNAMI!
GAGGGGGGG!
RUN LIKE A BASTARD!
JESUS! I AM UNCLEAN!
FECAL FACIAL!
$#!STURBATING!
THROB

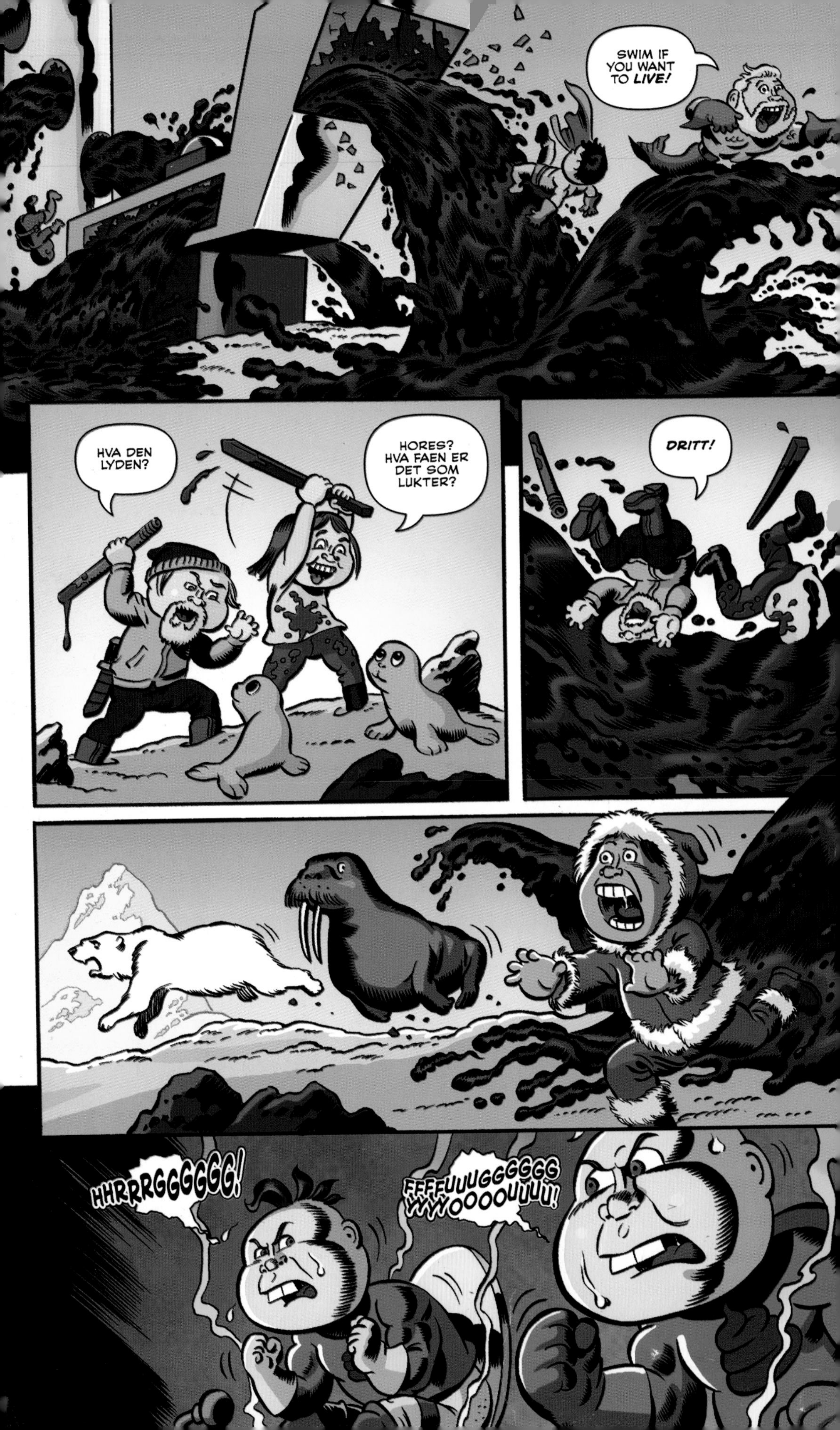
SWIM IF YOU WANT TO *LIVE!*
HVA DEN LYDEN?
HORES? HVA FAEN ER DET SOM LUKTER?
DRITT!
HHRRRGGGGGG!
FFFFUUUGGGGGG YYYOOOOUUUU!

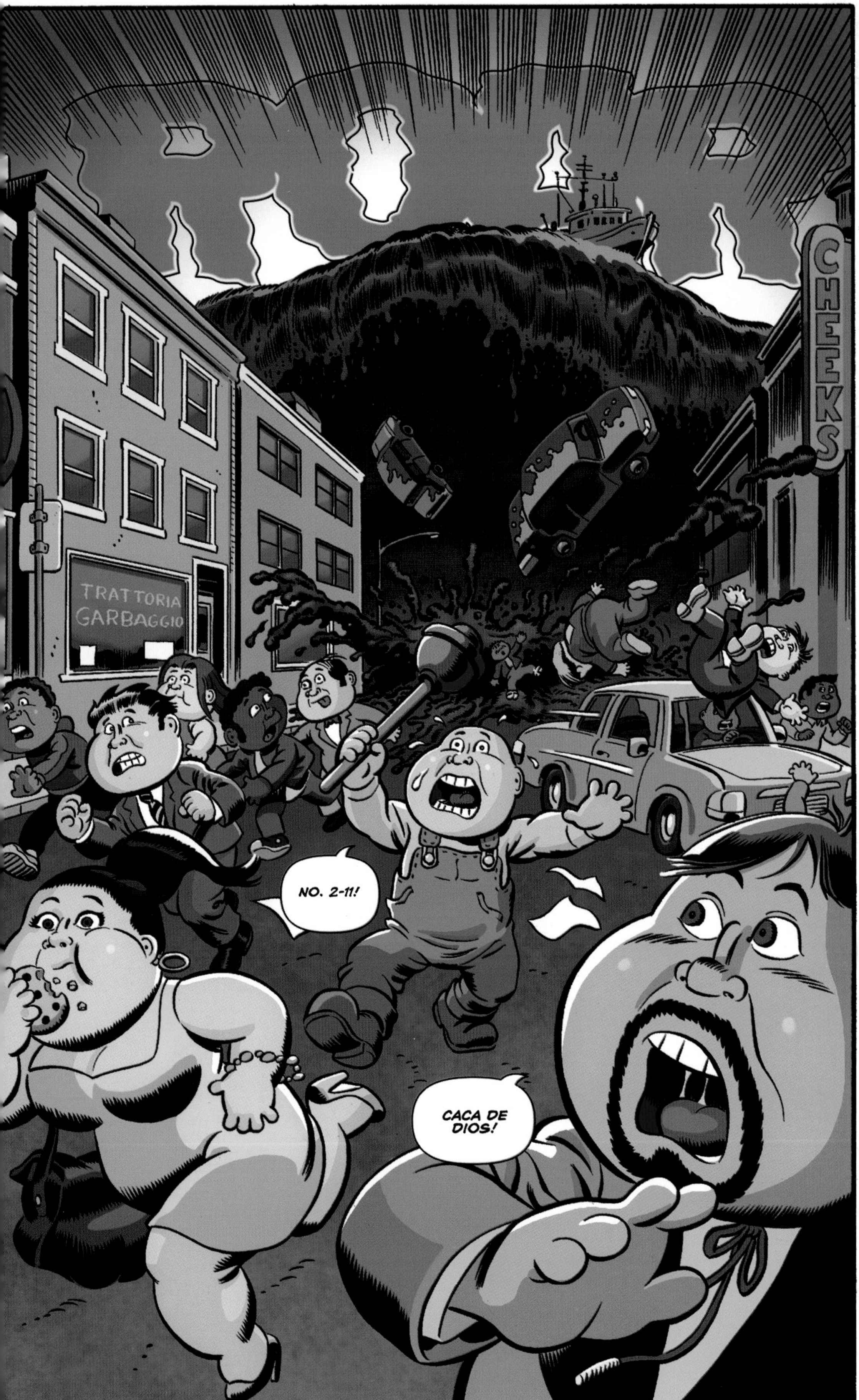
CHEEKS
TRATTORIA GARBAGGIO
NO. 2-11!
CACA DE DIOS!

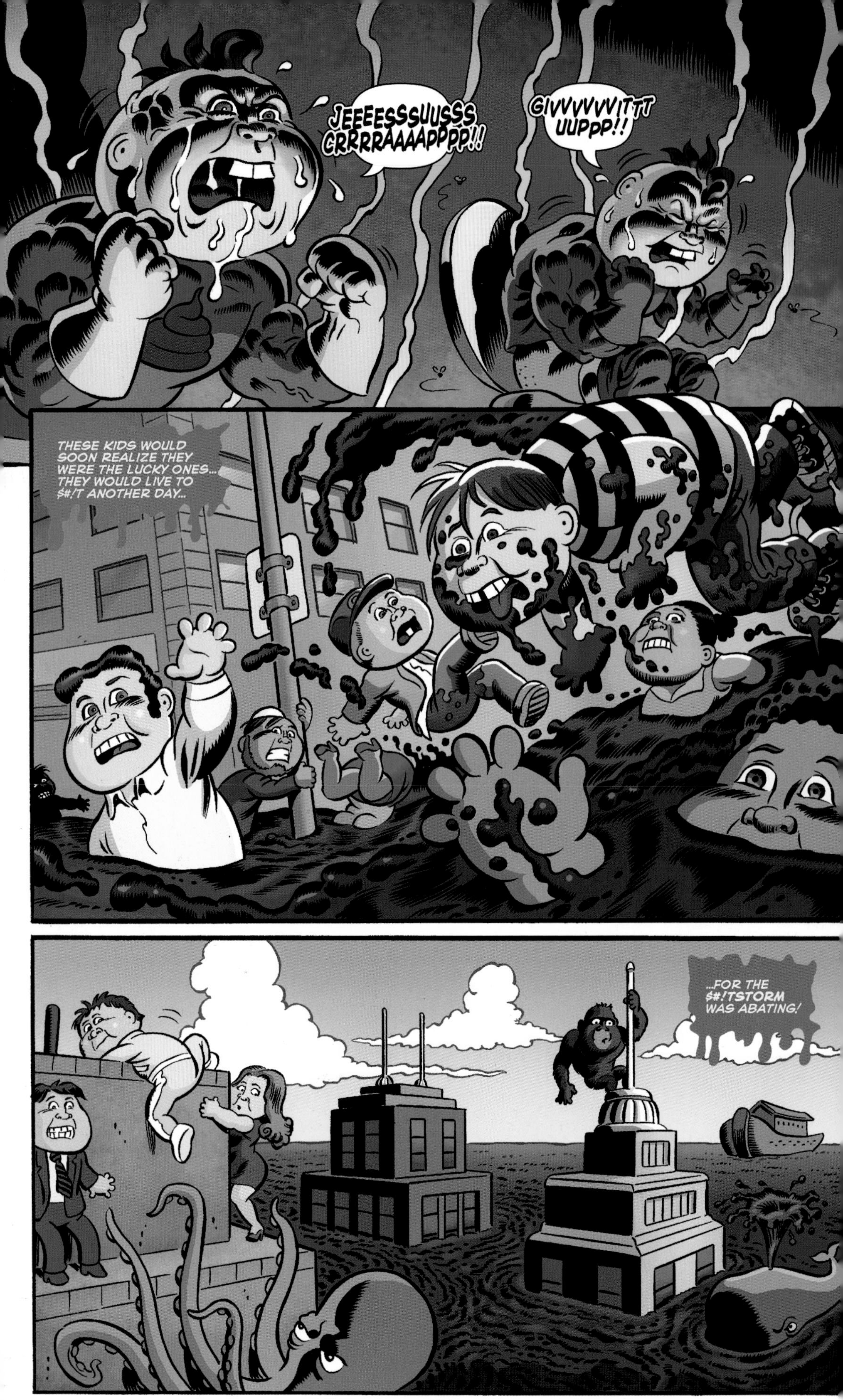

JEEEESSSUUSSS CRRRRAAAAPPPP!!
GIVVVVVVITTT UUPPP!!
THESE KIDS WOULD SOON REALIZE THEY WERE THE LUCKY ONES... THEY WOULD LIVE TO $#!T ANOTHER DAY...
...FOR THE $#!TSTORM WAS ABATING!

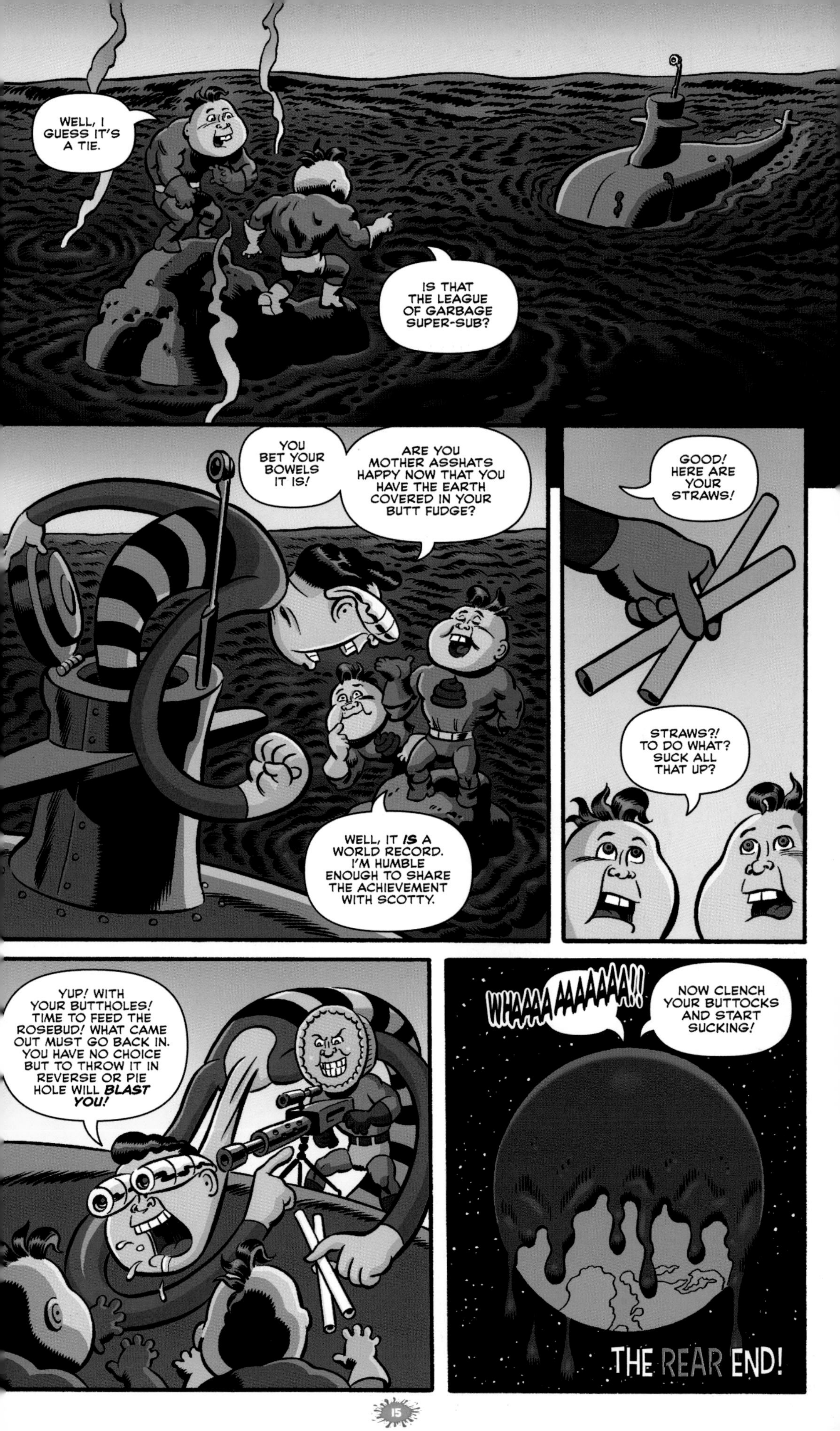

WELL, I GUESS IT'S A TIE.
IS THAT THE LEAGUE OF GARBAGE SUPER-SUB?
YOU BET YOUR BOWELS IT IS!
ARE YOU MOTHER ASSHATS HAPPY NOW THAT YOU HAVE THE EARTH COVERED IN YOUR BUTT FUDGE?
WELL, IT *IS* A WORLD RECORD. I'M HUMBLE ENOUGH TO SHARE THE ACHIEVEMENT WITH SCOTTY.
GOOD! HERE ARE YOUR STRAWS!
STRAWS?! TO DO WHAT? SUCK ALL THAT UP?
YUP! WITH YOUR BUTTHOLES! TIME TO FEED THE ROSEBUD! WHAT CAME OUT MUST GO BACK IN. YOU HAVE NO CHOICE BUT TO THROW IT IN REVERSE OR PIE HOLE WILL ***BLAST YOU!***
WHAAAA AAAAAAA!!
NOW CLENCH YOUR BUTTOCKS AND START SUCKING!
THE REAR END!

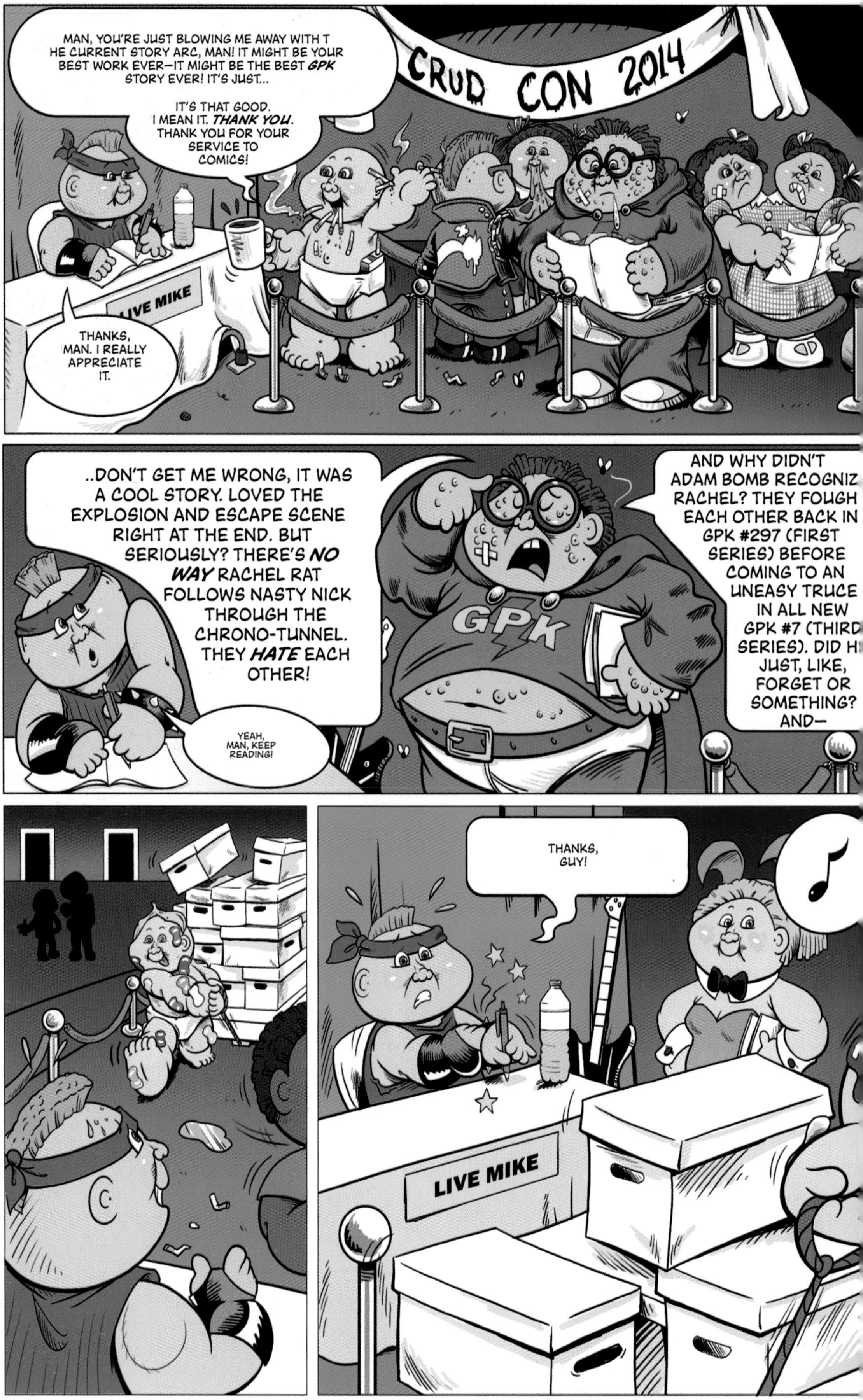
CRUD CON 2014
MAN, YOU'RE JUST BLOWING ME AWAY WITH T HE CURRENT STORY ARC, MAN! IT MIGHT BE YOUR BEST WORK EVER—IT MIGHT BE THE BEST GPK STORY EVER! IT'S JUST...
IT'S THAT GOOD. I MEAN IT. THANK YOU. THANK YOU FOR YOUR SERVICE TO COMICS!
LIVE MIKE
THANKS, MAN. I REALLY APPRECIATE IT.
..DON'T GET ME WRONG, IT WAS A COOL STORY. LOVED THE EXPLOSION AND ESCAPE SCENE RIGHT AT THE END. BUT SERIOUSLY? THERE'S NO WAY RACHEL RAT FOLLOWS NASTY NICK THROUGH THE CHRONO-TUNNEL. THEY HATE EACH OTHER!
AND WHY DIDN'T ADAM BOMB RECOGNIZ RACHEL? THEY FOUGH EACH OTHER BACK IN GPK #297 (FIRST SERIES) BEFORE COMING TO AN UNEASY TRUCE IN ALL NEW GPK #7 (THIRD SERIES). DID H JUST, LIKE, FORGET OR SOMETHING? AND—
GPK
YEAH, MAN, KEEP READING!
THANKS, GUY!
LIVE MIKE

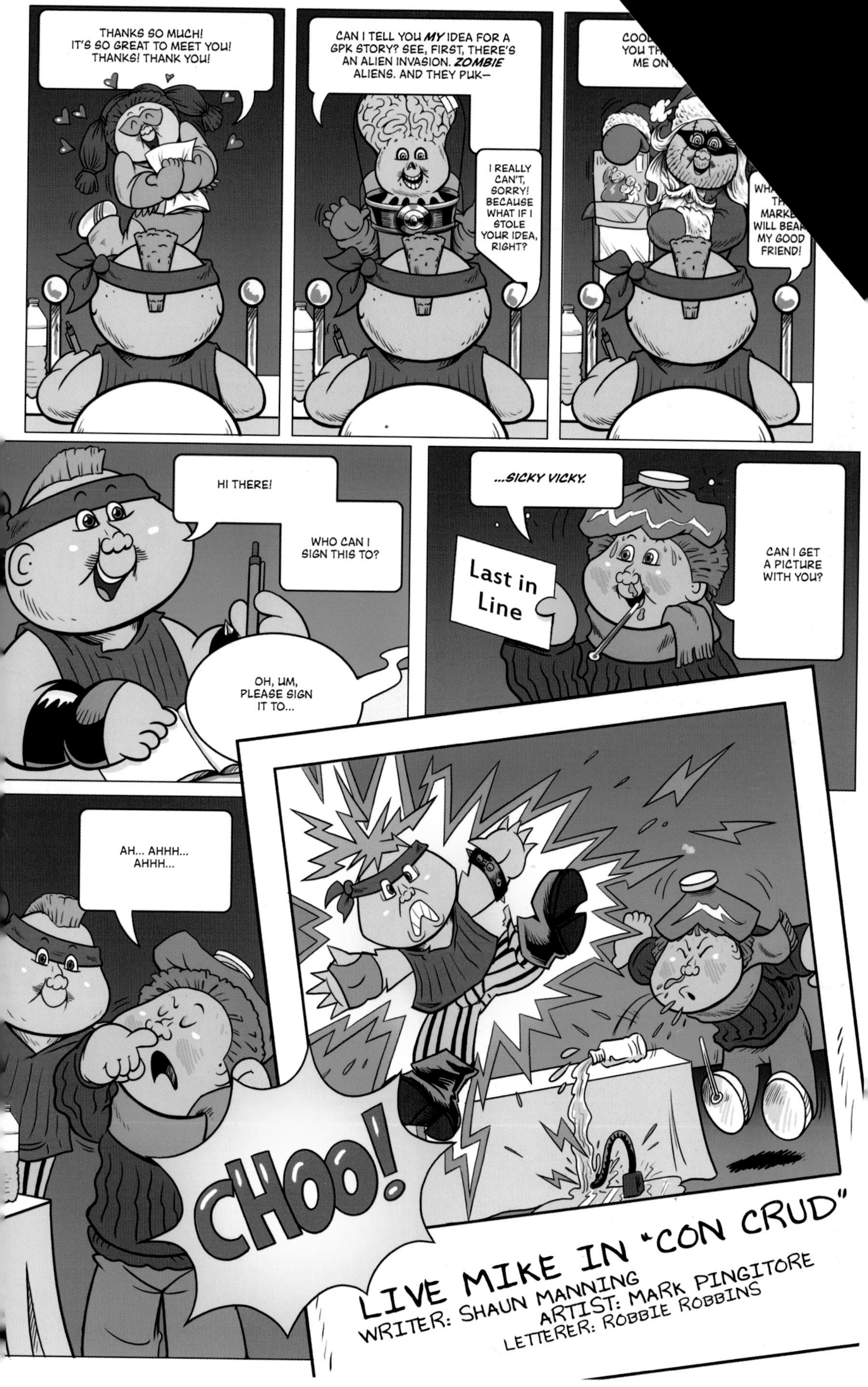
THANKS SO MUCH! IT'S SO GREAT TO MEET YOU! THANKS! THANK YOU!
CAN I TELL YOU *MY* IDEA FOR A GPK STORY? SEE, FIRST, THERE'S AN ALIEN INVASION. *ZOMBIE* ALIENS. AND THEY PUK—
I REALLY CAN'T, SORRY! BECAUSE WHAT IF I STOLE YOUR IDEA, RIGHT?
MY GOOD FRIEND!
HI THERE!
WHO CAN I SIGN THIS TO?
OH, UM, PLEASE SIGN IT TO...
...SICKY VICKY.
Last in Line
CAN I GET A PICTURE WITH YOU?
AH... AHHH... AHHH...
CHOO!
LIVE MIKE IN "CON CRUD"
WRITER: SHAUN MANNING
ARTIST: MARK PINGITORE
LETTERER: ROBBIE ROBBINS

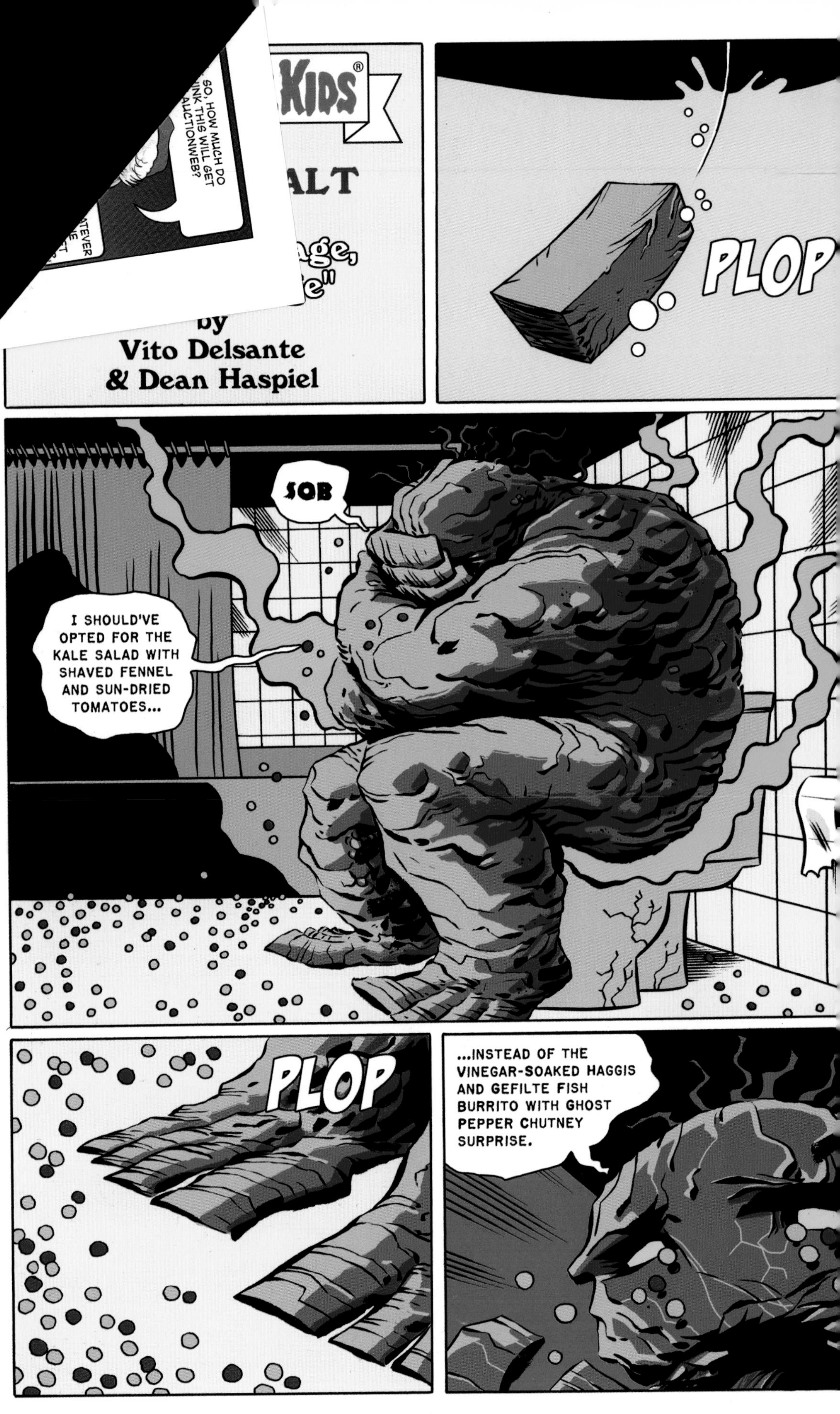
by
Vito Delsante
& Dean Haspiel
PLOP
SOB
I SHOULD'VE OPTED FOR THE KALE SALAD WITH SHAVED FENNEL AND SUN-DRIED TOMATOES...
PLOP
...INSTEAD OF THE VINEGAR-SOAKED HAGGIS AND GEFILTE FISH BURRITO WITH GHOST PEPPER CHUTNEY SURPRISE.

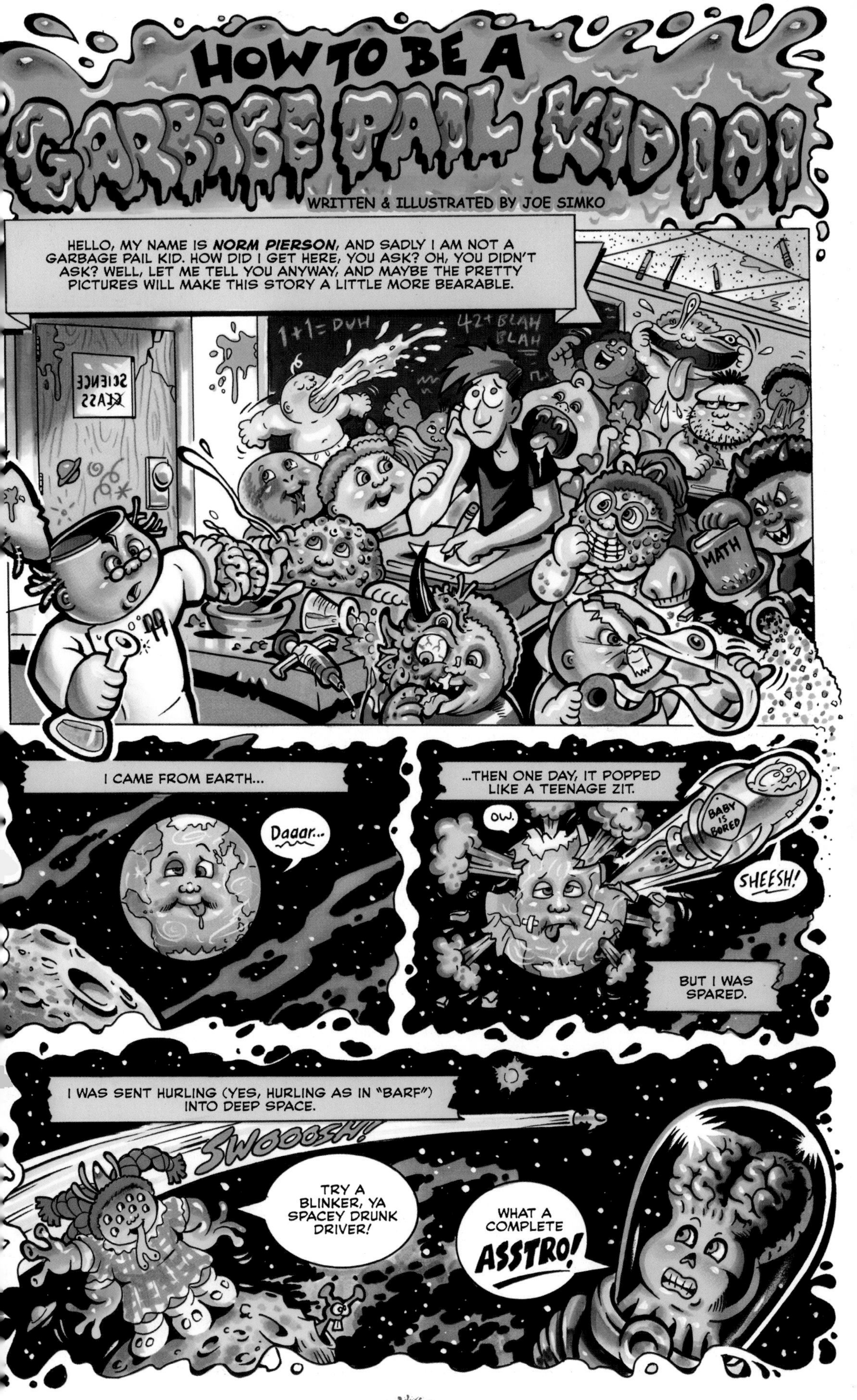
HOW TO BE A
GARBAGE PAIL KID 101
WRITTEN & ILLUSTRATED BY JOE SIMKO
HELLO, MY NAME IS NORM PIERSON, AND SADLY I AM NOT A GARBAGE PAIL KID. HOW DID I GET HERE, YOU ASK? OH, YOU DIDN'T ASK? WELL, LET ME TELL YOU ANYWAY, AND MAYBE THE PRETTY PICTURES WILL MAKE THIS STORY A LITTLE MORE BEARABLE.
1+1= DUH
42+ BLAH BLAH
SCIENCE CLASS
MATH
I CAME FROM EARTH...
Daaar...
...THEN ONE DAY, IT POPPED LIKE A TEENAGE ZIT.
OW.
BABY IS BORED
SHEESH!
BUT I WAS SPARED.
I WAS SENT HURLING (YES, HURLING AS IN "BARF") INTO DEEP SPACE.
SWOOOSH!
TRY A BLINKER, YA SPACEY DRUNK DRIVER!
WHAT A COMPLETE ASSTRO!

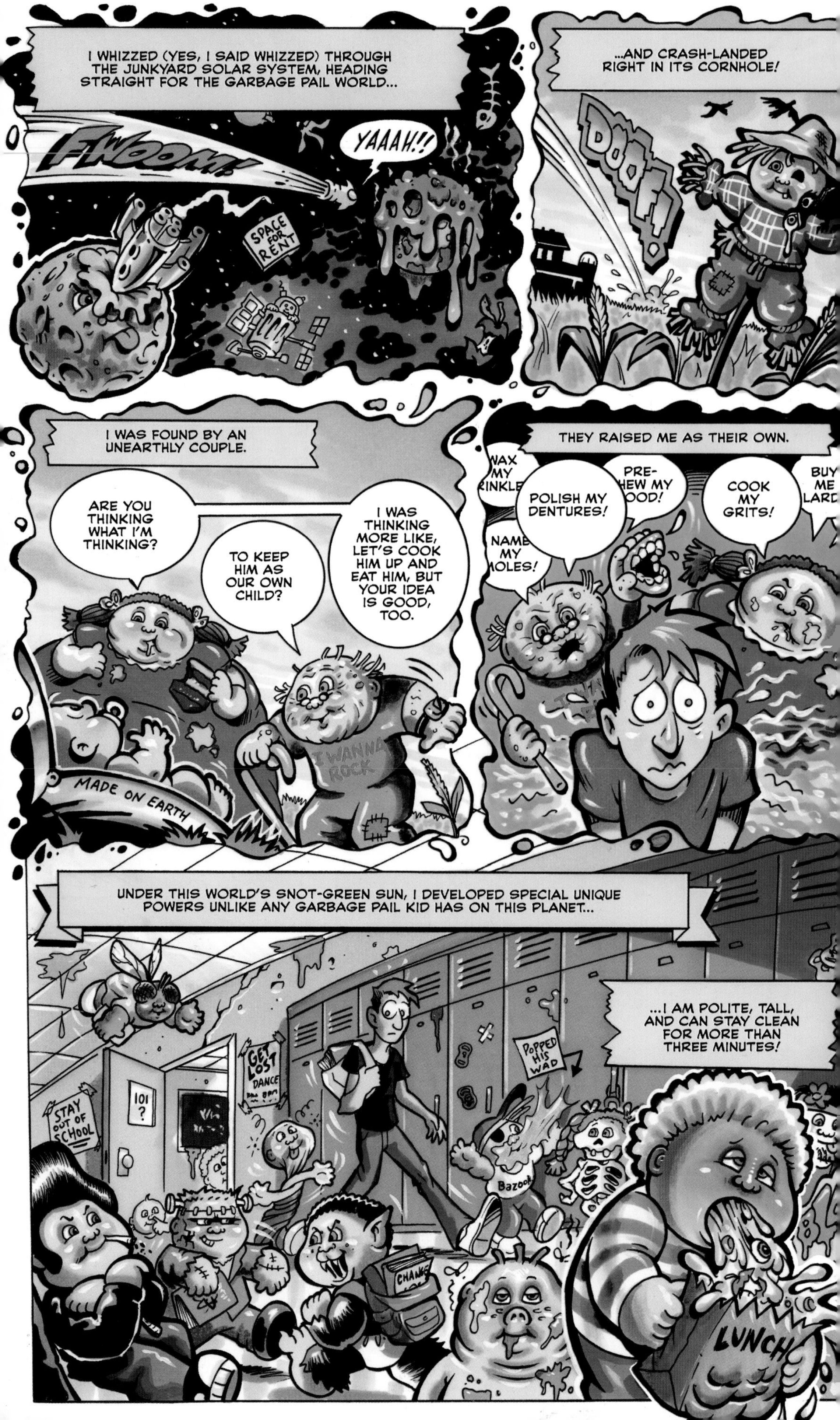
I WHIZZED (YES, I SAID WHIZZED) THROUGH THE JUNKYARD SOLAR SYSTEM, HEADING STRAIGHT FOR THE GARBAGE PAIL WORLD...
FWOOM!
YAAAH!!
SPACE FOR RENT
...AND CRASH-LANDED RIGHT IN ITS CORNHOLE!
DOOF!
I WAS FOUND BY AN UNEARTHLY COUPLE.
ARE YOU THINKING WHAT I'M THINKING?
TO KEEP HIM AS OUR OWN CHILD?
I WAS THINKING MORE LIKE, LET'S COOK HIM UP AND EAT HIM, BUT YOUR IDEA IS GOOD, TOO.
MADE ON EARTH
I WANNA ROCK
THEY RAISED ME AS THEIR OWN.
POLISH MY DENTURES!
COOK MY GRITS!
UNDER THIS WORLD'S SNOT-GREEN SUN, I DEVELOPED SPECIAL UNIQUE POWERS UNLIKE ANY GARBAGE PAIL KID HAS ON THIS PLANET...
...I AM POLITE, TALL, AND CAN STAY CLEAN FOR MORE THAN THREE MINUTES!
STAY OUT OF SCHOOL
101 ?
GET LOST DANCE
POPPED HIS WAD
Bazook
CHANGE
LUNCH

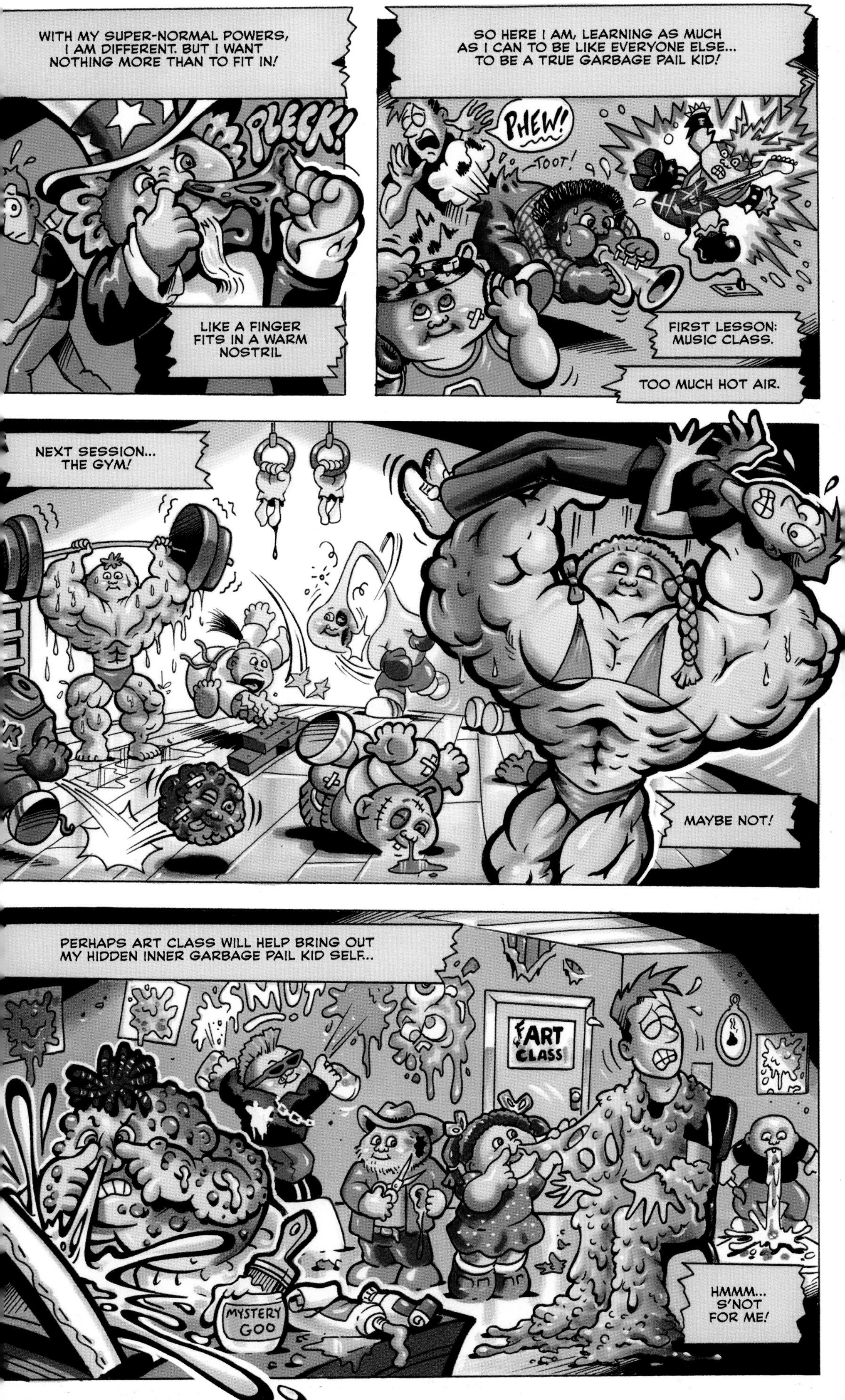
WITH MY SUPER-NORMAL POWERS, I AM DIFFERENT. BUT I WANT NOTHING MORE THAN TO FIT IN!
PLECK!
LIKE A FINGER FITS IN A WARM NOSTRIL
SO HERE I AM, LEARNING AS MUCH AS I CAN TO BE LIKE EVERYONE ELSE... TO BE A TRUE GARBAGE PAIL KID!
PHEW!
TOOT!
FIRST LESSON: MUSIC CLASS.
TOO MUCH HOT AIR.
NEXT SESSION... THE GYM!
MAYBE NOT!
PERHAPS ART CLASS WILL HELP BRING OUT MY HIDDEN INNER GARBAGE PAIL KID SELF...
SNOT
FART CLASS
MYSTERY GOO
HMMM... S'NOT FOR ME!

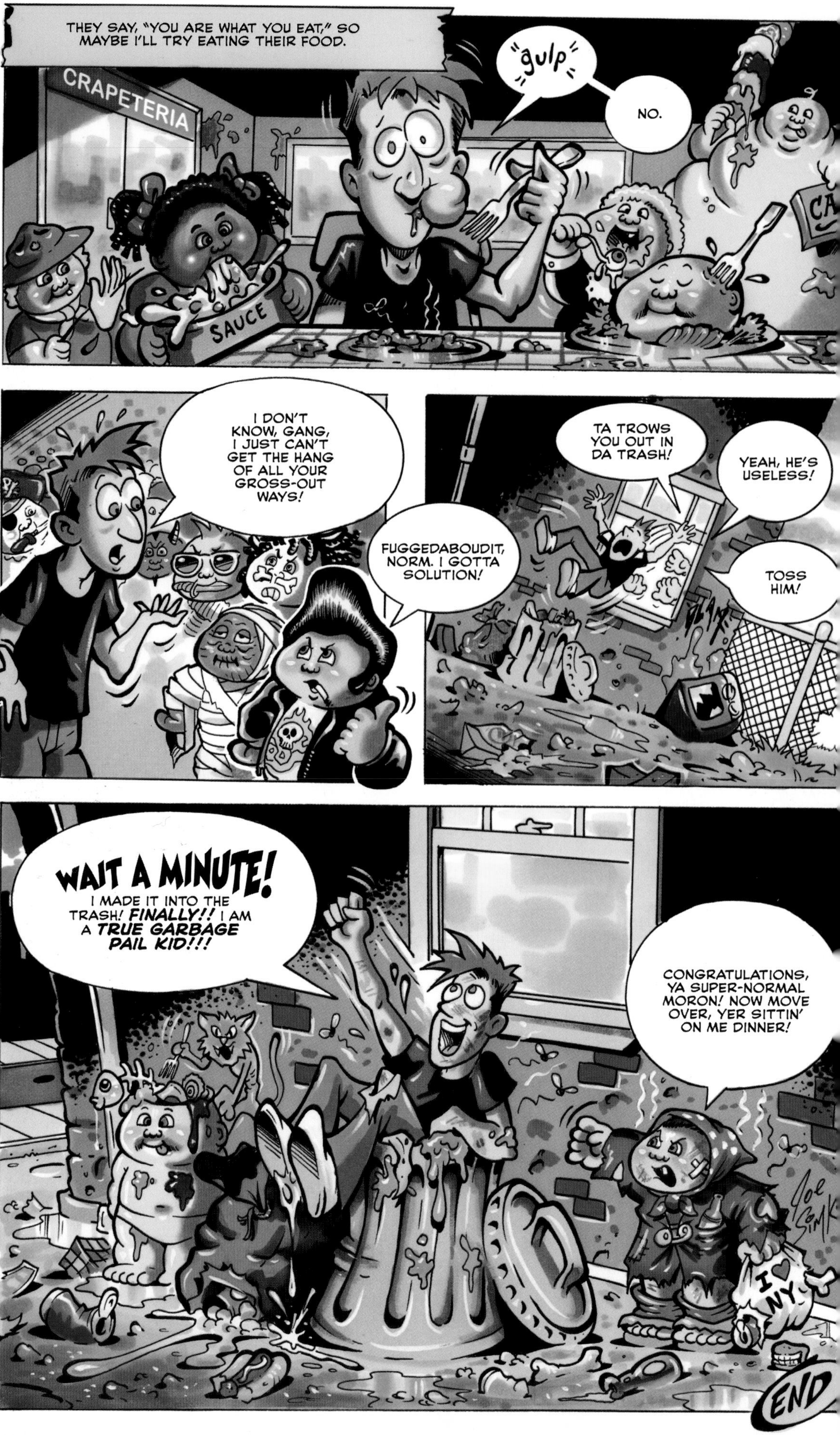
THEY SAY, "YOU ARE WHAT YOU EAT," SO MAYBE I'LL TRY EATING THEIR FOOD.
CRAPETERIA
SAUCE
"gulp"
NO.
I DON'T KNOW, GANG, I JUST CAN'T GET THE HANG OF ALL YOUR GROSS-OUT WAYS!
FUGGEDABOUDIT, NORM. I GOTTA SOLUTION!
TA TROWS YOU OUT IN DA TRASH!
YEAH, HE'S USELESS!
TOSS HIM!
WAIT A MINUTE! I MADE IT INTO THE TRASH! FINALLY!! I AM A TRUE GARBAGE PAIL KID!!!
CONGRATULATIONS, YA SUPER-NORMAL MORON! NOW MOVE OVER, YER SITTIN' ON ME DINNER!
I ♥ NY
END

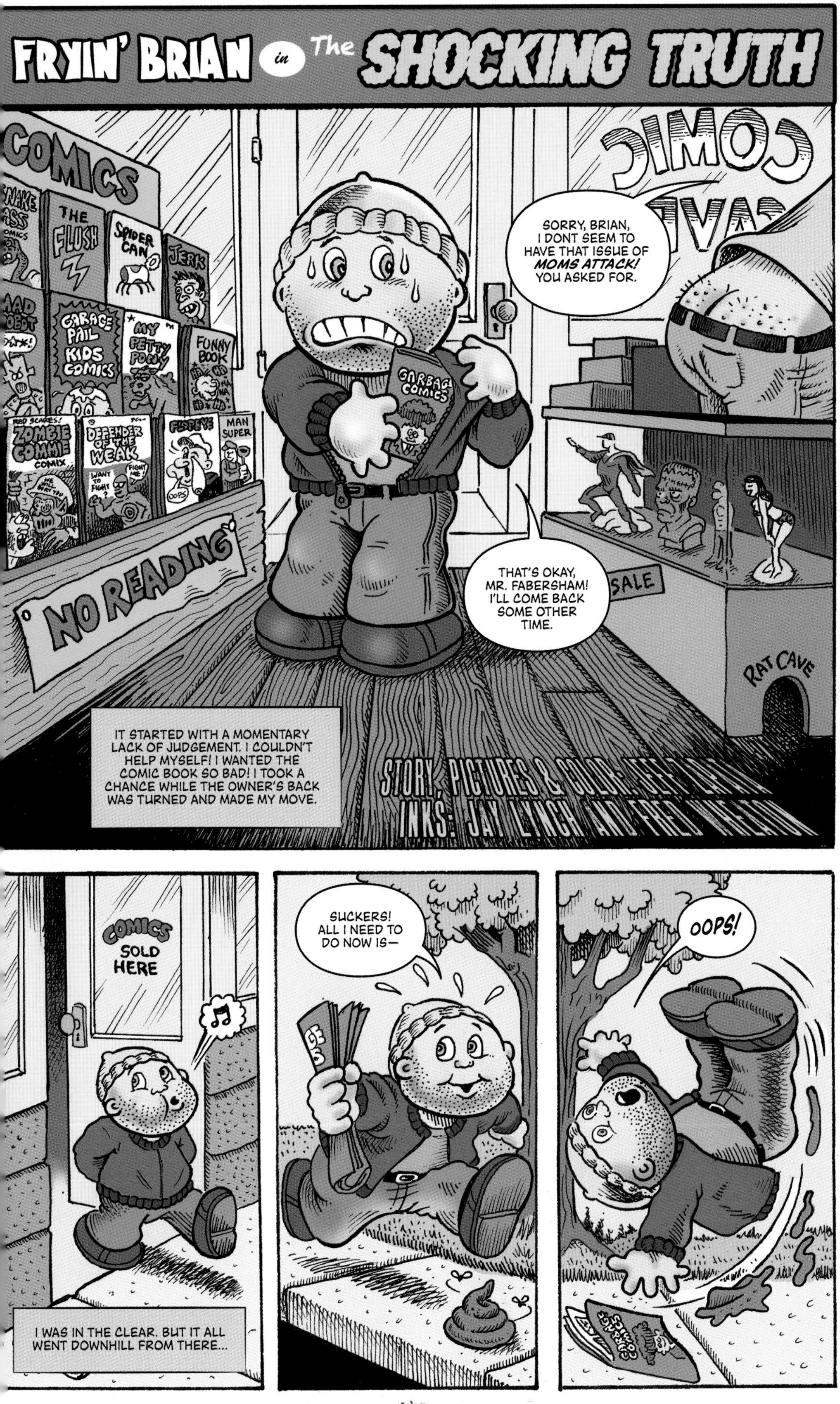
FRYIN' BRIAN in The SHOCKING TRUTH
COMICS
SNAKE ASS COMICS
THE FLUSH
SPIDER CAN
JERK
GARAGE PAIL KIDS COMICS
MY PETTY PONY
FUNNY BOOK
RED SCARES! ZOMBIE COMMIE COMIX
DEFENDER OF THE WEAK
WANT TO FIGHT?
FIGHT ME!
MAN SUPER
OOPS
NO READING
COMIC CAVE
GARBAGE COMICS
SORRY, BRIAN, I DONT SEEM TO HAVE THAT ISSUE OF *MOMS ATTACK!* YOU ASKED FOR.
THAT'S OKAY, MR. FABERSHAM! I'LL COME BACK SOME OTHER TIME.
SALE
RAT CAVE
IT STARTED WITH A MOMENTARY LACK OF JUDGEMENT. I COULDN'T HELP MYSELF! I WANTED THE COMIC BOOK SO BAD! I TOOK A CHANCE WHILE THE OWNER'S BACK WAS TURNED AND MADE MY MOVE.
STORY, PICTURES &
INKS: JAY LYNCH
COMICS SOLD HERE
I WAS IN THE CLEAR. BUT IT ALL WENT DOWNHILL FROM THERE...
SUCKERS! ALL I NEED TO DO NOW IS—
OOPS!
GARBAGE COMICS

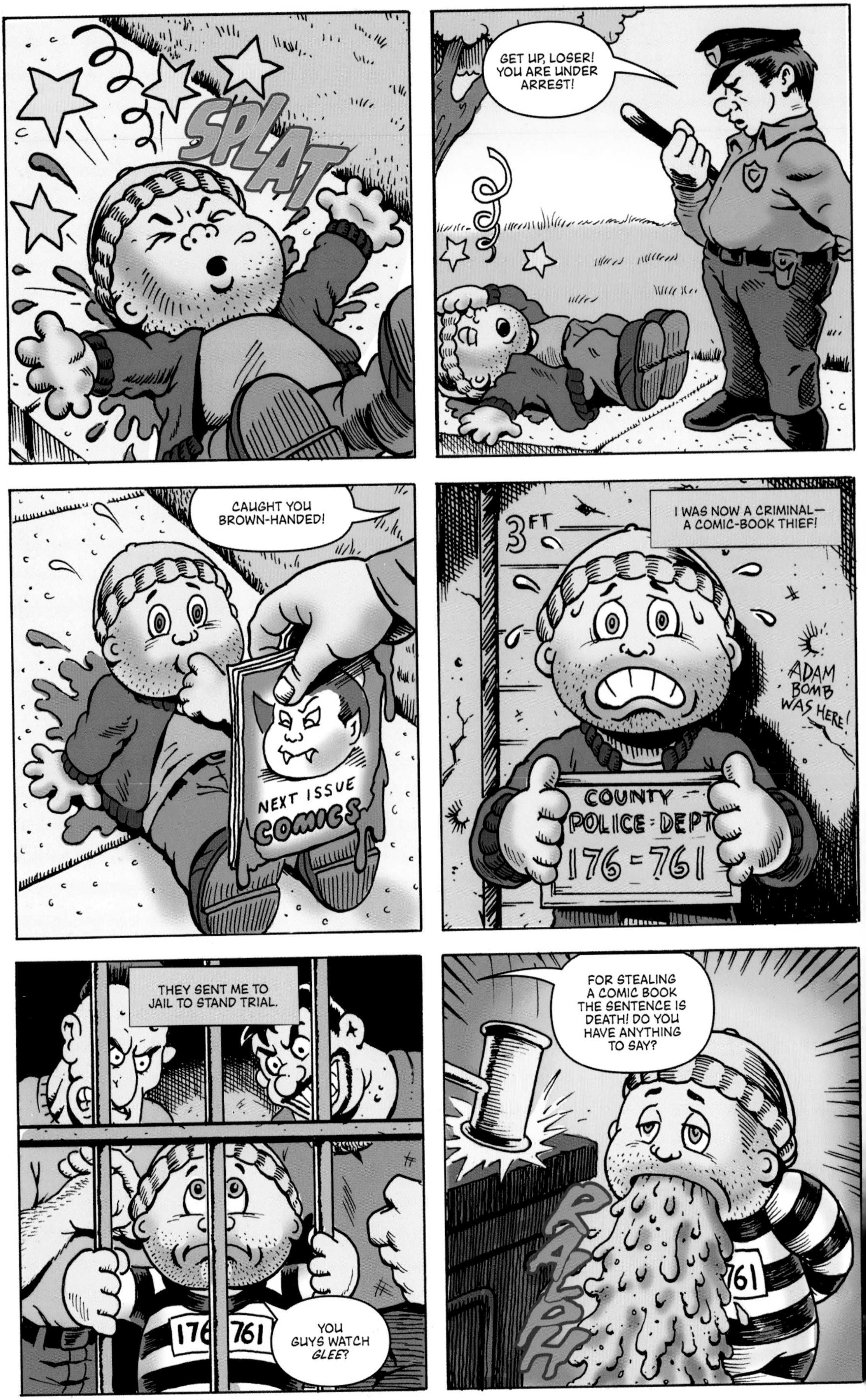
SPLAT
GET UP, LOSER! YOU ARE UNDER ARREST!
CAUGHT YOU BROWN-HANDED!
NEXT ISSUE
COMICS
I WAS NOW A CRIMINAL— A COMIC-BOOK THIEF!
3 FT
ADAM BOMB WAS HERE!
COUNTY POLICE DEPT 176-761
THEY SENT ME TO JAIL TO STAND TRIAL.
176 761
YOU GUYS WATCH *GLEE*?
FOR STEALING A COMIC BOOK THE SENTENCE IS DEATH! DO YOU HAVE ANYTHING TO SAY?
RALPH
761

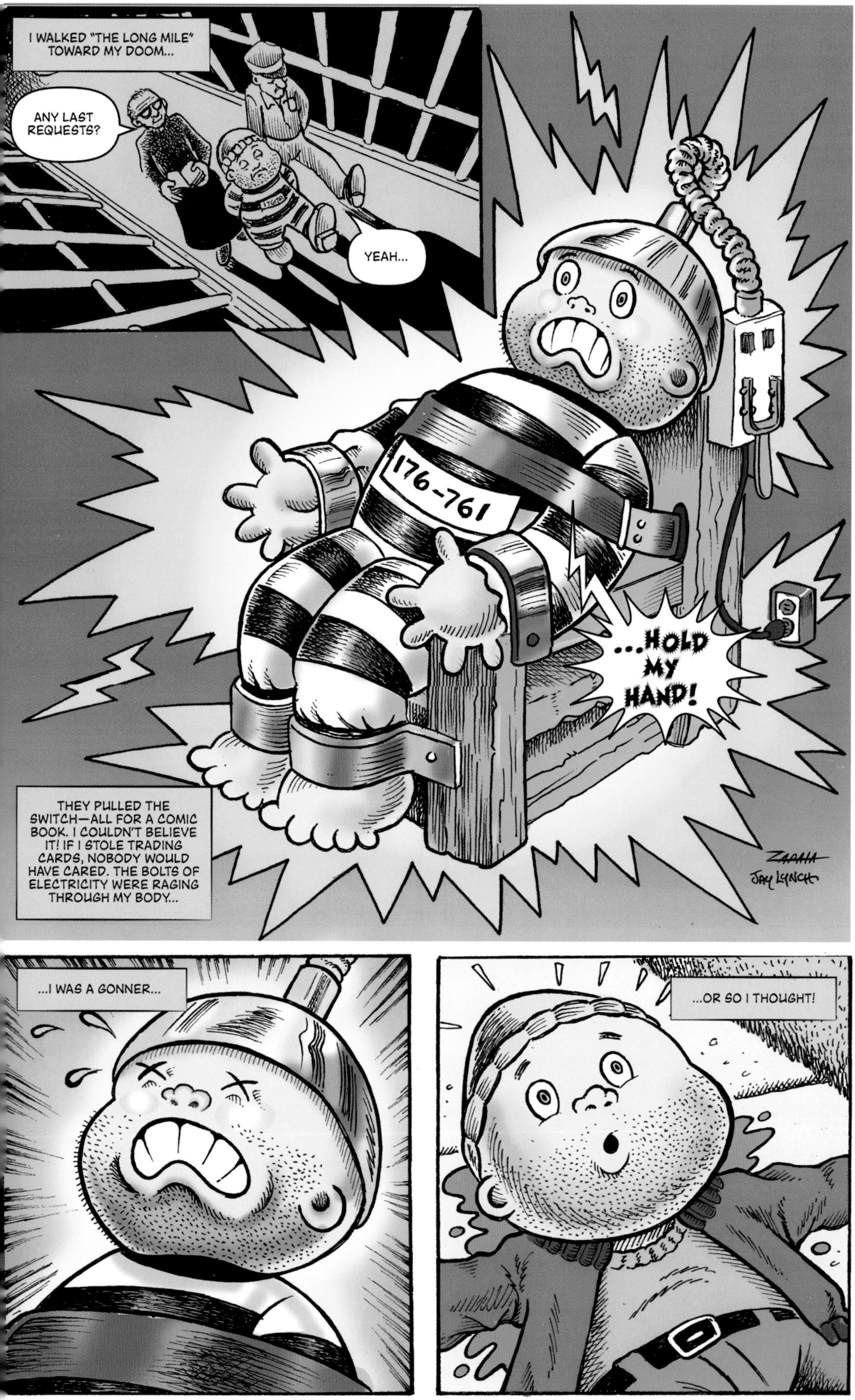
I WALKED "THE LONG MILE" TOWARD MY DOOM...
ANY LAST REQUESTS?
YEAH...
176-761
...HOLD MY HAND!
THEY PULLED THE SWITCH—ALL FOR A COMIC BOOK. I COULDN'T BELIEVE IT! IF I STOLE TRADING CARDS, NOBODY WOULD HAVE CARED. THE BOLTS OF ELECTRICITY WERE RAGING THROUGH MY BODY...
JAY LYNCH
...I WAS A GONNER...
...OR SO I THOUGHT!

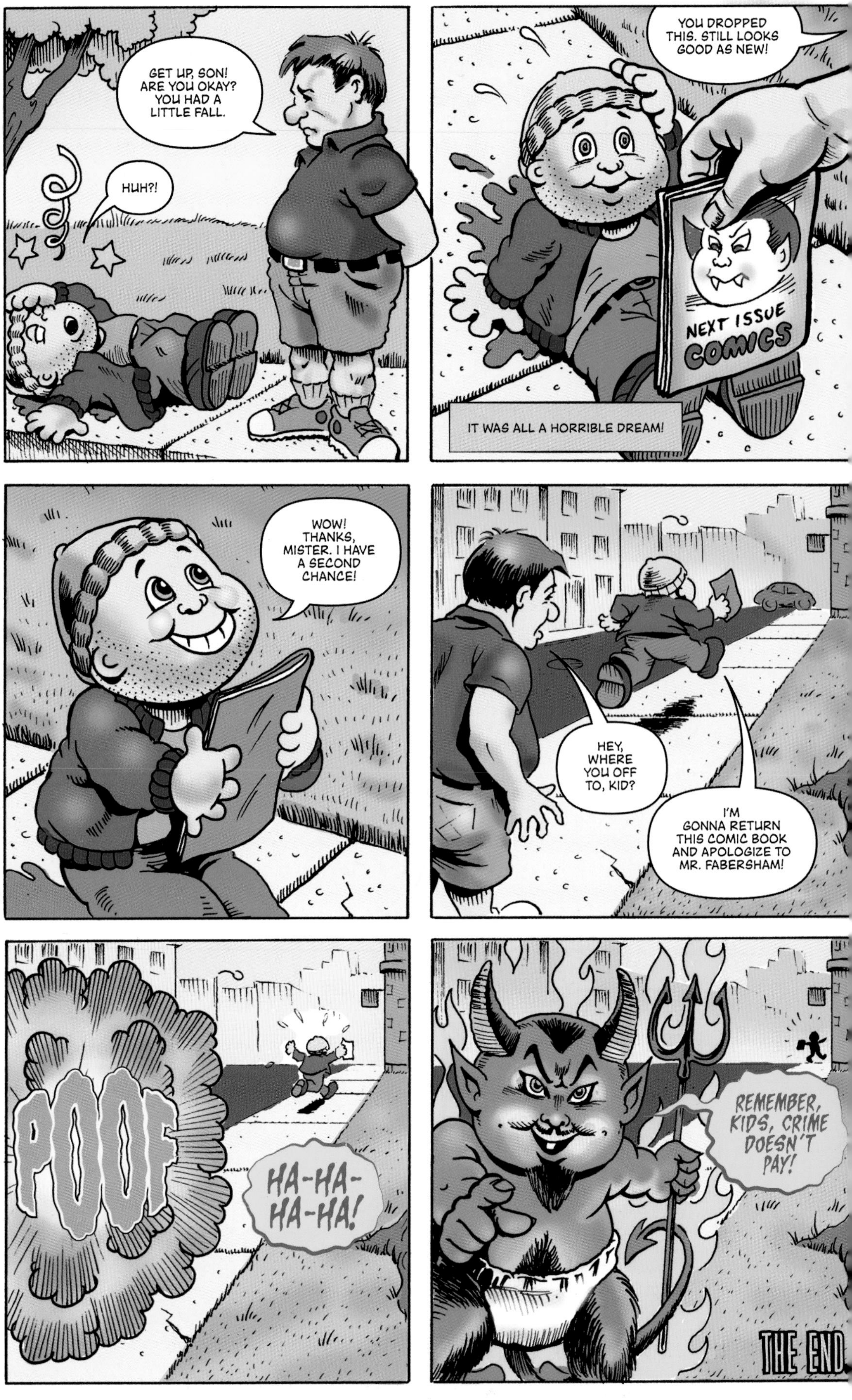
GET UP, SON! ARE YOU OKAY? YOU HAD A LITTLE FALL.
HUH?!
YOU DROPPED THIS. STILL LOOKS GOOD AS NEW!
NEXT ISSUE COMICS
IT WAS ALL A HORRIBLE DREAM!
WOW! THANKS, MISTER. I HAVE A SECOND CHANCE!
HEY, WHERE YOU OFF TO, KID?
I'M GONNA RETURN THIS COMIC BOOK AND APOLOGIZE TO MR. FABERSHAM!
POOF
HA-HA-HA-HA!
REMEMBER, KIDS, CRIME DOESN'T PAY!
THE END

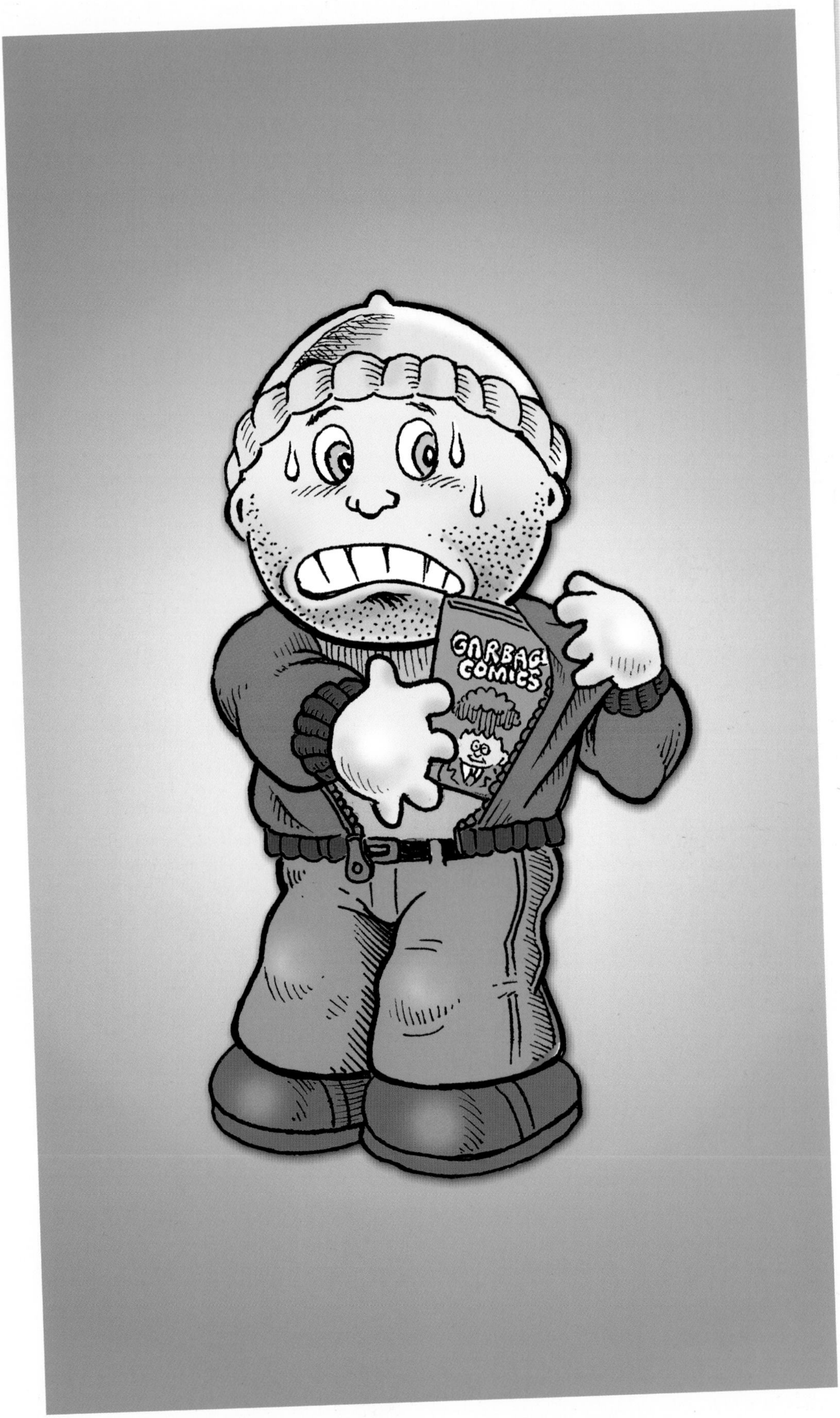
GARBAGE
COMICS

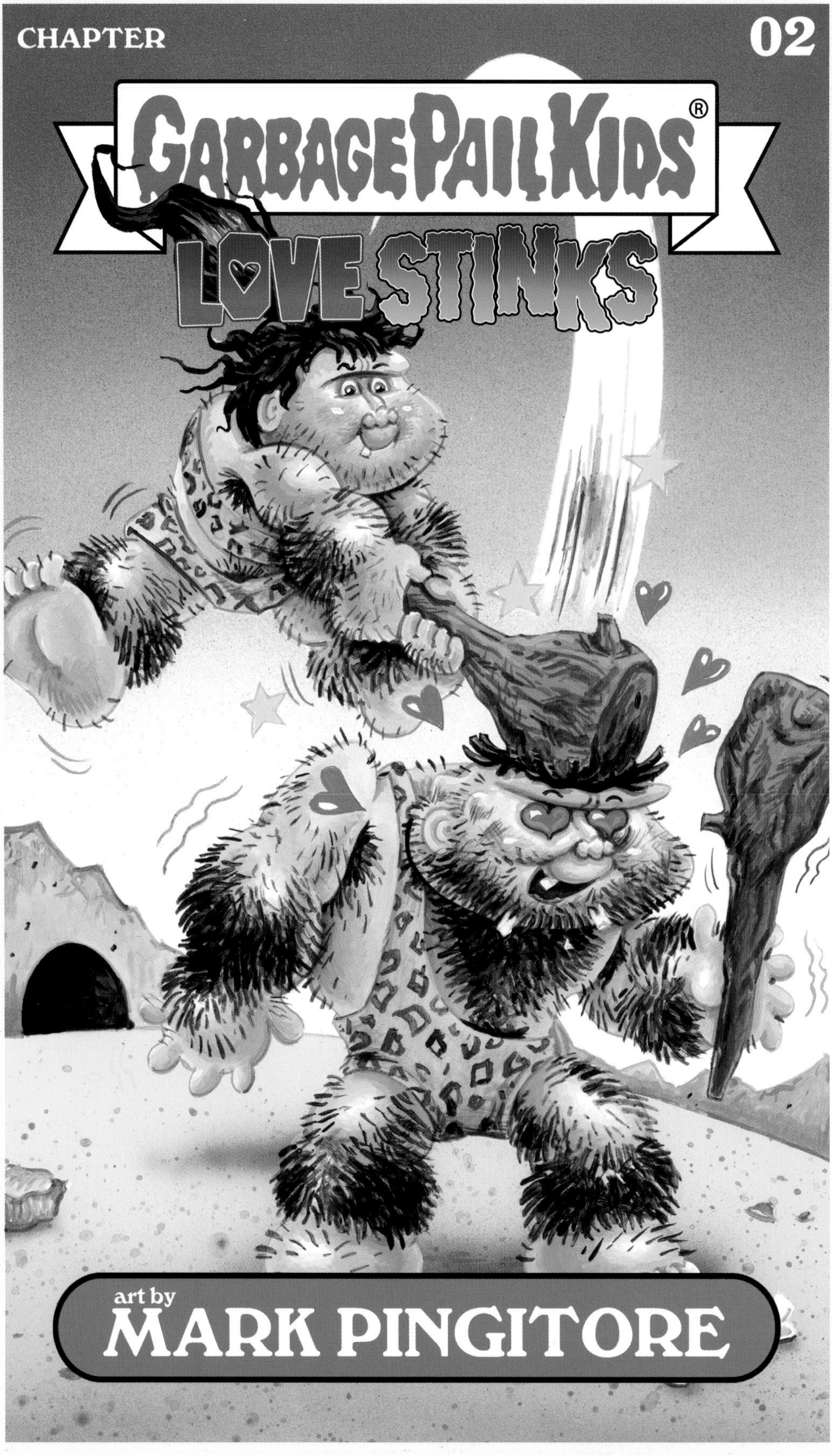
CHAPTER
02
GARBAGE PAIL KIDS®
LOVE STINKS
art by
MARK PINGITORE

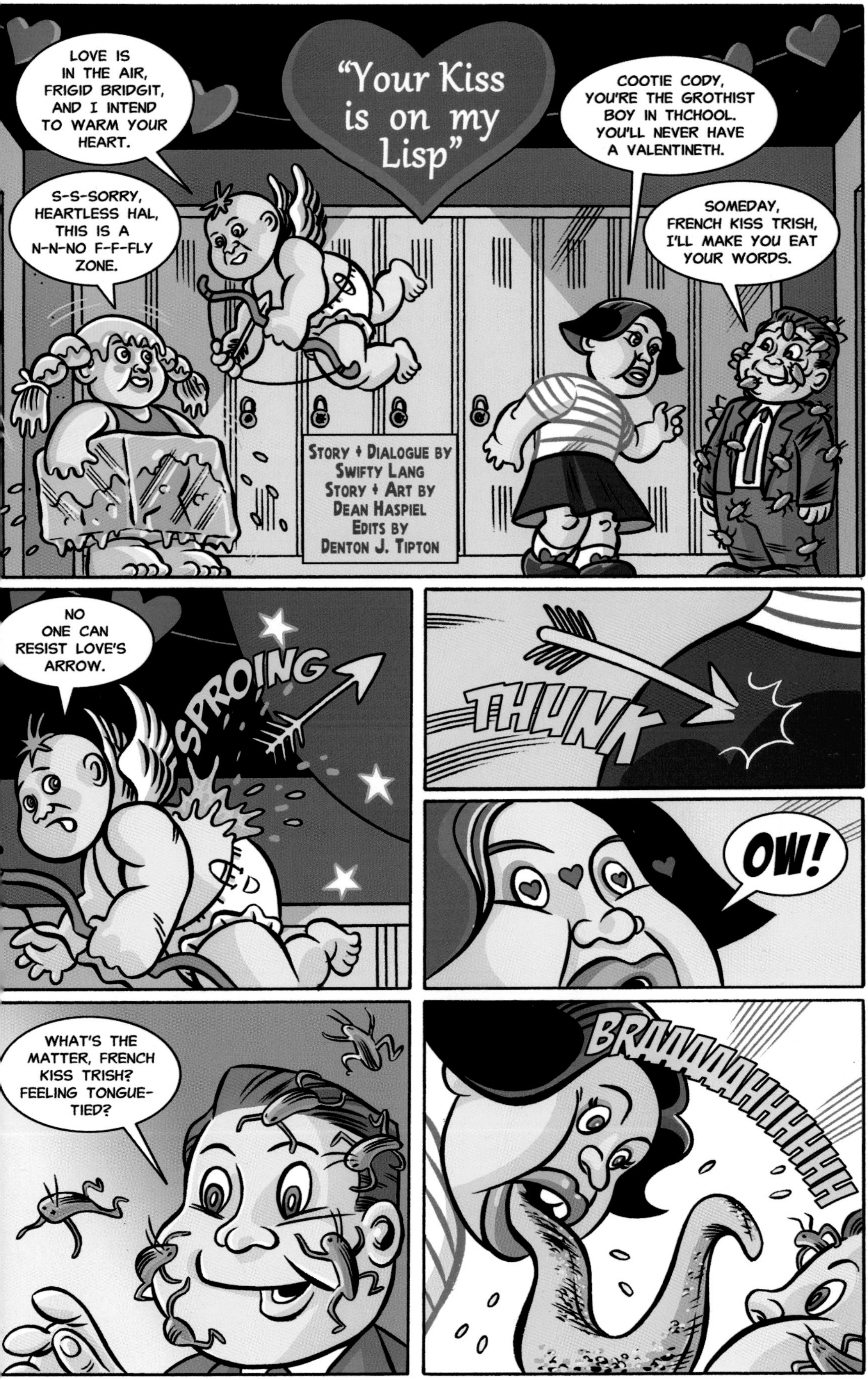
"Your Kiss is on my Lisp"
LOVE IS IN THE AIR, FRIGID BRIDGIT, AND I INTEND TO WARM YOUR HEART.
S-S-SORRY, HEARTLESS HAL, THIS IS A N-N-NO F-F-FLY ZONE.
COOTIE CODY, YOU'RE THE GROTHIST BOY IN THCHOOL. YOU'LL NEVER HAVE A VALENTINETH.
SOMEDAY, FRENCH KISS TRISH, I'LL MAKE YOU EAT YOUR WORDS.
STORY + DIALOGUE BY SWIFTY LANG
STORY + ART BY DEAN HASPIEL
EDITS BY DENTON J. TIPTON
NO ONE CAN RESIST LOVE'S ARROW.
SPROING
THUNK
OW!
WHAT'S THE MATTER, FRENCH KISS TRISH? FEELING TONGUE-TIED?
BRAAAAAHHHHHH

--GUESS LUST IS BLIND, TOO.

SLIIIIITHP

THEEEWWWP

WOAH! L-L-LOOK AT CODY. IF HE WAS M-M-MY TYPE, HE'D S-S-SURE M-M-MAKE ME THAW.

TING

I CAN'T CONTROL LOVE'S PATH, BUT AT LEAST I KNOW IT STILL FLOWS.

OH MY GAWD, COOTIE CODY'S A REAL HEART-THROB!

I THOULD'VE KEPT MY MOUTH THUT!

Y-Y-YOU SHOULD P-P-PUT S-S-SOME ICE ON TH-TH-THAT.

SHAGGIE AGGIE?

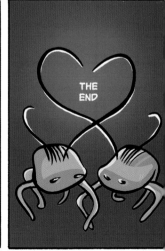

THE END

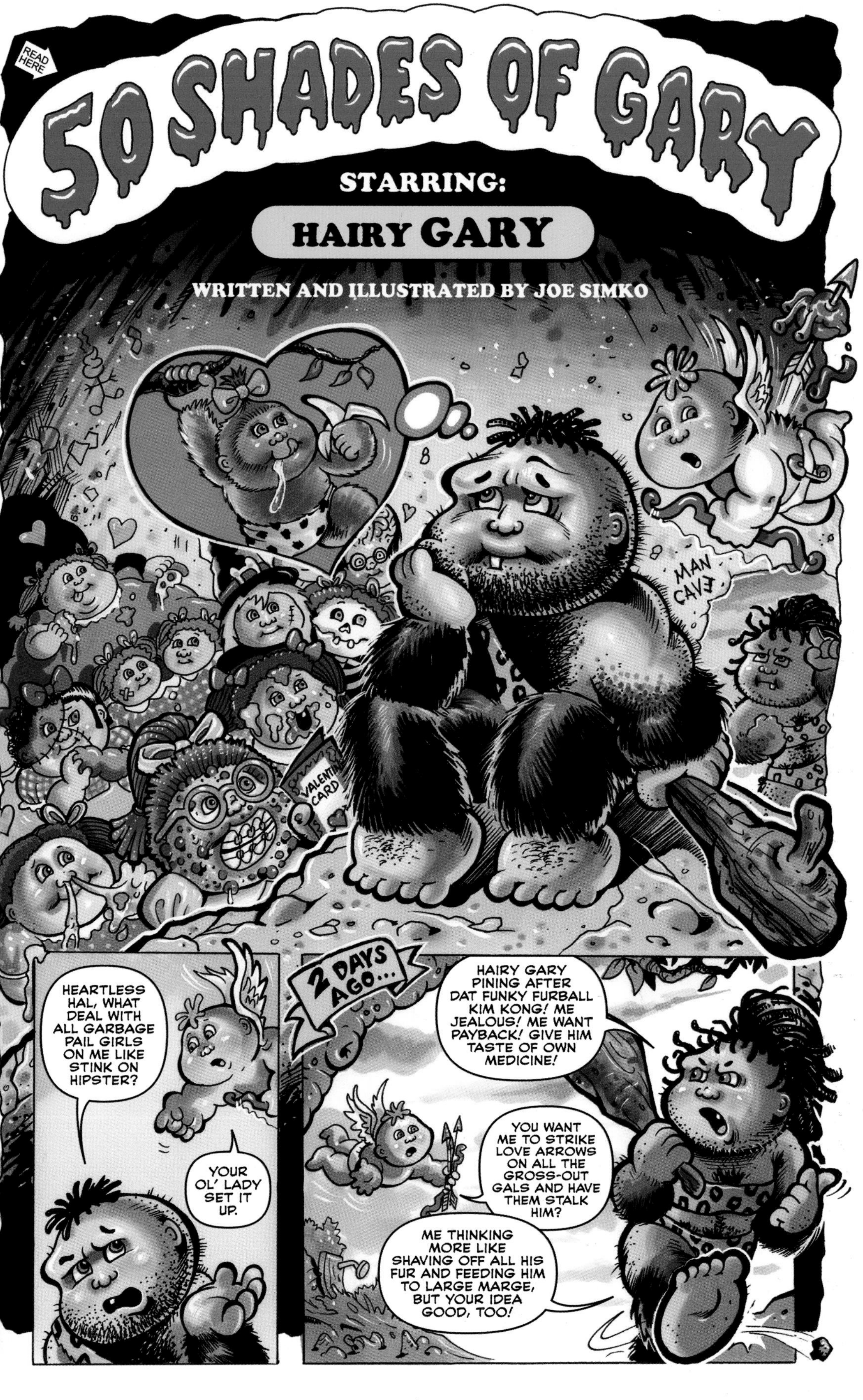
READ HERE
50 SHADES OF GARY
STARRING:
HAIRY GARY
WRITTEN AND ILLUSTRATED BY JOE SIMKO
B
MAN CAVE
VALENTINE CARD
HEARTLESS HAL, WHAT DEAL WITH ALL GARBAGE PAIL GIRLS ON ME LIKE STINK ON HIPSTER?
YOUR OL' LADY SET IT UP.
2 DAYS AGO...
HAIRY GARY PINING AFTER DAT FUNKY FURBALL KIM KONG! ME JEALOUS! ME WANT PAYBACK! GIVE HIM TASTE OF OWN MEDICINE!
YOU WANT ME TO STRIKE LOVE ARROWS ON ALL THE GROSS-OUT GALS AND HAVE THEM STALK HIM?
ME THINKING MORE LIKE SHAVING OFF ALL HIS FUR AND FEEDING HIM TO LARGE MARGE, BUT YOUR IDEA GOOD, TOO!

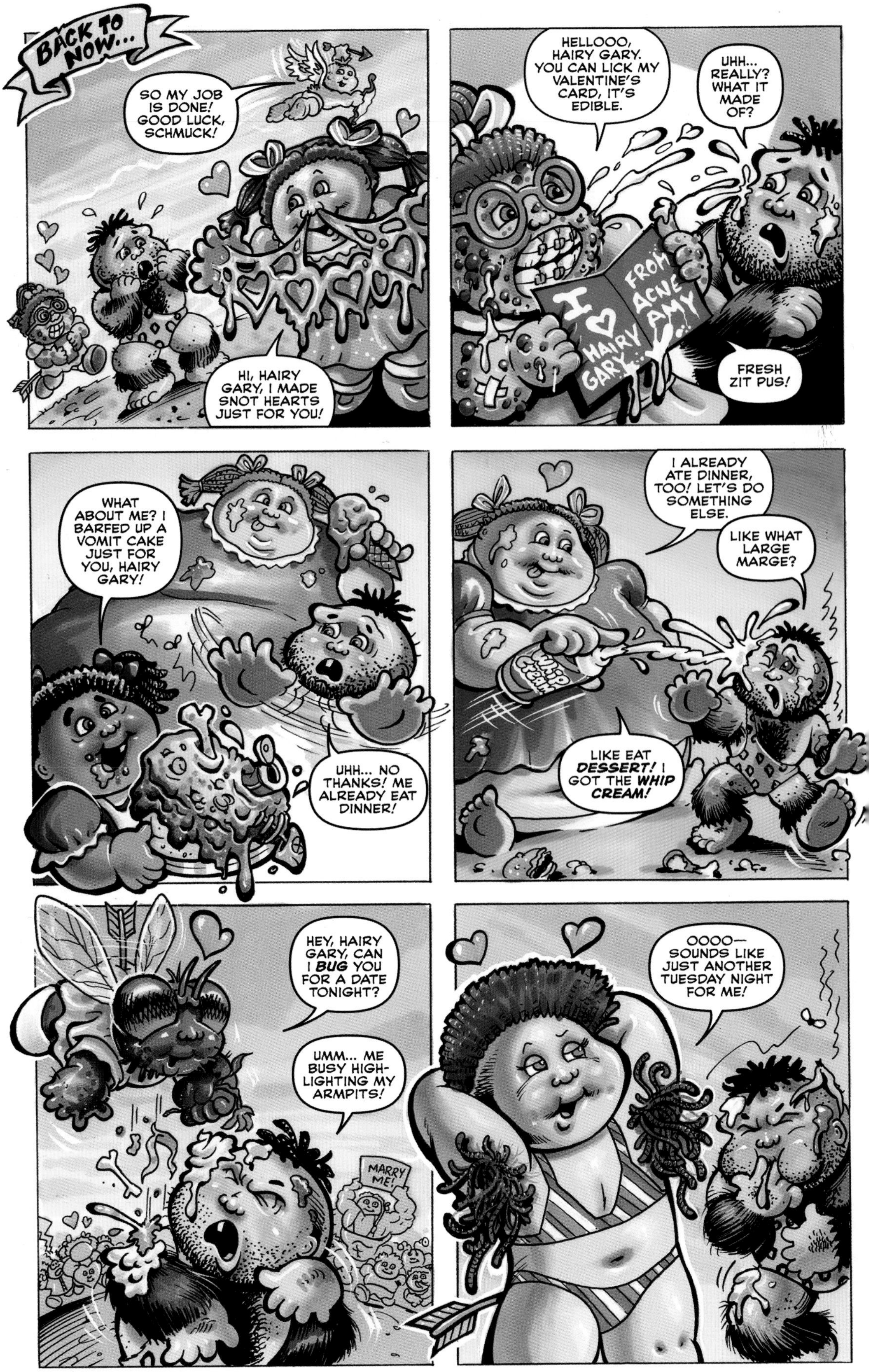
BACK TO NOW...
SO MY JOB IS DONE! GOOD LUCK, SCHMUCK!
HI, HAIRY GARY, I MADE SNOT HEARTS JUST FOR YOU!
HELLOOO, HAIRY GARY. YOU CAN LICK MY VALENTINE'S CARD, IT'S EDIBLE.
UHH... REALLY? WHAT IT MADE OF?
I ♥ HAIRY GARY...
FROM ACNE AMY
FRESH ZIT PUS!
WHAT ABOUT ME? I BARFED UP A VOMIT CAKE JUST FOR YOU, HAIRY GARY!
UHH... NO THANKS! ME ALREADY EAT DINNER!
I ALREADY ATE DINNER, TOO! LET'S DO SOMETHING ELSE.
LIKE WHAT LARGE MARGE?
WHIP CREAM
LIKE EAT **DESSERT!** I GOT THE **WHIP CREAM!**
HEY, HAIRY GARY, CAN I **BUG** YOU FOR A DATE TONIGHT?
UMM... ME BUSY HIGH-LIGHTING MY ARMPITS!
MARRY ME!
OOOO— SOUNDS LIKE JUST ANOTHER TUESDAY NIGHT FOR ME!

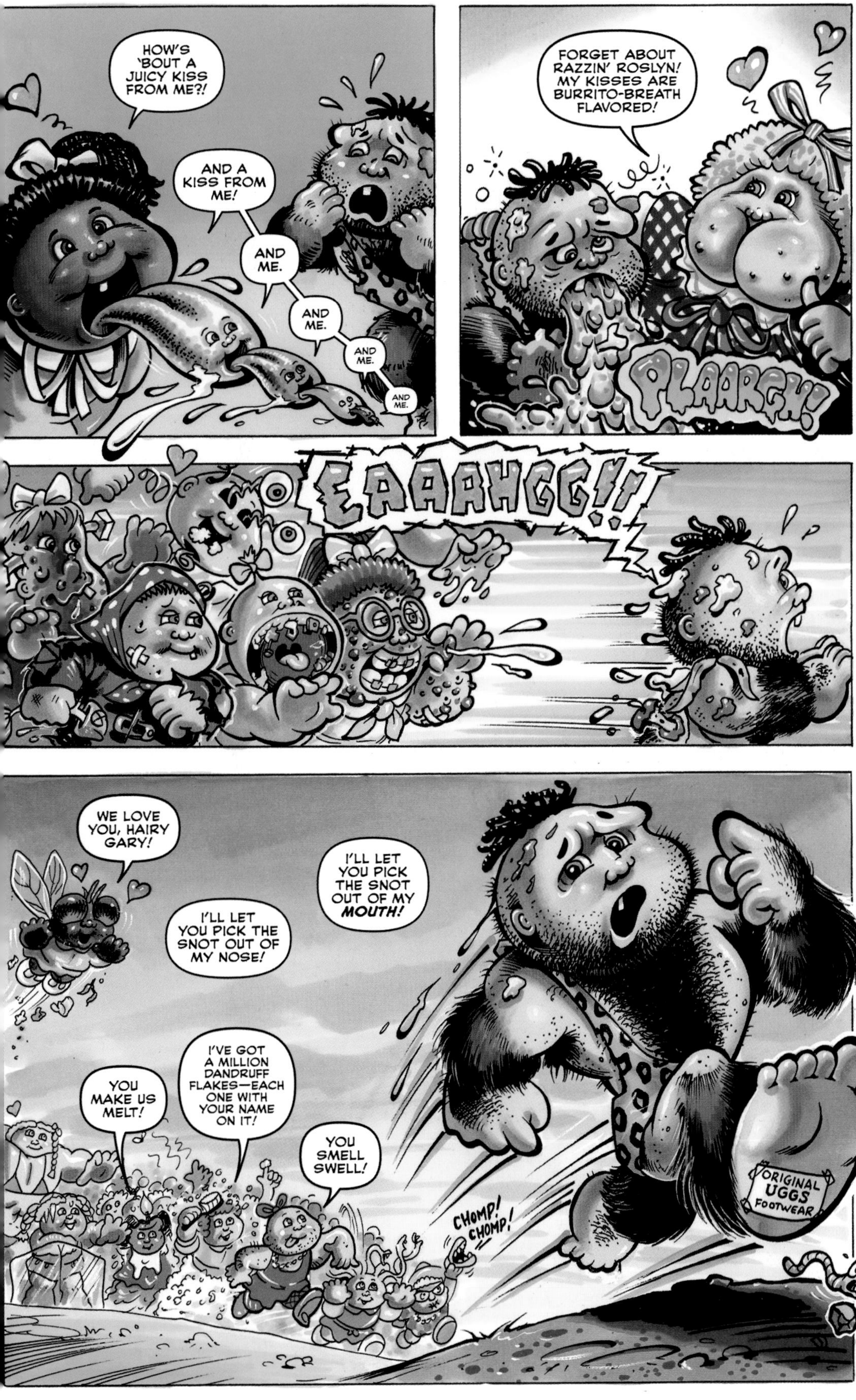
HOW'S 'BOUT A JUICY KISS FROM ME?!
AND A KISS FROM ME!
AND ME.
AND ME.
AND ME.
AND ME.
FORGET ABOUT RAZZIN' ROSLYN! MY KISSES ARE BURRITO-BREATH FLAVORED!
PLAARGH!
EAAAHGG!!
WE LOVE YOU, HAIRY GARY!
I'LL LET YOU PICK THE SNOT OUT OF MY NOSE!
I'LL LET YOU PICK THE SNOT OUT OF MY *MOUTH!*
YOU MAKE US MELT!
I'VE GOT A MILLION DANDRUFF FLAKES—EACH ONE WITH YOUR NAME ON IT!
YOU SMELL SWELL!
CHOMP! CHOMP!
ORIGINAL UGGS FOOTWEAR

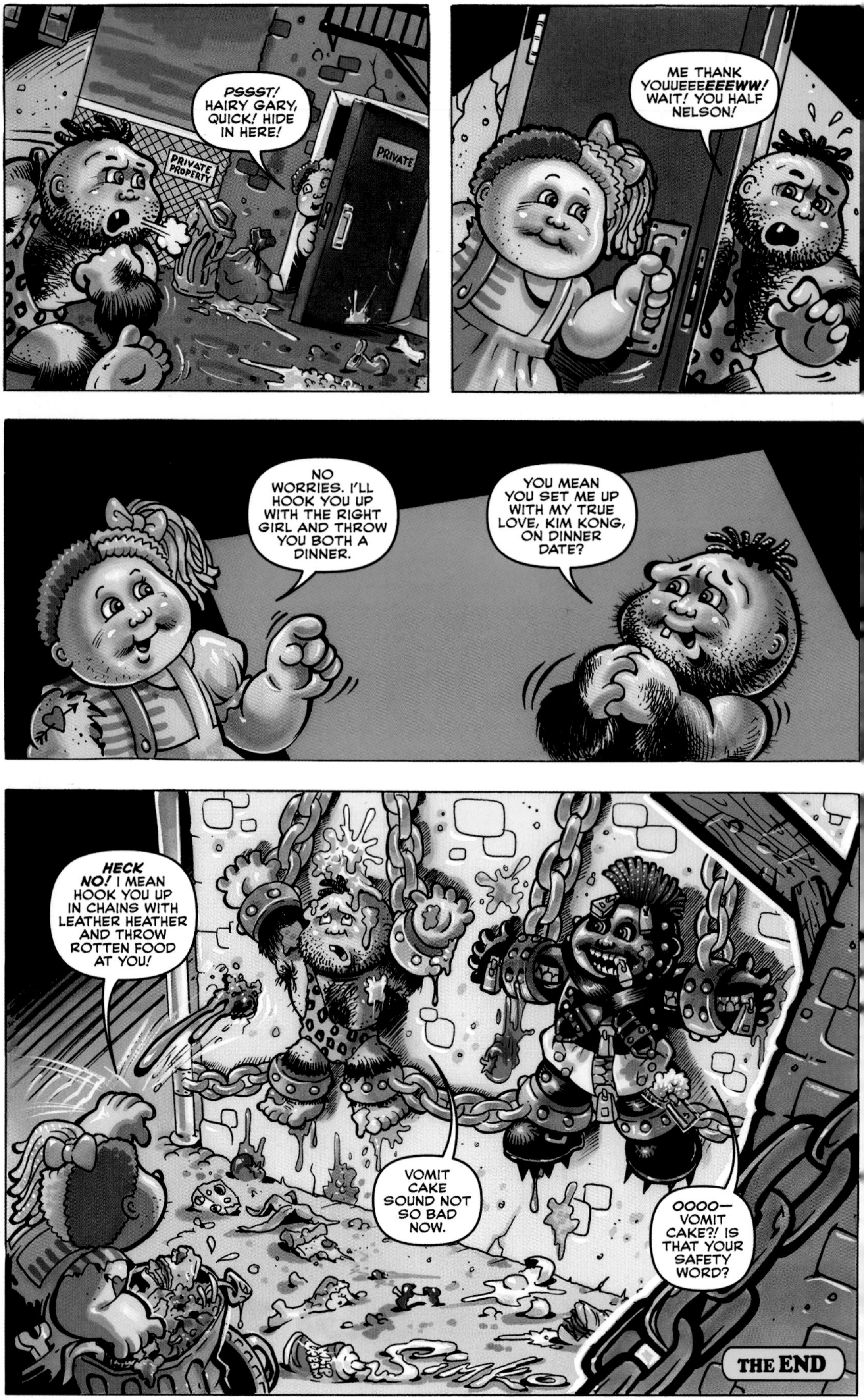
PSSST! HAIRY GARY, QUICK! HIDE IN HERE!
PRIVATE PROPERTY
PRIVATE
ME THANK YOUUEEEEEEWW! WAIT! YOU HALF NELSON!
NO WORRIES. I'LL HOOK YOU UP WITH THE RIGHT GIRL AND THROW YOU BOTH A DINNER.
YOU MEAN YOU SET ME UP WITH MY TRUE LOVE, KIM KONG, ON DINNER DATE?
HECK NO! I MEAN HOOK YOU UP IN CHAINS WITH LEATHER HEATHER AND THROW ROTTEN FOOD AT YOU!
VOMIT CAKE SOUND NOT SO BAD NOW.
OOOO— VOMIT CAKE?! IS THAT YOUR SAFETY WORD?
SIMKO
THE END

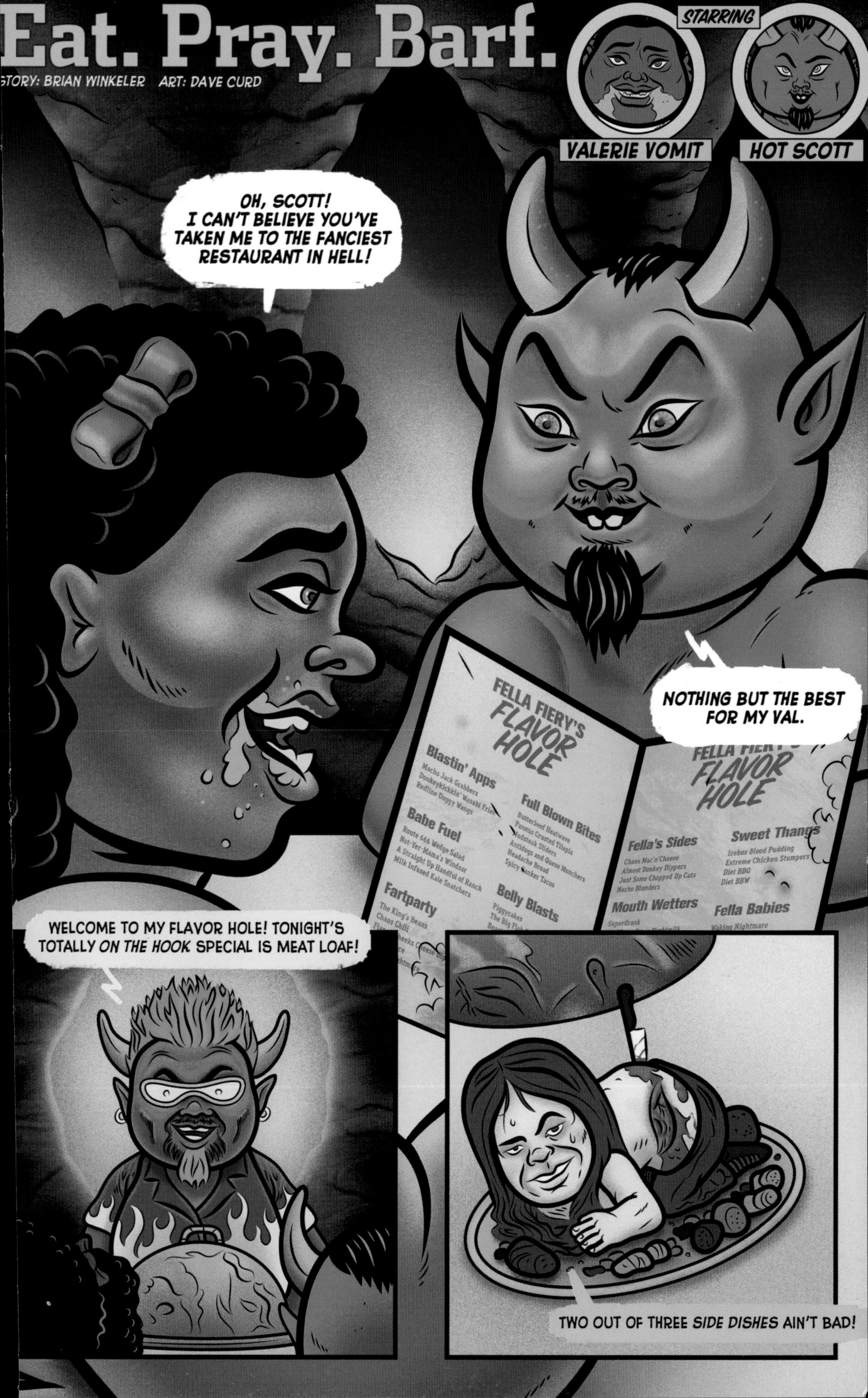
Eat. Pray. Barf.
STORY: BRIAN WINKELER ART: DAVE CURD
STARRING
VALERIE VOMIT
HOT SCOTT
OH, SCOTT! I CAN'T BELIEVE YOU'VE TAKEN ME TO THE FANCIEST RESTAURANT IN HELL!
NOTHING BUT THE BEST FOR MY VAL.
FELLA FIERY'S FLAVOR HOLE
Blastin' Apps
Full Blown Bites
Babe Fuel
Fartparty
Belly Blasts
FLAVOR HOLE
Fella's Sides
Sweet Thangs
Mouth Wetters
Fella Babies
WELCOME TO MY FLAVOR HOLE! TONIGHT'S TOTALLY ON THE HOOK SPECIAL IS MEAT LOAF!
TWO OUT OF THREE SIDE DISHES AIN'T BAD!

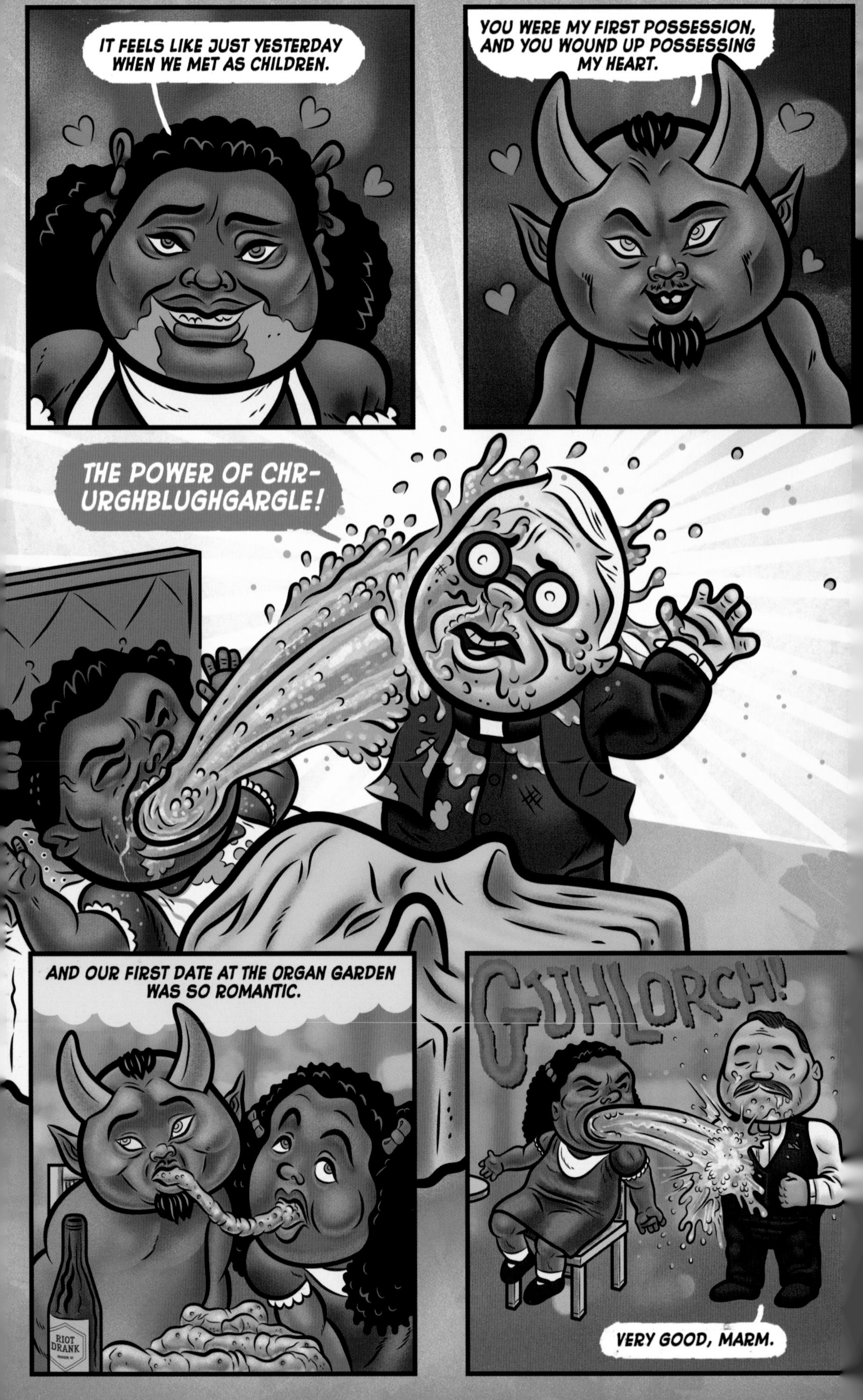
IT FEELS LIKE JUST YESTERDAY WHEN WE MET AS CHILDREN.
YOU WERE MY FIRST POSSESSION, AND YOU WOUND UP POSSESSING MY HEART.
THE POWER OF CHR-URGHBLUGHGARGLE!
AND OUR FIRST DATE AT THE ORGAN GARDEN WAS SO ROMANTIC.
RIOT DRANK
GUHLORCH!
VERY GOOD, MARM.

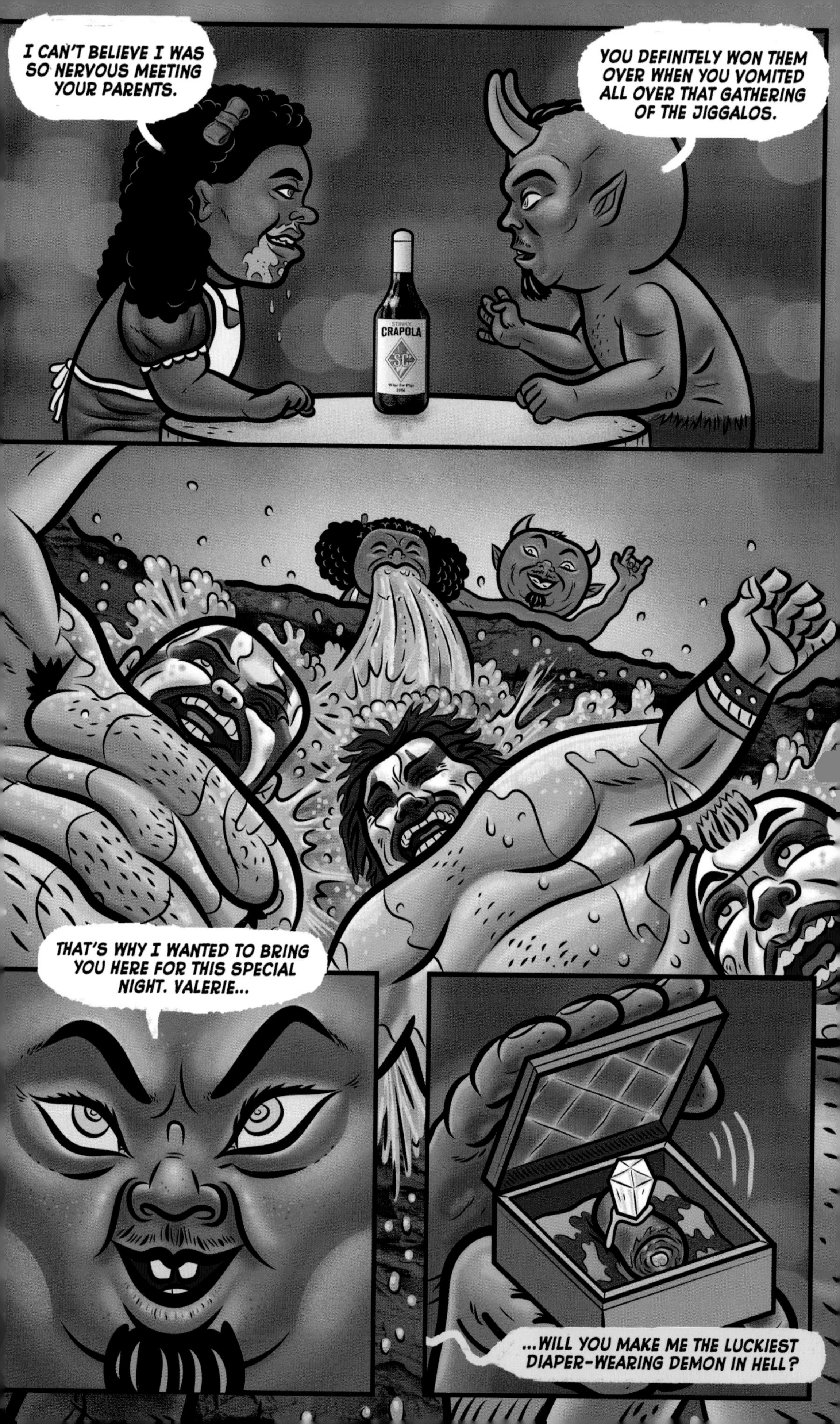
I CAN'T BELIEVE I WAS SO NERVOUS MEETING YOUR PARENTS.
YOU DEFINITELY WON THEM OVER WHEN YOU VOMITED ALL OVER THAT GATHERING OF THE JIGGALOS.
STINKY CRAPOLA
SC
Wine for Pigs 2006
THAT'S WHY I WANTED TO BRING YOU HERE FOR THIS SPECIAL NIGHT. VALERIE...
...WILL YOU MAKE ME THE LUCKIEST DIAPER-WEARING DEMON IN HELL?

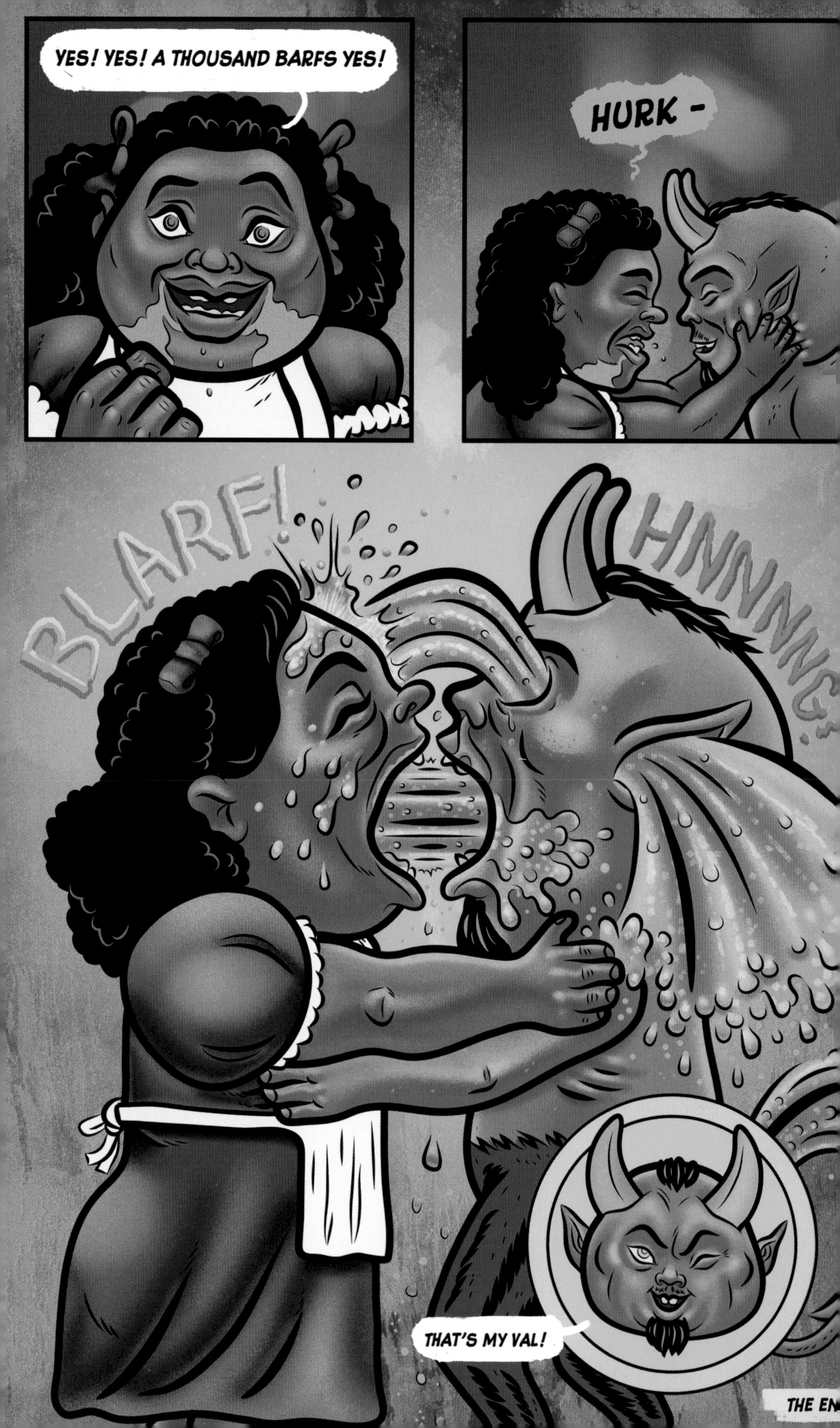
YES! YES! A THOUSAND BARFS YES!
HURK -
BLARF!
HNNNNNG!
THAT'S MY VAL!
THE EN

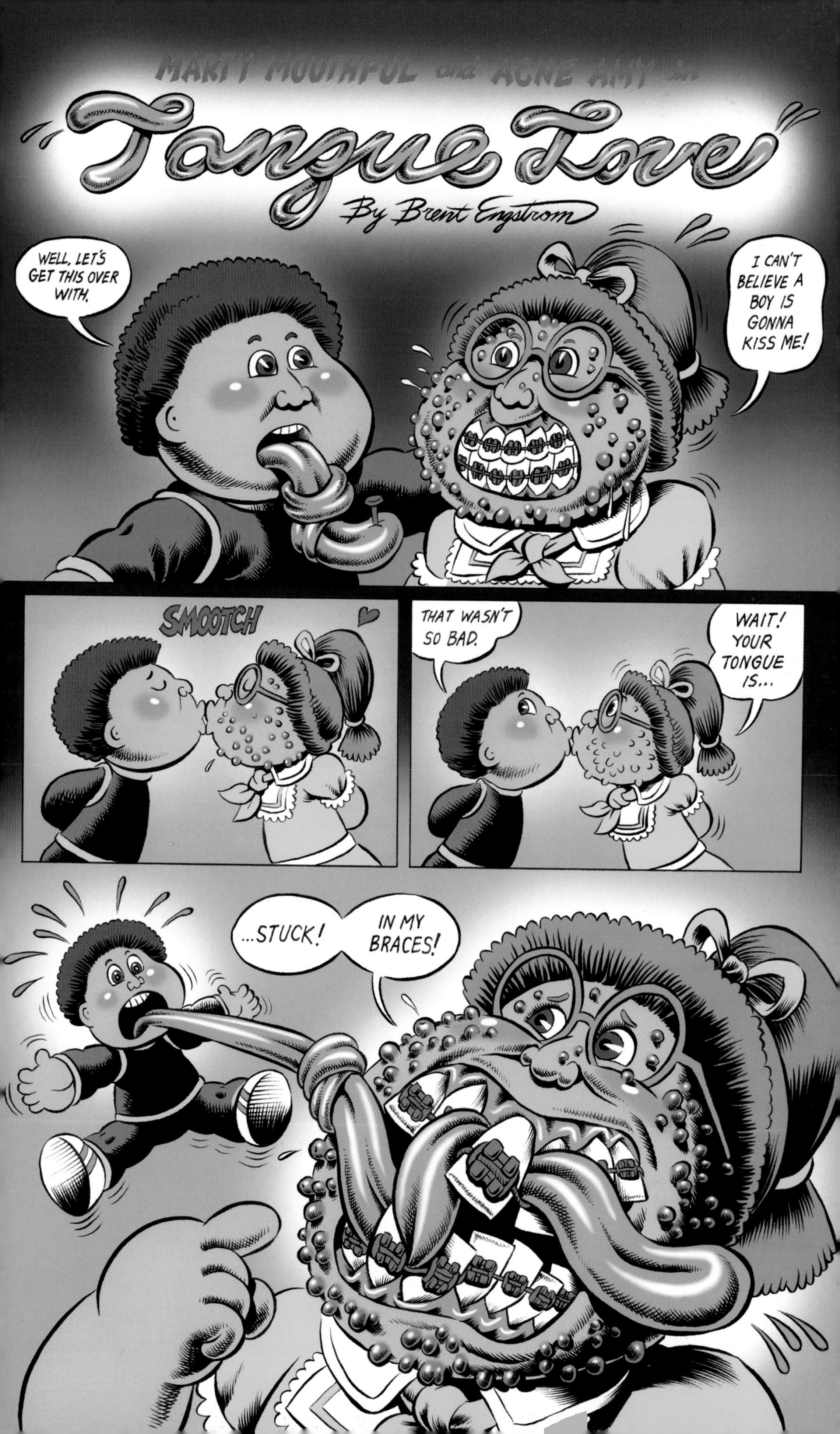
MARTY MOUTHFUL and ACNE AMY in
Tongue Love
By Brent Engstrom
WELL, LET'S GET THIS OVER WITH.
I CAN'T BELIEVE A BOY IS GONNA KISS ME!
SMOOTCH
THAT WASN'T SO BAD.
WAIT! YOUR TONGUE IS...
...STUCK!
IN MY BRACES!

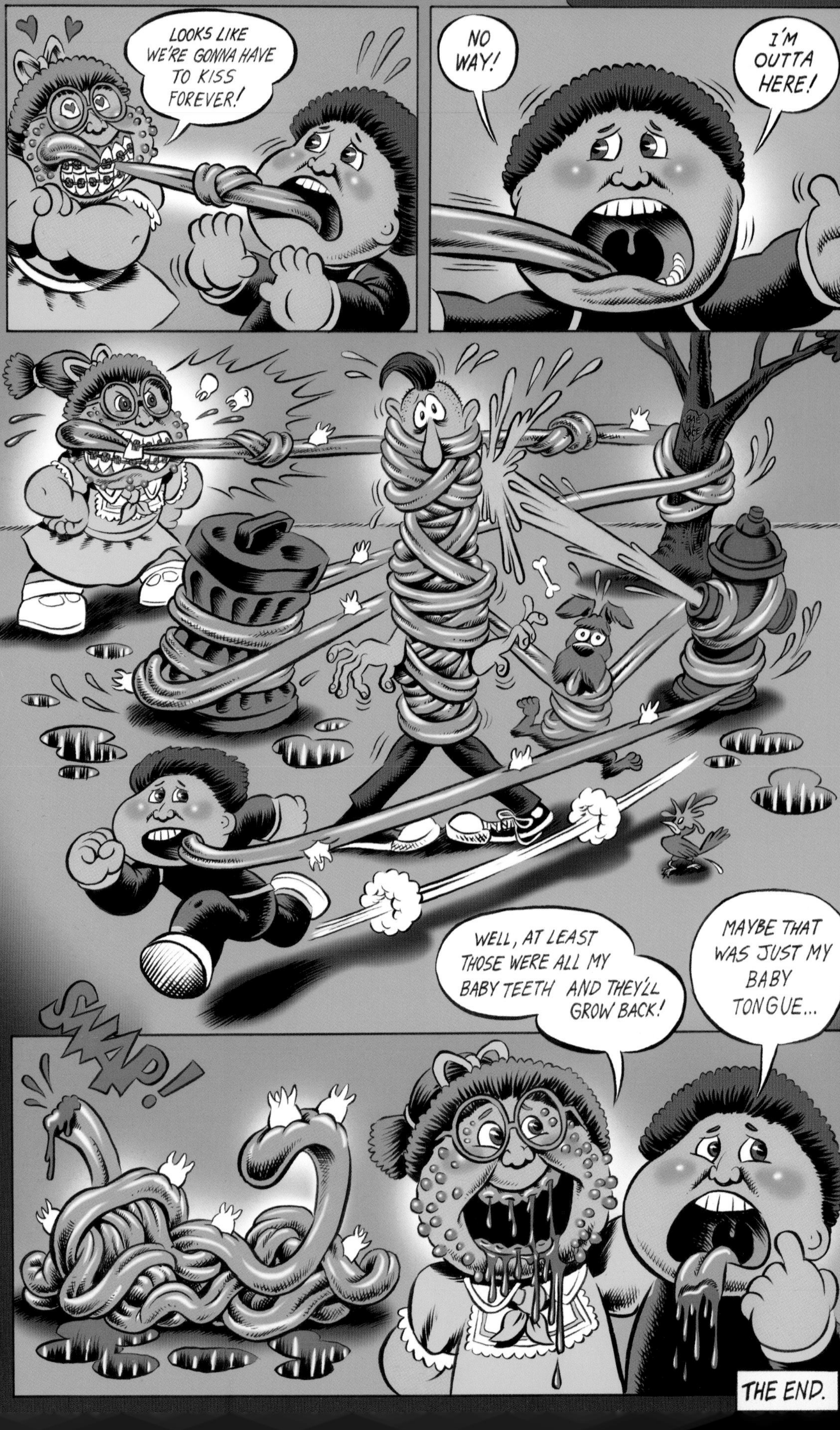
LOOKS LIKE WE'RE GONNA HAVE TO KISS FOREVER!
NO WAY!
I'M OUTTA HERE!
SNAP!
WELL, AT LEAST THOSE WERE ALL MY BABY TEETH AND THEY'LL GROW BACK!
MAYBE THAT WAS JUST MY BABY TONGUE...
THE END.

vertisement by MERRILY CHOPP and MIRAN KIM

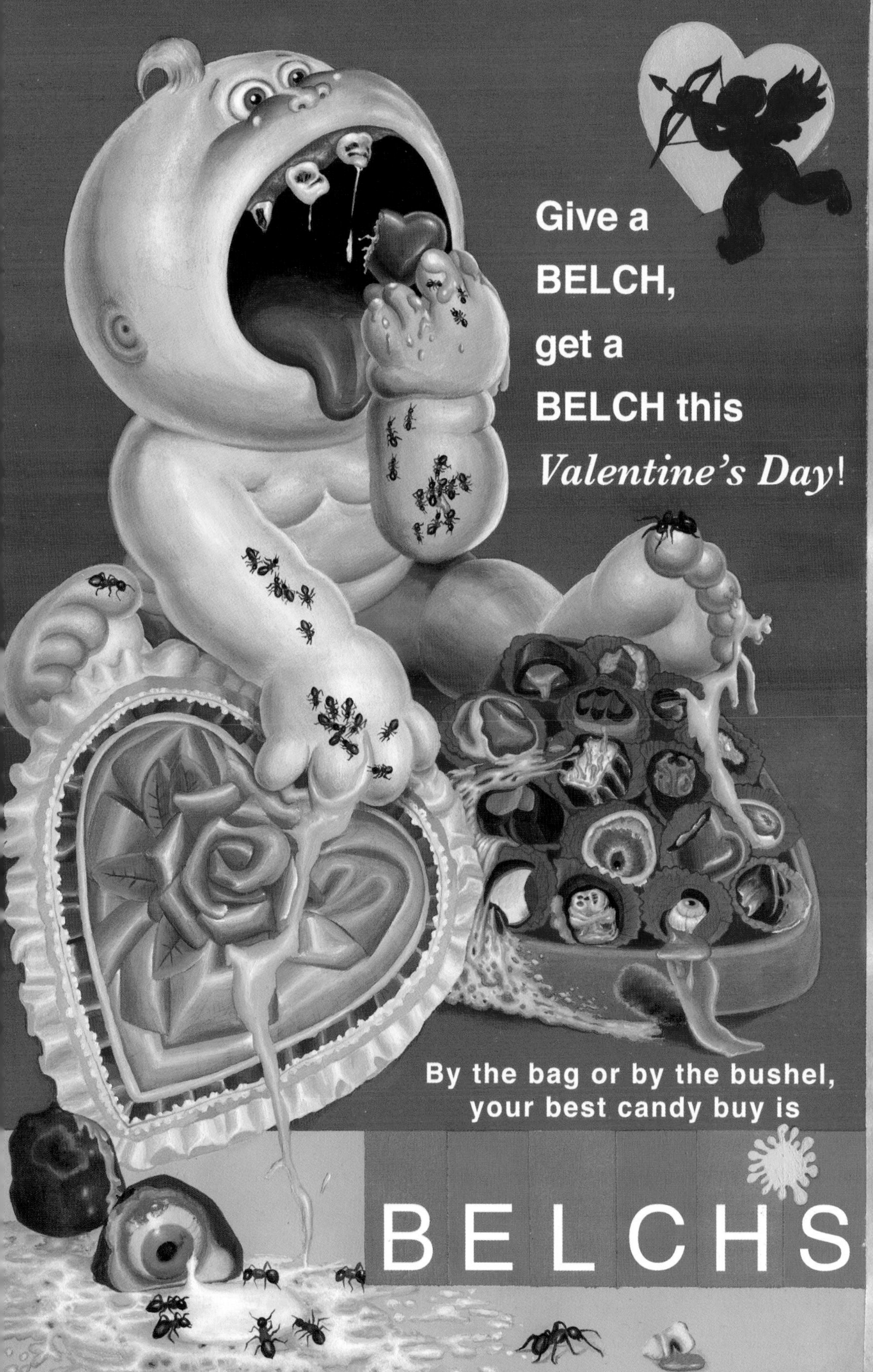
Give a
BELCH,
get a
BELCH this
Valentine's Day!
By the bag or by the bushel,
your best candy buy is
BELCHS

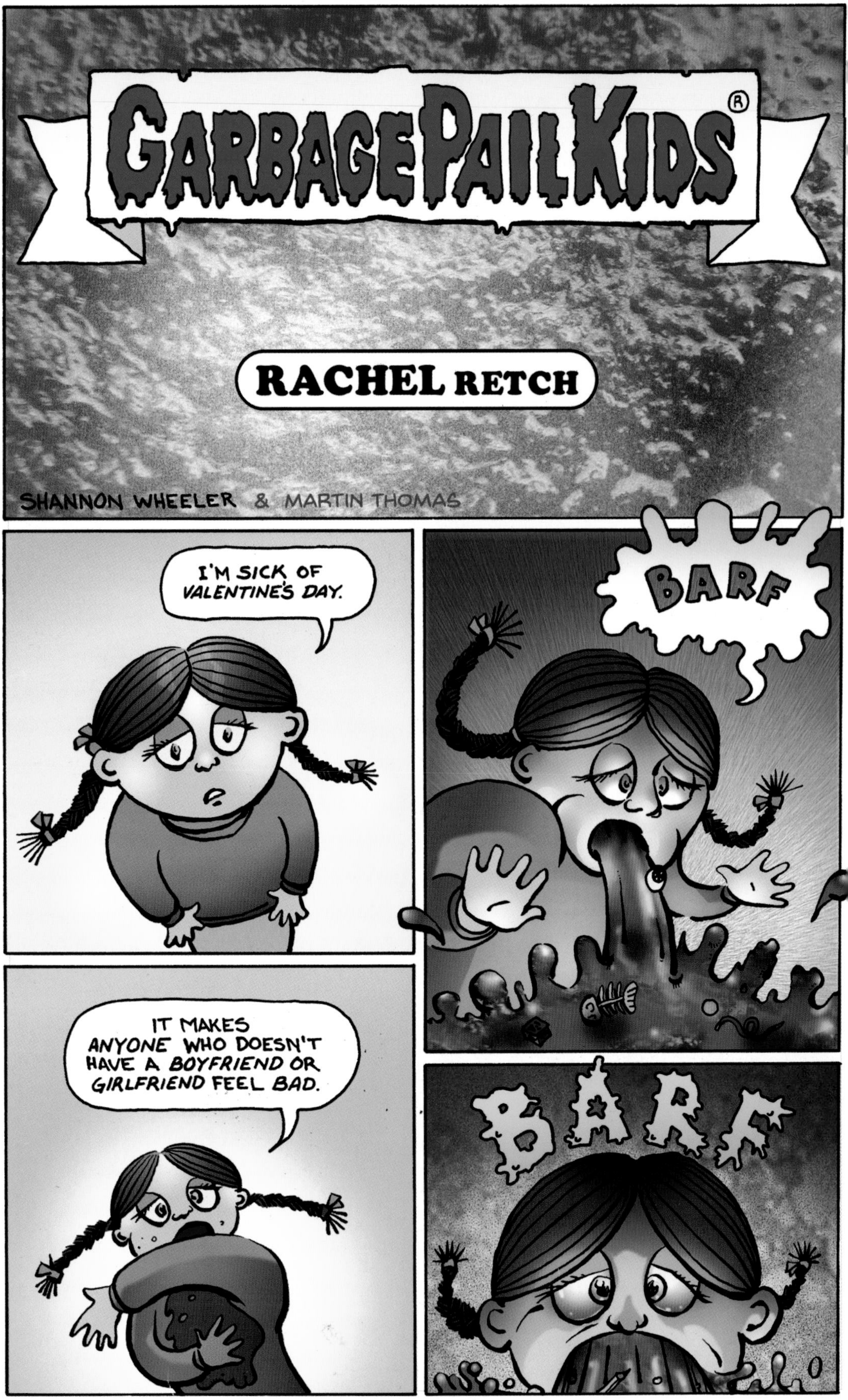
GARBAGE PAIL KIDS®
RACHEL RETCH
SHANNON WHEELER & MARTIN THOMAS
I'M SICK OF VALENTINE'S DAY.
BARF
IT MAKES ANYONE WHO DOESN'T HAVE A *BOYFRIEND* OR GIRLFRIEND FEEL BAD.
BARF

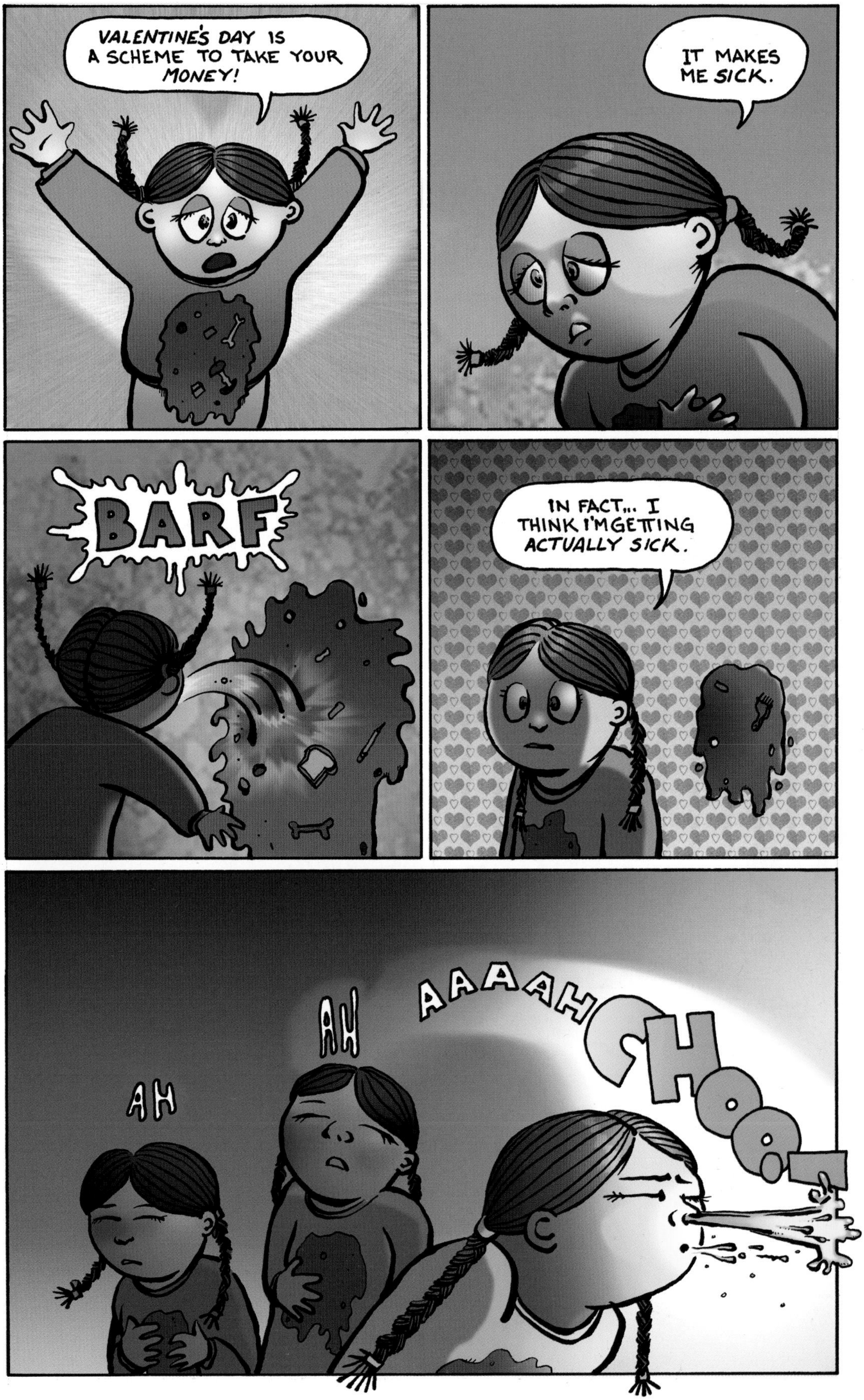
VALENTINE'S DAY IS A SCHEME TO TAKE YOUR MONEY!
IT MAKES ME SICK.
BARF
IN FACT... I THINK I'M GETTING ACTUALLY SICK.
AH
AH
AAAAHCHOO!

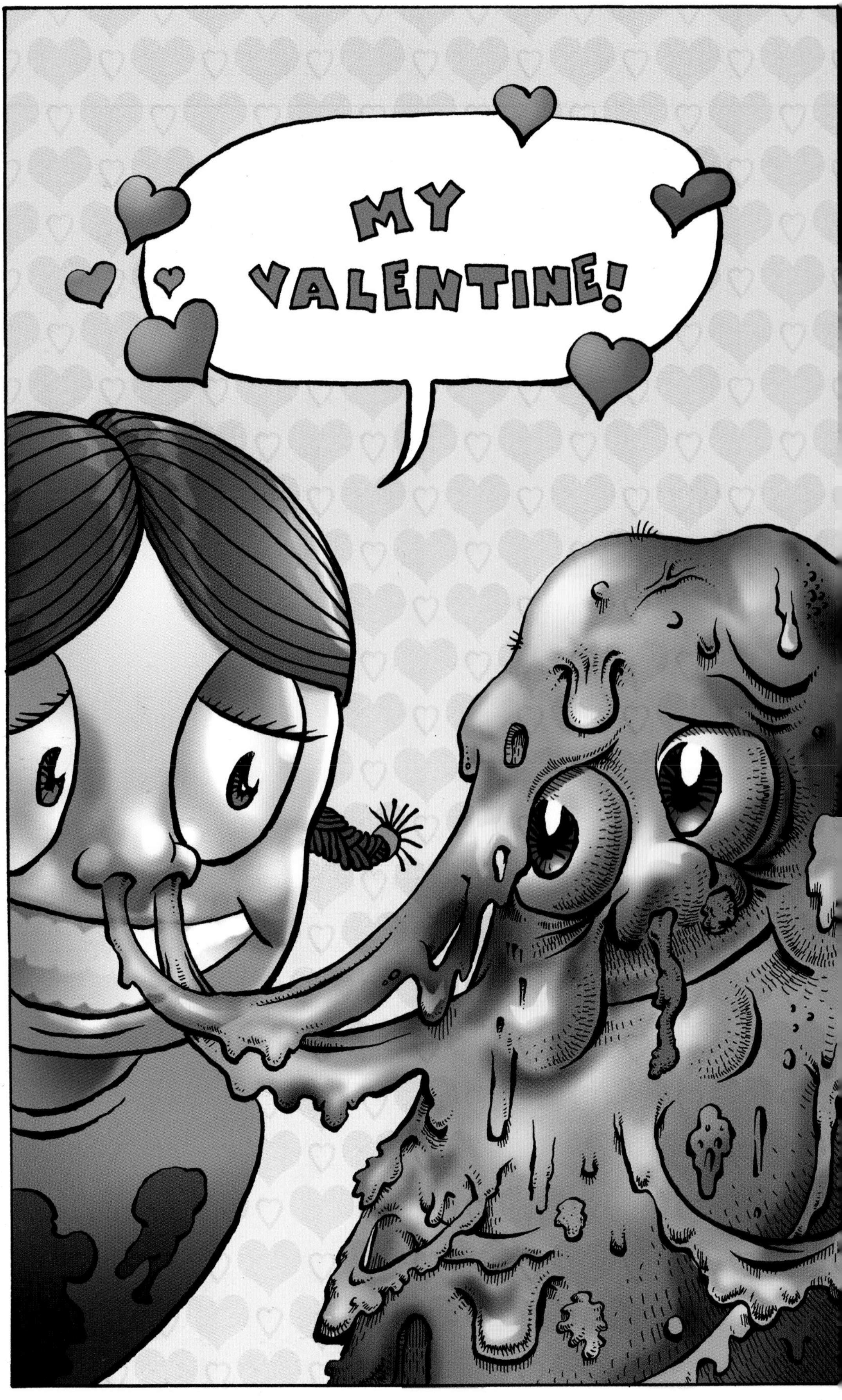
MY VALENTINE!

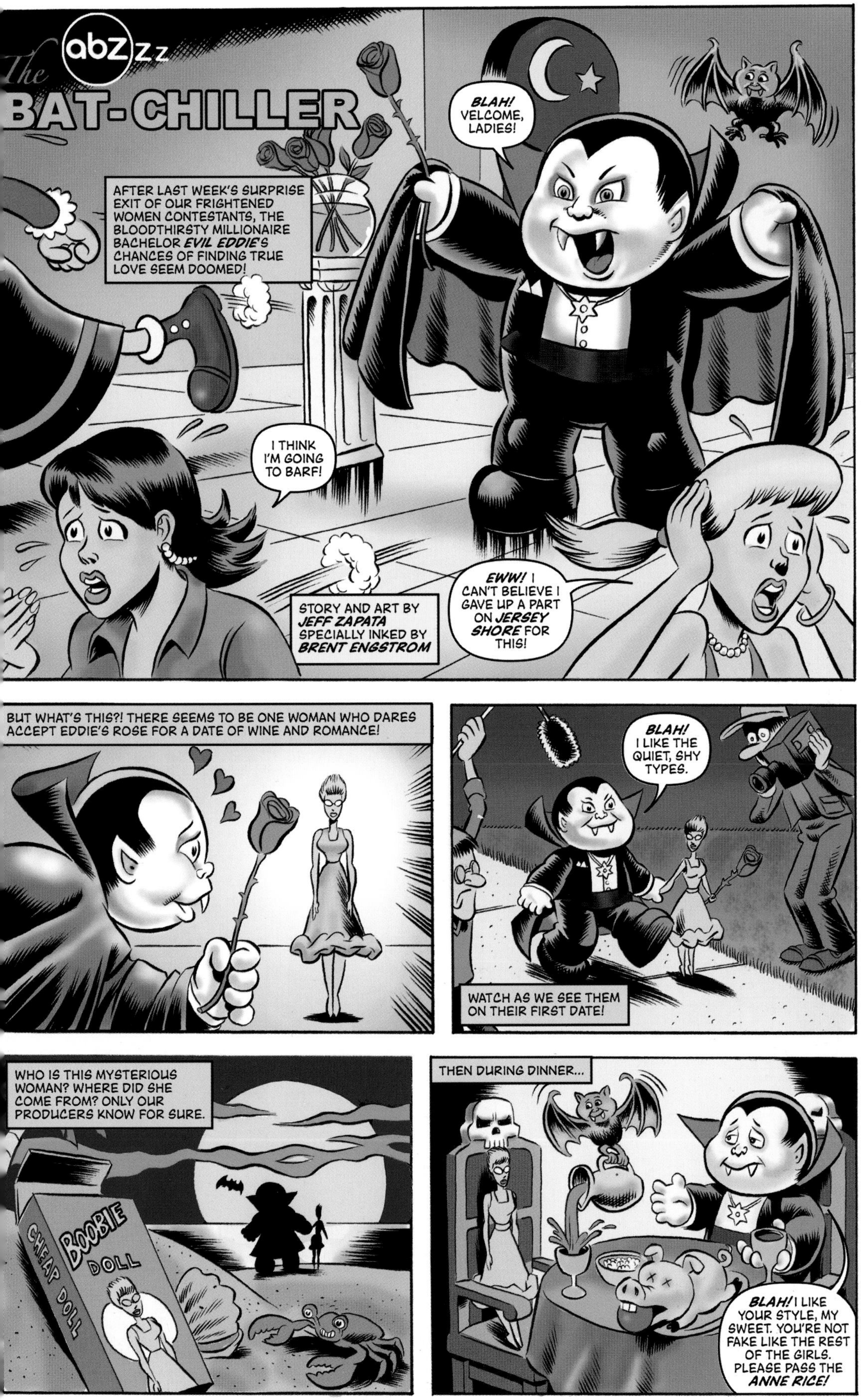
abzzz
The BAT-CHILLER
AFTER LAST WEEK'S SURPRISE EXIT OF OUR FRIGHTENED WOMEN CONTESTANTS, THE BLOODTHIRSTY MILLIONAIRE BACHELOR EVIL EDDIE'S CHANCES OF FINDING TRUE LOVE SEEM DOOMED!
BLAH! VELCOME, LADIES!
I THINK I'M GOING TO BARF!
STORY AND ART BY JEFF ZAPATA SPECIALLY INKED BY BRENT ENGSTROM
EWW! I CAN'T BELIEVE I GAVE UP A PART ON JERSEY SHORE FOR THIS!
BUT WHAT'S THIS?! THERE SEEMS TO BE ONE WOMAN WHO DARES ACCEPT EDDIE'S ROSE FOR A DATE OF WINE AND ROMANCE!
BLAH! I LIKE THE QUIET, SHY TYPES.
WATCH AS WE SEE THEM ON THEIR FIRST DATE!
WHO IS THIS MYSTERIOUS WOMAN? WHERE DID SHE COME FROM? ONLY OUR PRODUCERS KNOW FOR SURE.
BOOBIE DOLL
CHEAP DOLL
THEN DURING DINNER...
BLAH! I LIKE YOUR STYLE, MY SWEET. YOU'RE NOT FAKE LIKE THE REST OF THE GIRLS. PLEASE PASS THE ANNE RICE!

FINALLY, THE LOVERS TAKE A MOONLIT STROLL BY A CEMETERY.

RIP DEAD TED

BLAH! I'M SO ENCHANTED BY YOU, MY LOVE!

I CAN'T HELP MYSELF! I MUST KISS YOU!

SMOOCH

SMOOCH

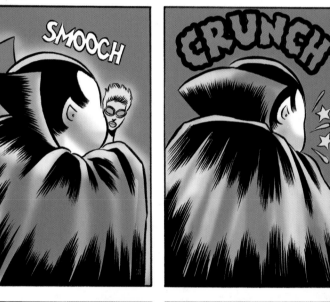

CRUNCH

I'VE HEARD OF PLASTIC SURGERY, BUT THIS IS RIDICULOUS!

SHE'S JUST A LIFELESS DOLL! I HATE THIS SHOW!

THOK!

WILL EDDIE EVER FIND TRUE LOVE? FIND OUT ON THE NEXT BAT-CHILLER!

≶SOB≶

THE END.

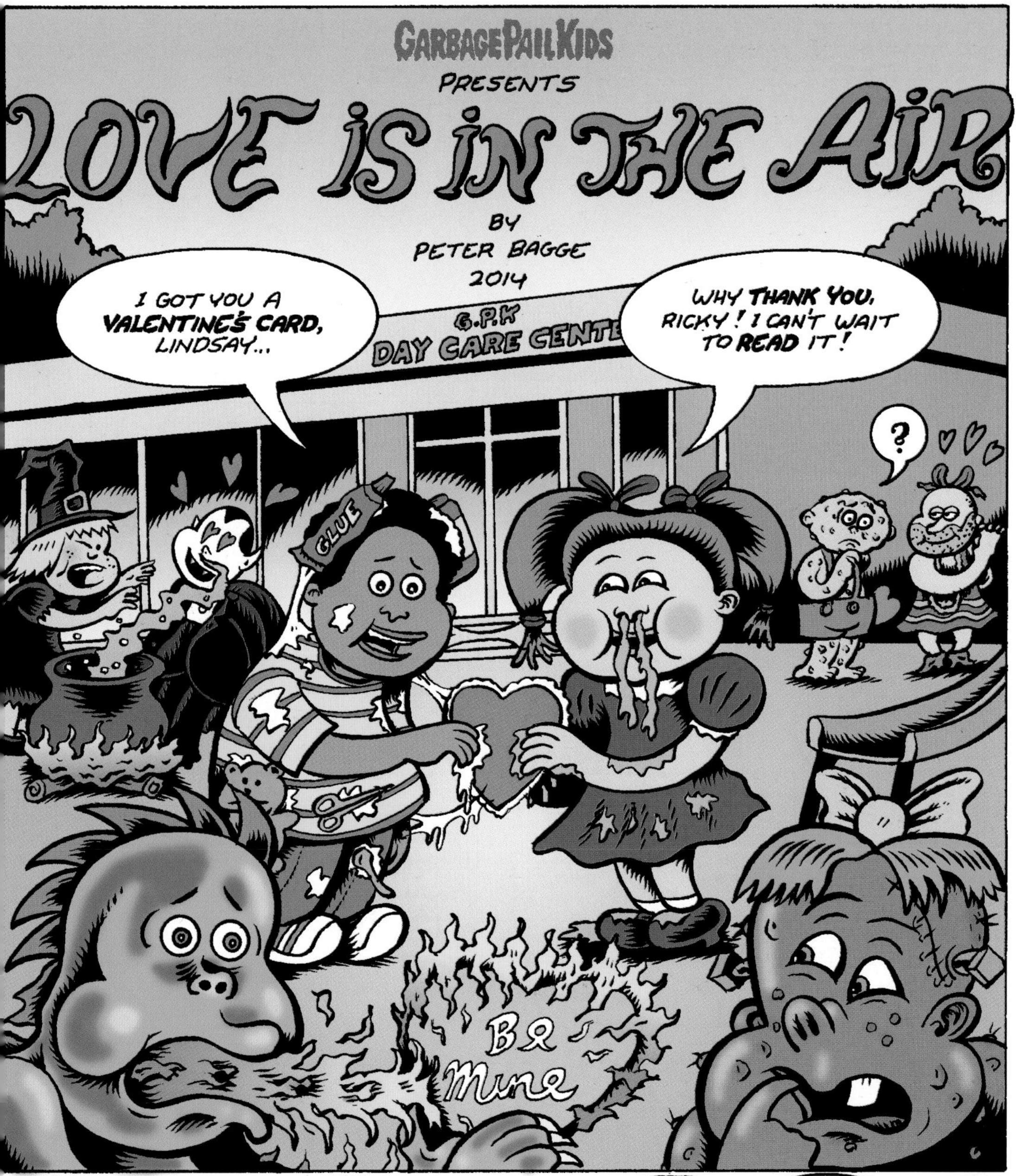
GARBAGE PAIL KIDS
PRESENTS
LOVE IS IN THE AIR
BY
PETER BAGGE
2014
I GOT YOU A VALENTINE'S CARD, LINDSAY...
G.P.K
DAY CARE CENTE
WHY THANK YOU, RICKY! I CAN'T WAIT TO READ IT!
?
GLUE
Be Mine

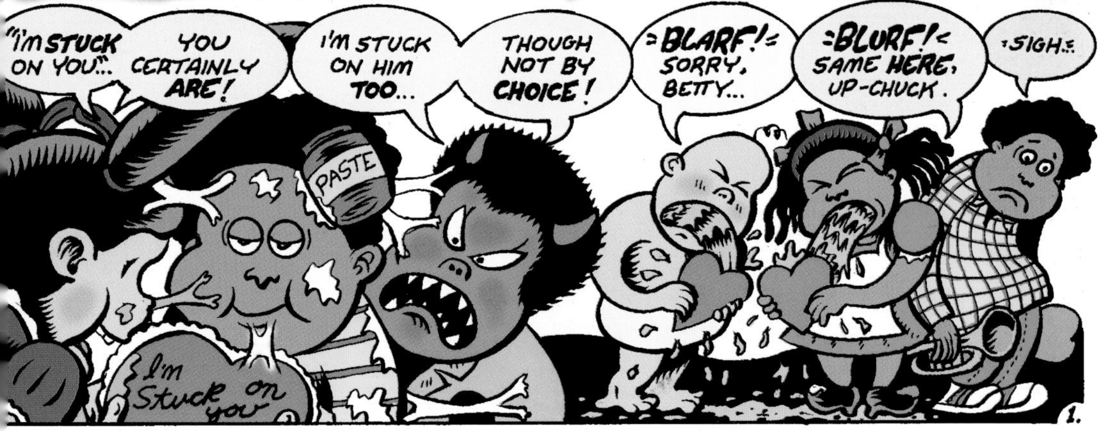
"I'M STUCK ON YOU"...
YOU CERTAINLY ARE!
I'M STUCK ON HIM TOO...
THOUGH NOT BY CHOICE!
BLARF! SORRY, BETTY...
BLURF! SAME HERE, UP-CHUCK.
SIGH
PASTE
I'm Stuck on you
1.

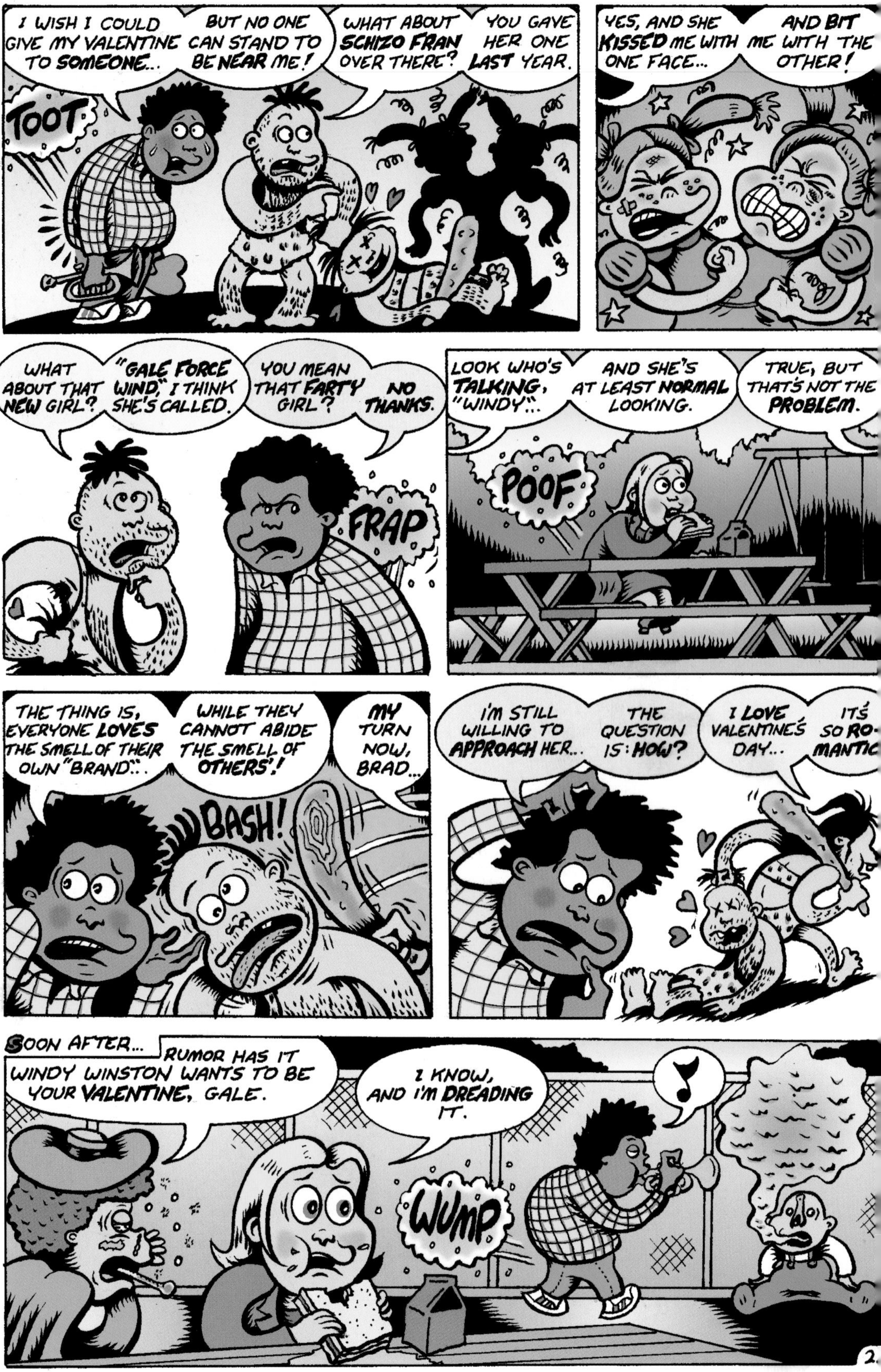
I WISH I COULD GIVE MY VALENTINE TO SOMEONE...
BUT NO ONE CAN STAND TO BE NEAR ME!
WHAT ABOUT SCHIZO FRAN OVER THERE?
YOU GAVE HER ONE LAST YEAR.
TOOT
YES, AND SHE KISSED ME WITH ONE FACE...
AND BIT ME WITH THE OTHER!
WHAT ABOUT THAT NEW GIRL?
"GALE FORCE WIND," I THINK SHE'S CALLED.
YOU MEAN THAT FARTY GIRL?
NO THANKS.
FRAP
LOOK WHO'S TALKING, "WINDY"...
AND SHE'S AT LEAST NORMAL LOOKING.
TRUE, BUT THAT'S NOT THE PROBLEM.
POOF
THE THING IS, EVERYONE LOVES THE SMELL OF THEIR OWN "BRAND"...
WHILE THEY CANNOT ABIDE THE SMELL OF OTHERS'!
MY TURN NOW, BRAD...
BASH!
I'M STILL WILLING TO APPROACH HER...
THE QUESTION IS: HOW?
I LOVE VALENTINE'S DAY...
IT'S SO RO-MANTIC
SOON AFTER...
RUMOR HAS IT WINDY WINSTON WANTS TO BE YOUR VALENTINE, GALE.
I KNOW, AND I'M DREADING IT.
WUMP
2

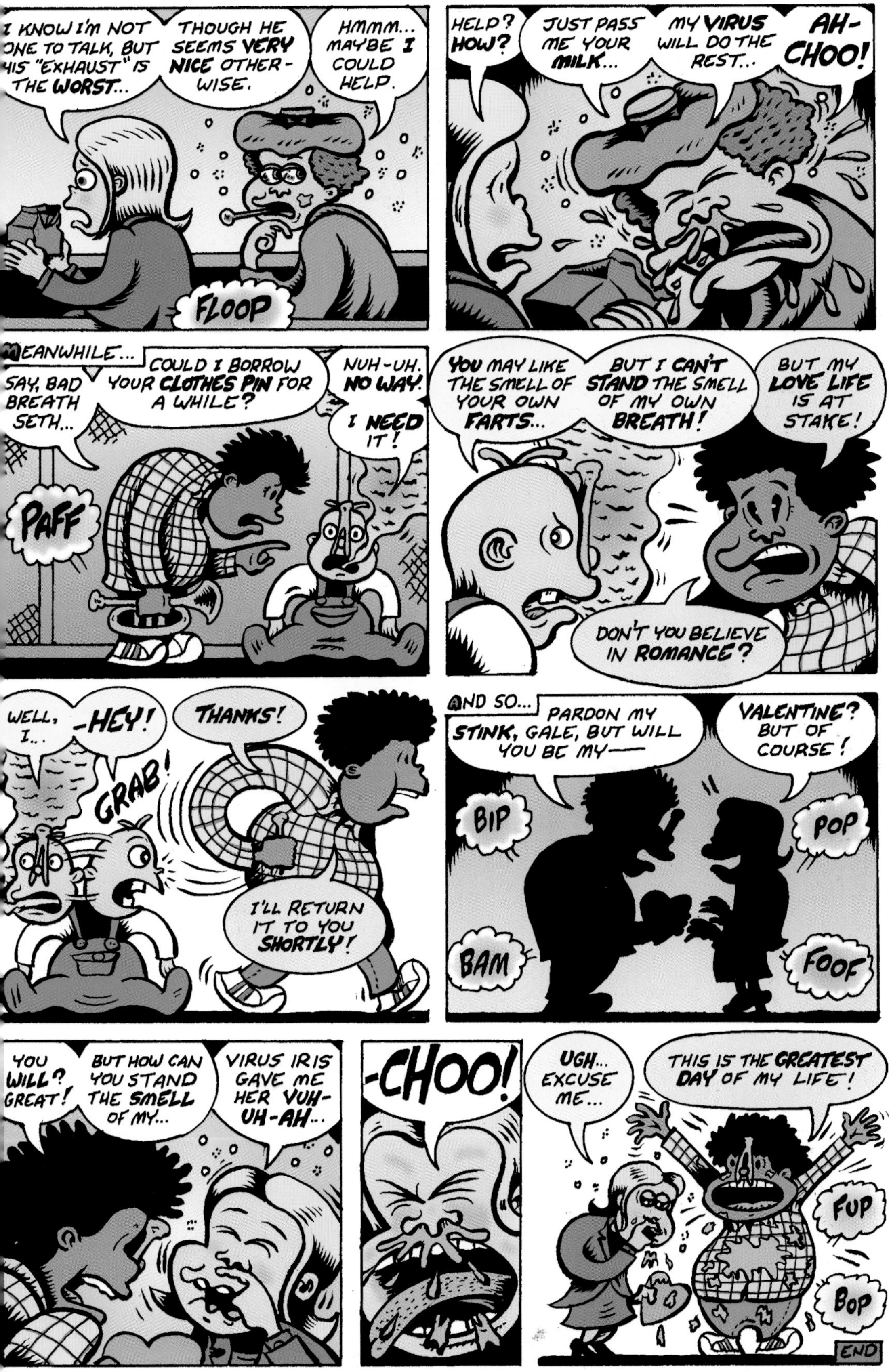
I KNOW I'M NOT ONE TO TALK, BUT HIS "EXHAUST" IS THE WORST...
THOUGH HE SEEMS VERY NICE OTHERWISE.
HMMM... MAYBE I COULD HELP.
FLOOP
HELP? HOW?
JUST PASS ME YOUR MILK...
MY VIRUS WILL DO THE REST...
AH-CHOO!
MEANWHILE...
SAY, BAD BREATH SETH...
COULD I BORROW YOUR CLOTHES PIN FOR A WHILE?
NUH-UH. NO WAY.
I NEED IT!
PAFF
YOU MAY LIKE THE SMELL OF YOUR OWN FARTS...
BUT I CAN'T STAND THE SMELL OF MY OWN BREATH!
BUT MY LOVE LIFE IS AT STAKE!
DON'T YOU BELIEVE IN ROMANCE?
WELL, I...
-HEY!
GRAB!
THANKS!
I'LL RETURN IT TO YOU SHORTLY!
AND SO...
PARDON MY STINK, GALE, BUT WILL YOU BE MY—
VALENTINE? BUT OF COURSE!
BIP
POP
BAM
FOOF
YOU WILL? GREAT!
BUT HOW CAN YOU STAND THE SMELL OF MY...
VIRUS IRIS GAVE ME HER VUH-UH-AH...
-CHOO!
UGH... EXCUSE ME...
THIS IS THE GREATEST DAY OF MY LIFE!
FUP
BOP
END

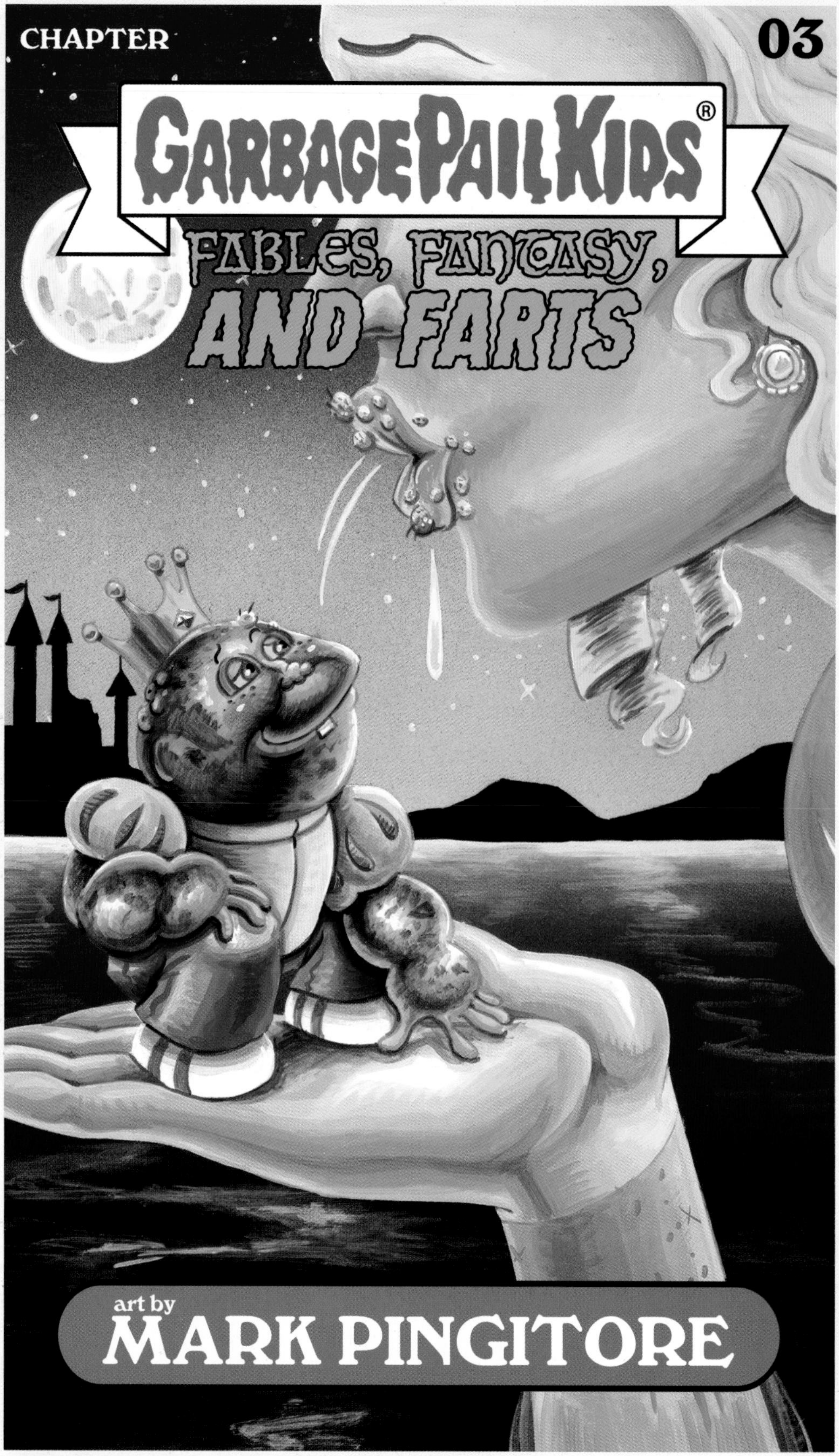
CHAPTER
03
GARBAGE PAIL KIDS®
FABLES, FANTASY, AND FARTS
art by
MARK PINGITORE

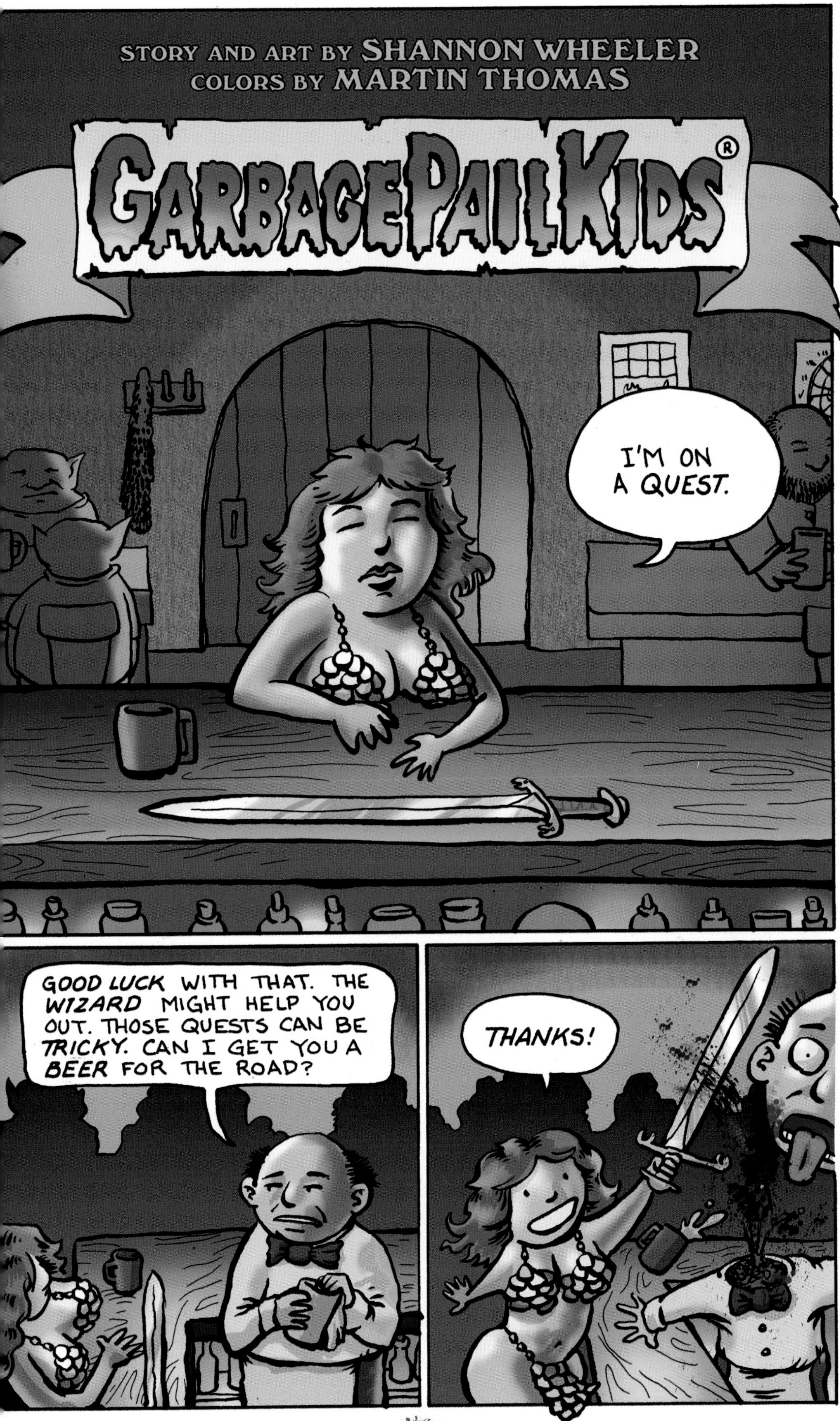
STORY AND ART BY SHANNON WHEELER
COLORS BY MARTIN THOMAS
GARBAGE PAIL KIDS®
I'M ON A QUEST.
GOOD LUCK WITH THAT. THE WIZARD MIGHT HELP YOU OUT. THOSE QUESTS CAN BE TRICKY. CAN I GET YOU A BEER FOR THE ROAD?
THANKS!

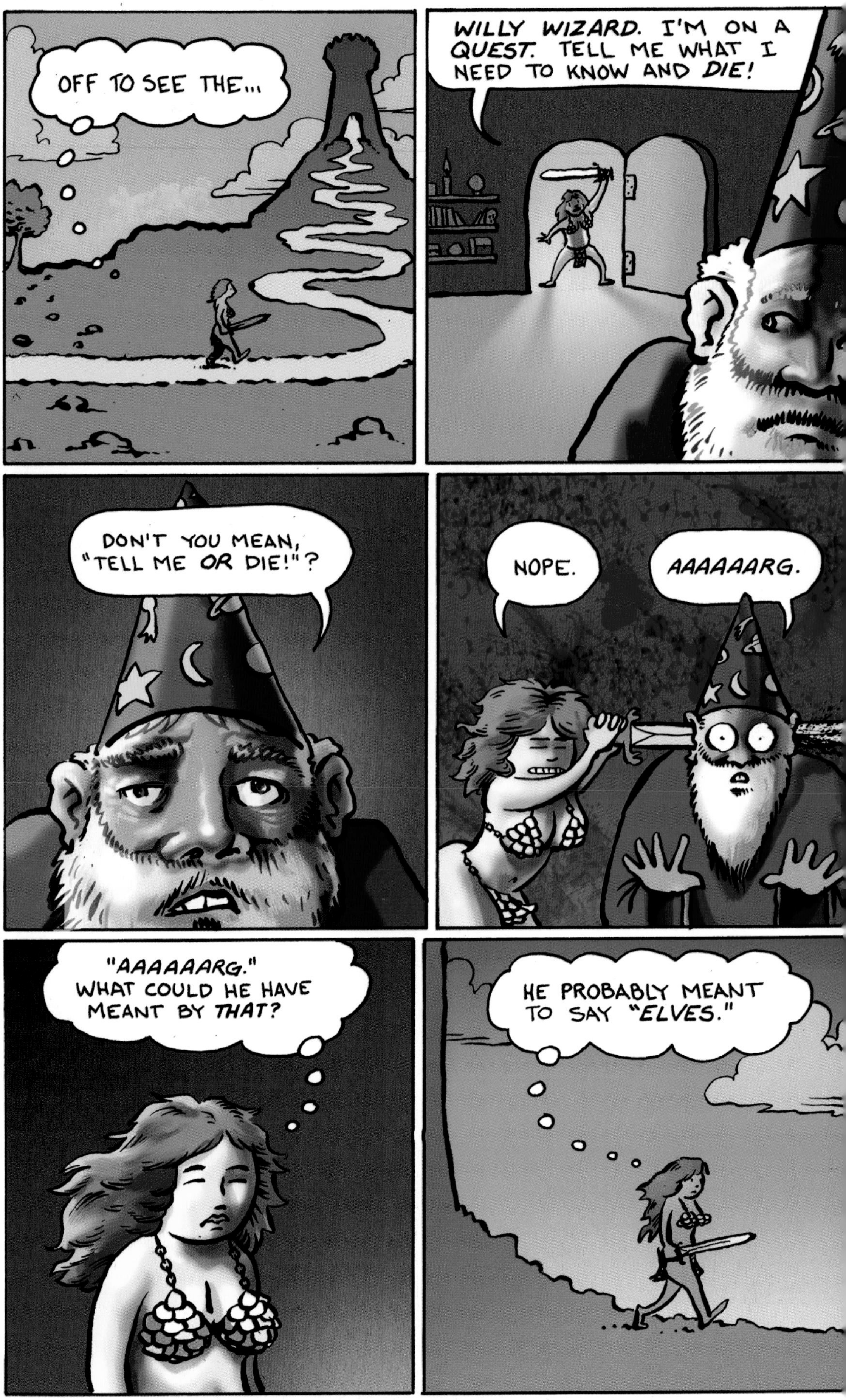
OFF TO SEE THE...
WILLY WIZARD. I'M ON A QUEST. TELL ME WHAT I NEED TO KNOW AND DIE!
DON'T YOU MEAN, "TELL ME OR DIE!"?
NOPE.
AAAAAARG.
"AAAAAARG." WHAT COULD HE HAVE MEANT BY THAT?
HE PROBABLY MEANT TO SAY "ELVES."

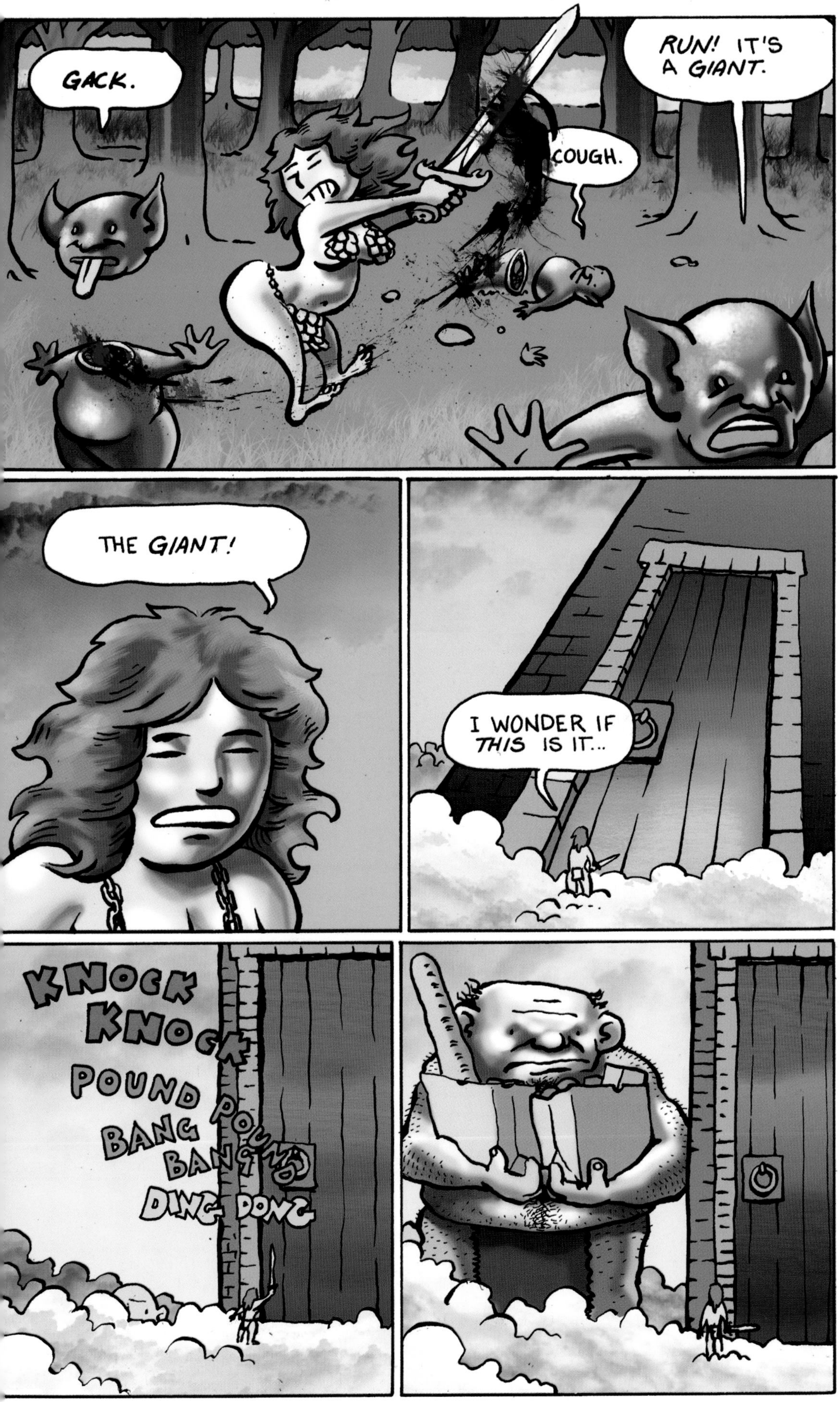
GACK.
COUGH.
RUN! IT'S A GIANT.
THE GIANT!
I WONDER IF THIS IS IT...
KNOCK KNOCK
POUND POUND
BANG BANG
DING DONG

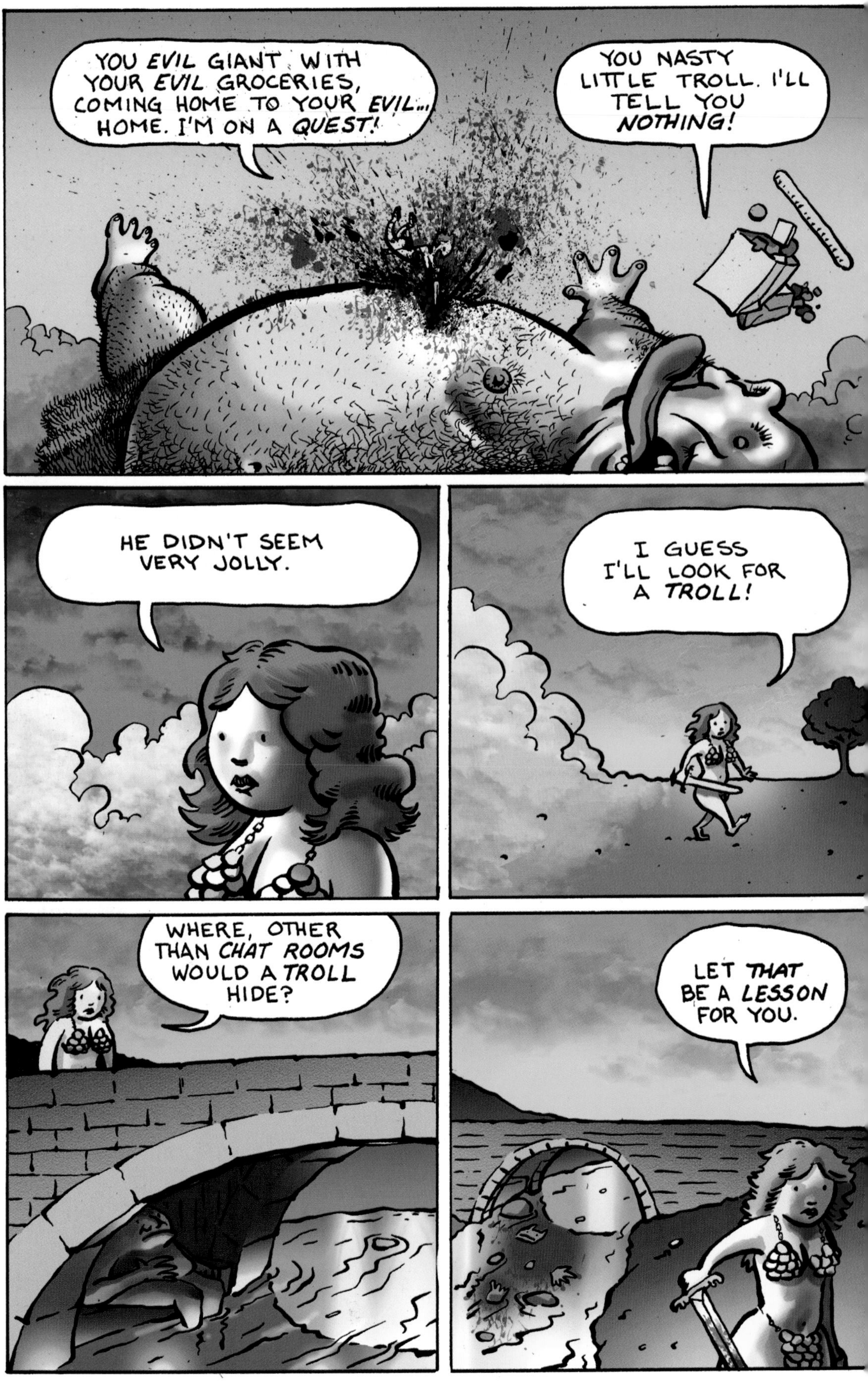
YOU EVIL GIANT WITH YOUR EVIL GROCERIES, COMING HOME TO YOUR EVIL... HOME. I'M ON A QUEST!
YOU NASTY LITTLE TROLL. I'LL TELL YOU NOTHING!
HE DIDN'T SEEM VERY JOLLY.
I GUESS I'LL LOOK FOR A TROLL!
WHERE, OTHER THAN CHAT ROOMS WOULD A TROLL HIDE?
LET THAT BE A LESSON FOR YOU.

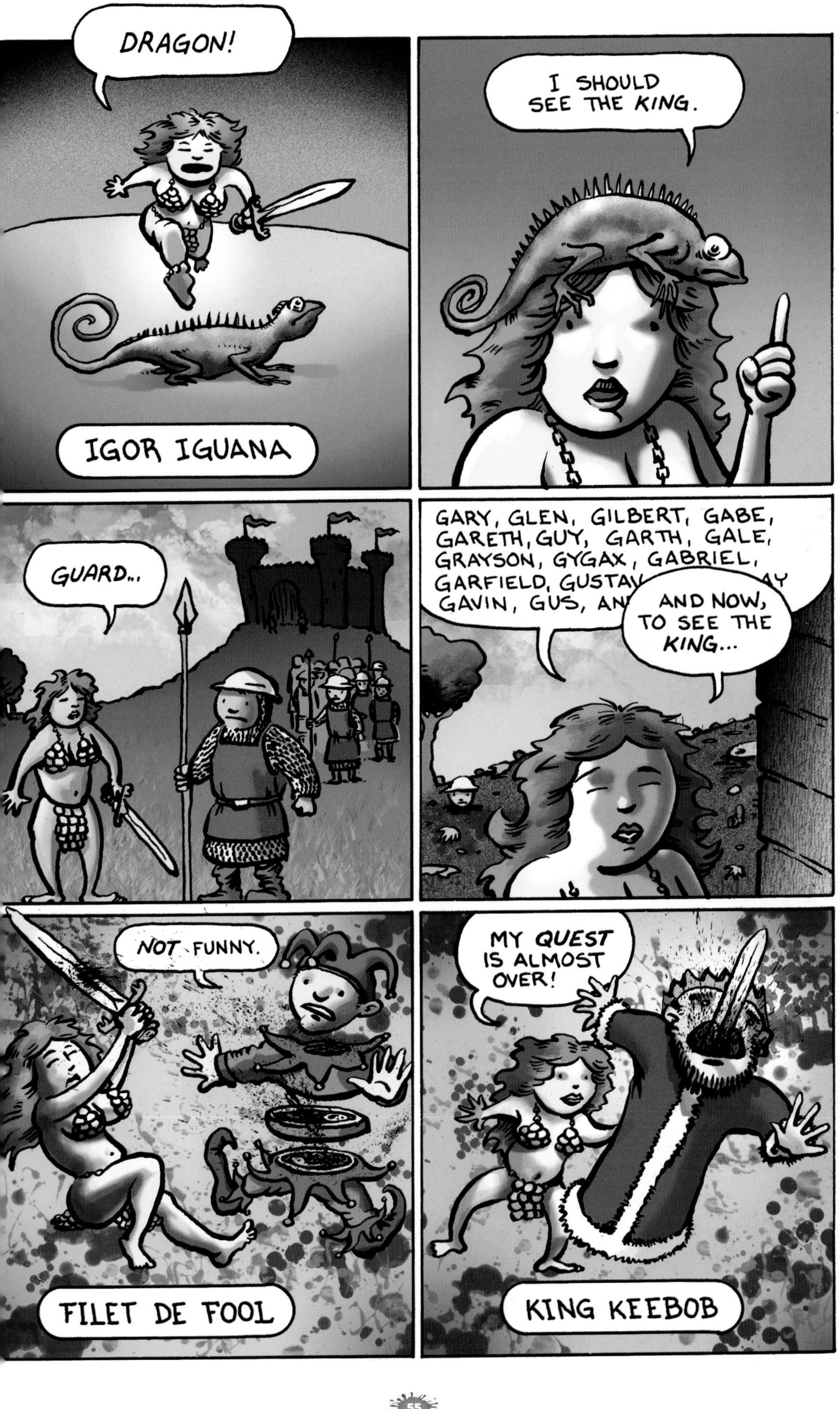
DRAGON!
IGOR IGUANA
I SHOULD SEE THE KING.
GUARD...
GARY, GLEN, GILBERT, GABE, GARETH, GUY, GARTH, GALE, GRAYSON, GYGAX, GABRIEL, GARFIELD, GUSTAV
GAVIN, GUS,
AND NOW, TO SEE THE KING...
NOT FUNNY.
FILET DE FOOL
MY QUEST IS ALMOST OVER!
KING KEEBOB

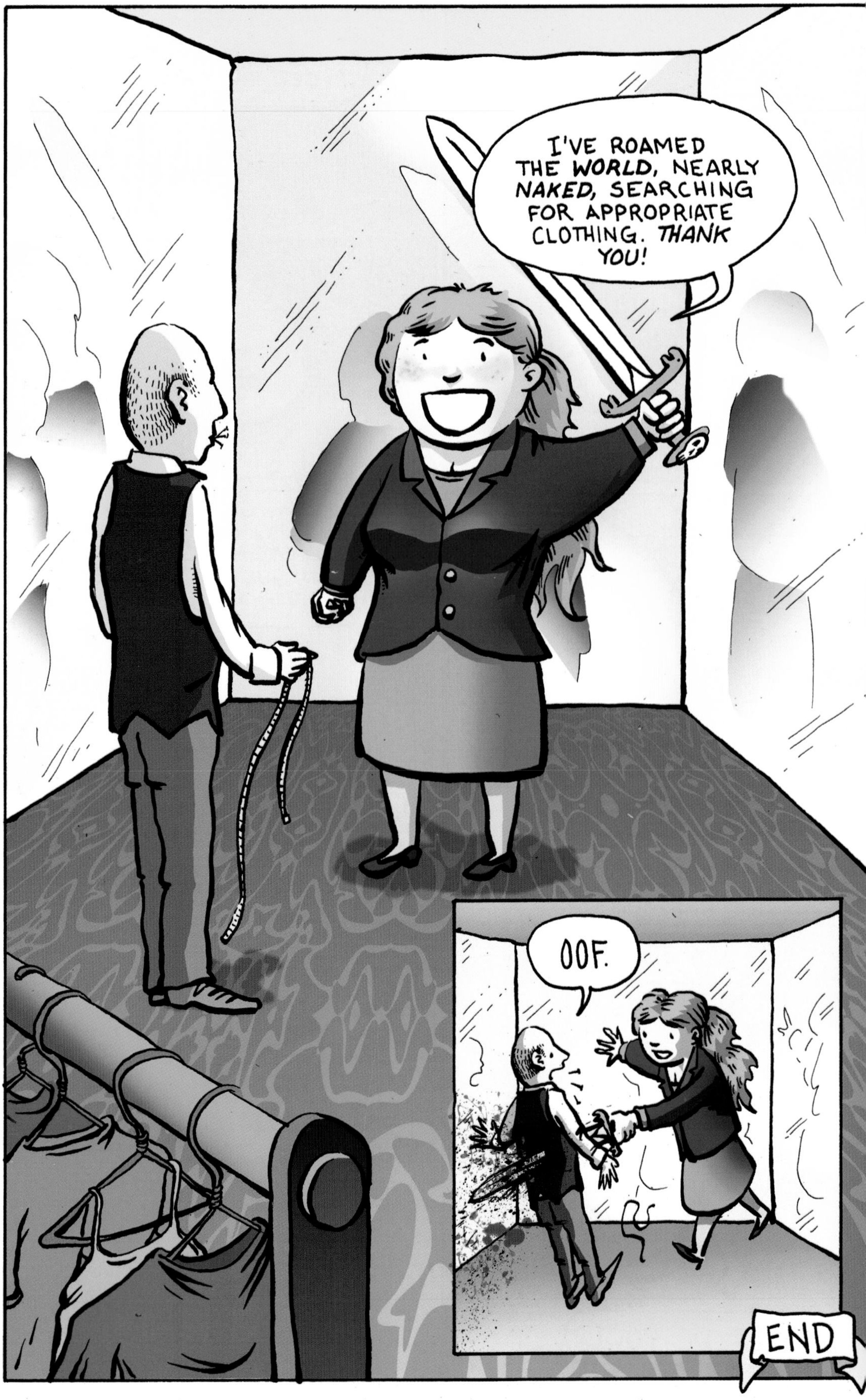
I'VE ROAMED THE WORLD, NEARLY NAKED, SEARCHING FOR APPROPRIATE CLOTHING. THANK YOU!
OOF.
END

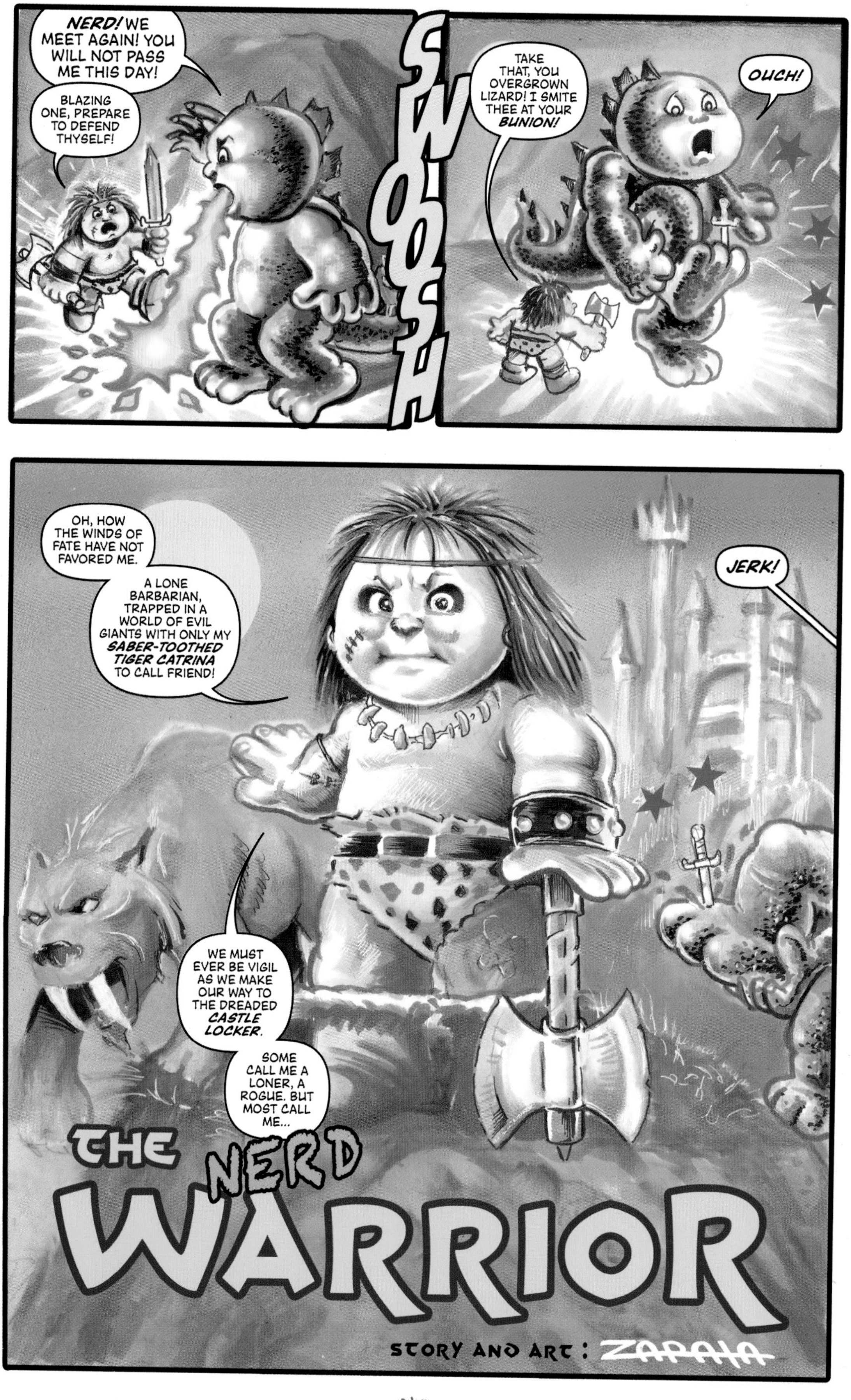
NERD! WE MEET AGAIN! YOU WILL NOT PASS ME THIS DAY!
BLAZING ONE, PREPARE TO DEFEND THYSELF!
SWOOSH
TAKE THAT, YOU OVERGROWN LIZARD! I SMITE THEE AT YOUR BUNION!
OUCH!
OH, HOW THE WINDS OF FATE HAVE NOT FAVORED ME.
A LONE BARBARIAN, TRAPPED IN A WORLD OF EVIL GIANTS WITH ONLY MY SABER-TOOTHED TIGER CATRINA TO CALL FRIEND!
JERK!
WE MUST EVER BE VIGIL AS WE MAKE OUR WAY TO THE DREADED CASTLE LOCKER.
SOME CALL ME A LONER, A ROGUE. BUT MOST CALL ME...
THE NERD WARRIOR
STORY AND ART: ZAPATA

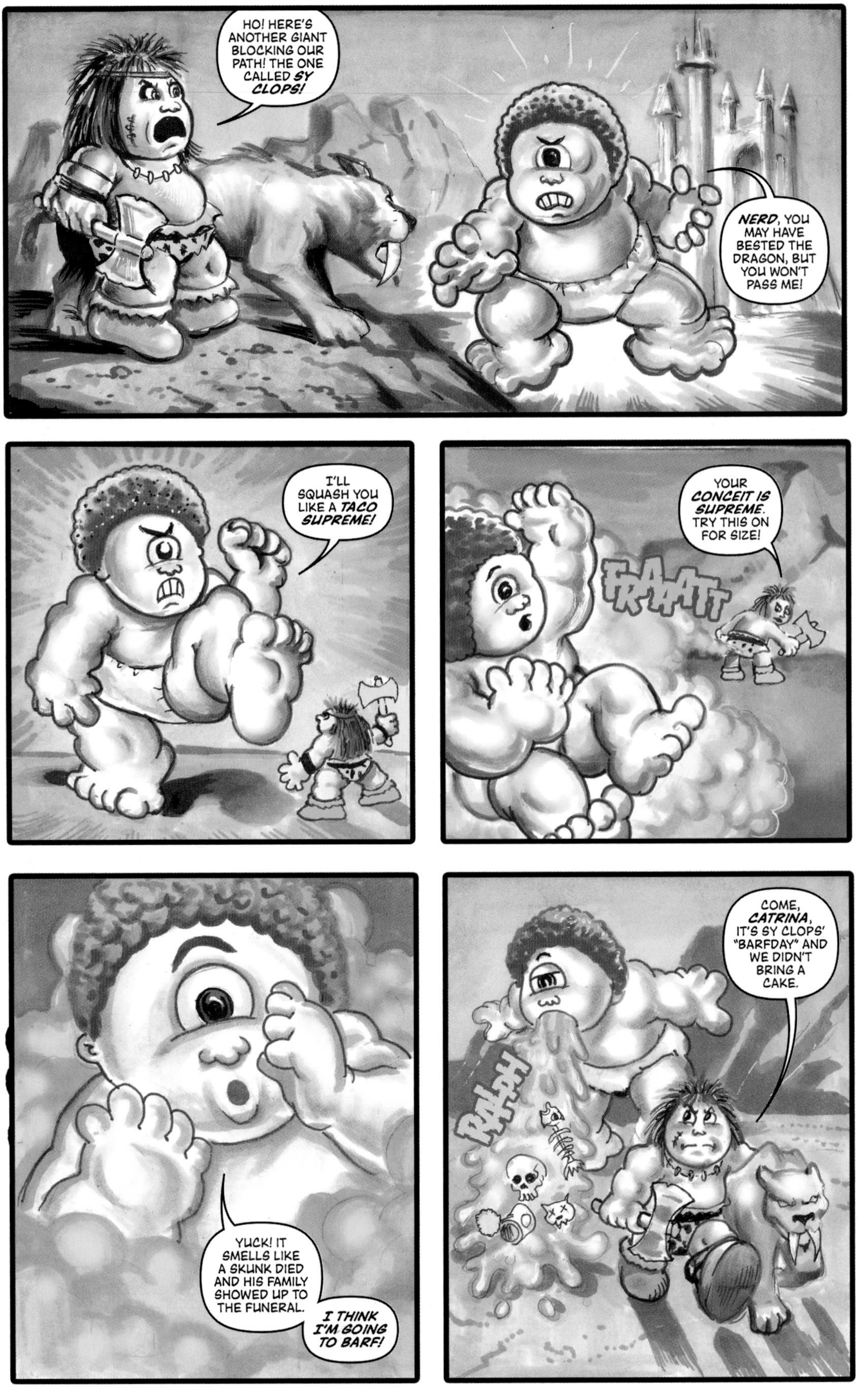

HO! HERE'S ANOTHER GIANT BLOCKING OUR PATH! THE ONE CALLED *SY CLOPS!*
NERD, YOU MAY HAVE BESTED THE DRAGON, BUT YOU WON'T PASS ME!
I'LL SQUASH YOU LIKE A *TACO SUPREME!*
YOUR *CONCEIT IS SUPREME*. TRY THIS ON FOR SIZE!
FRAAATT
YUCK! IT SMELLS LIKE A SKUNK DIED AND HIS FAMILY SHOWED UP TO THE FUNERAL.
I THINK I'M GOING TO BARF!
RALPH
COME, *CATRINA*, IT'S SY CLOPS' "BARFDAY" AND WE DIDN'T BRING A CAKE.

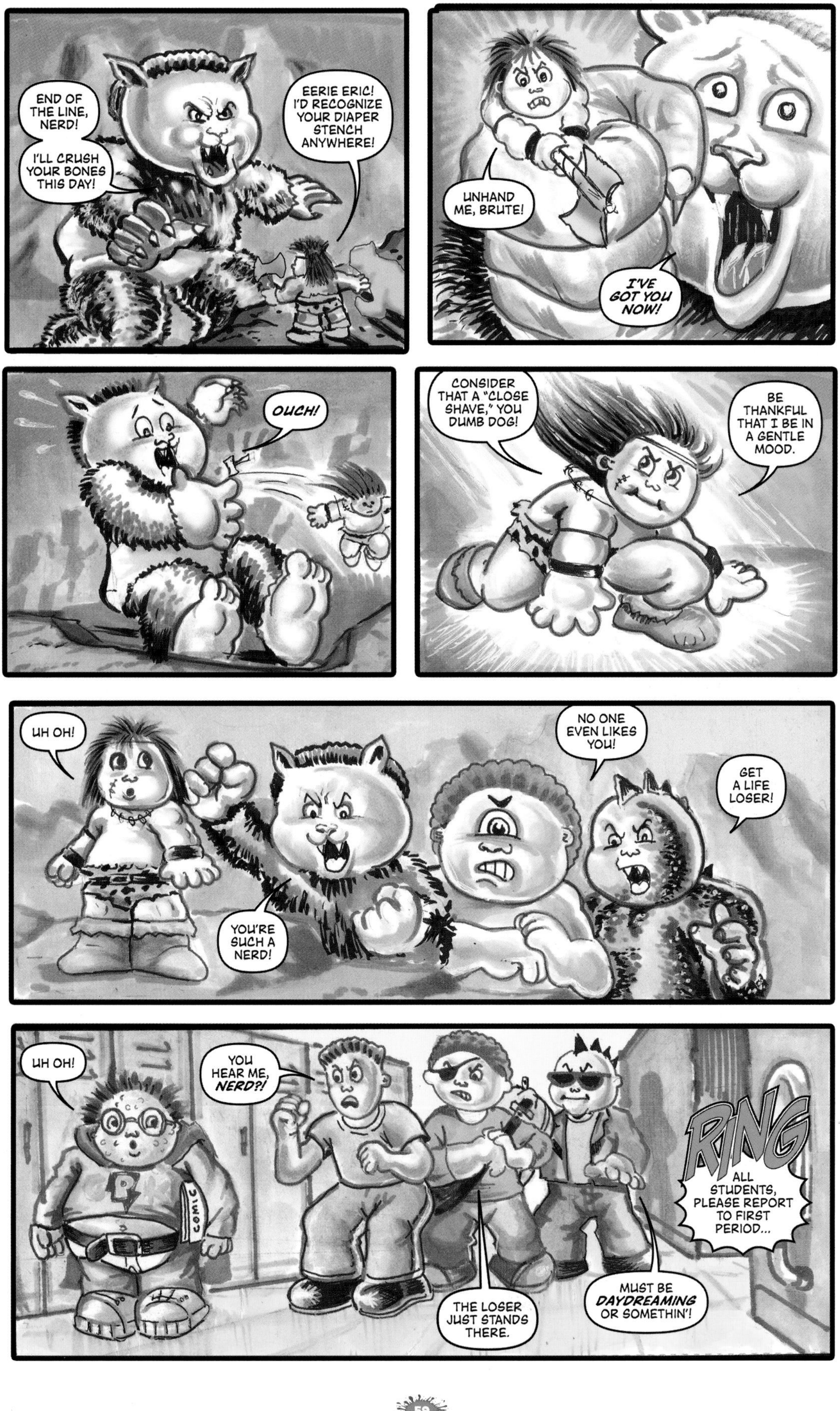
END OF THE LINE, NERD!
I'LL CRUSH YOUR BONES THIS DAY!
EERIE ERIC! I'D RECOGNIZE YOUR DIAPER STENCH ANYWHERE!
UNHAND ME, BRUTE!
I'VE GOT YOU NOW!
OUCH!
CONSIDER THAT A "CLOSE SHAVE," YOU DUMB DOG!
BE THANKFUL THAT I BE IN A GENTLE MOOD.
UH OH!
YOU'RE SUCH A NERD!
NO ONE EVEN LIKES YOU!
GET A LIFE LOSER!
UH OH!
YOU HEAR ME, NERD?!
COMIC
THE LOSER JUST STANDS THERE.
MUST BE DAYDREAMING OR SOMETHIN'!
RING
ALL STUDENTS, PLEASE REPORT TO FIRST PERIOD...

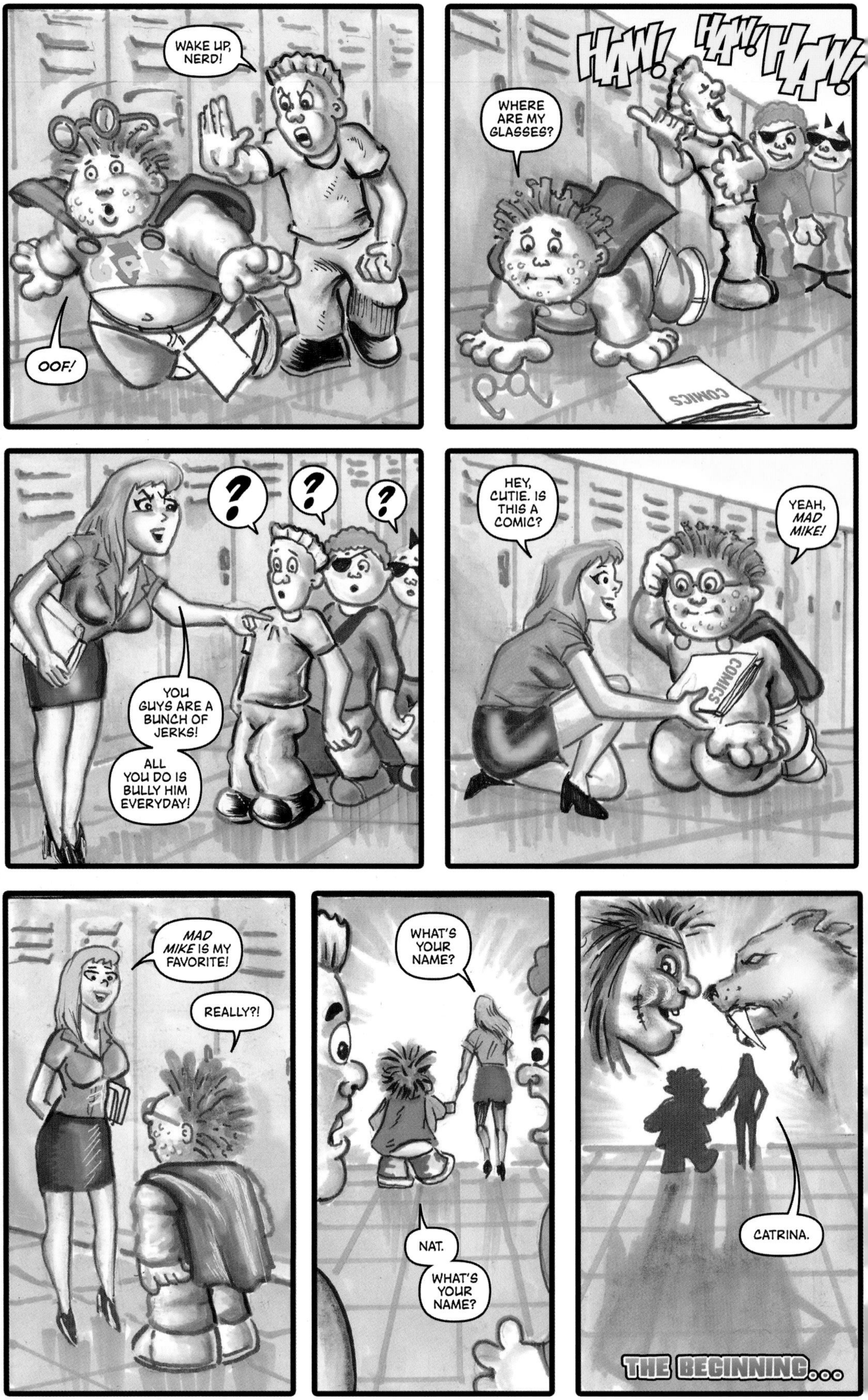

WAKE UP, NERD!
OOF!
WHERE ARE MY GLASSES?
HAW! HAW! HAW!
COMICS
YOU GUYS ARE A BUNCH OF JERKS!
ALL YOU DO IS BULLY HIM EVERYDAY!
HEY, CUTIE. IS THIS A COMIC?
YEAH, MAD MIKE!
COMICS
MAD MIKE IS MY FAVORITE!
REALLY?!
WHAT'S YOUR NAME?
NAT.
WHAT'S YOUR NAME?
CATRINA.
THE BEGINNING...

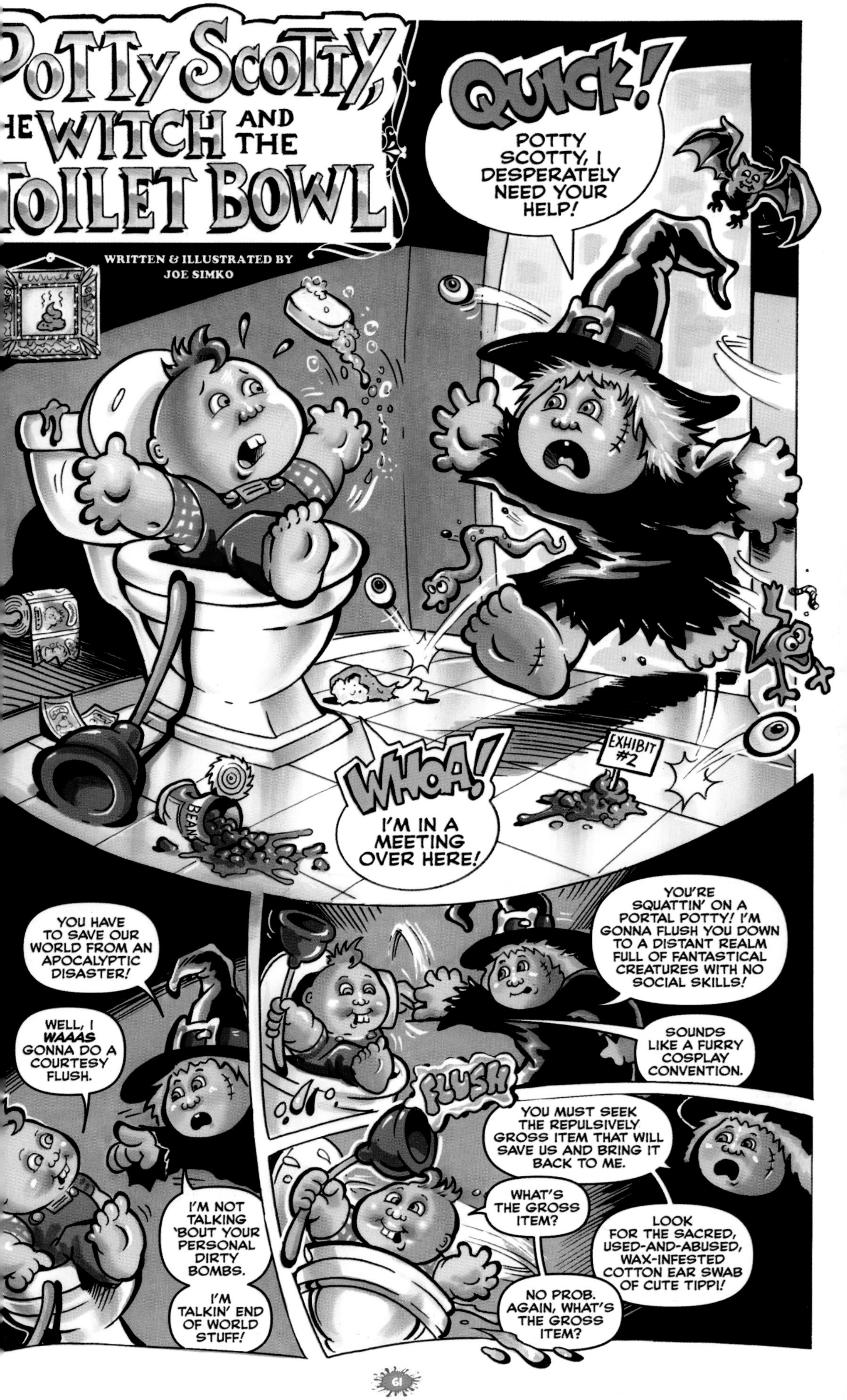

POTTY SCOTTY, THE WITCH AND THE TOILET BOWL
WRITTEN & ILLUSTRATED BY JOE SIMKO
QUICK! POTTY SCOTTY, I DESPERATELY NEED YOUR HELP!
WHOA! I'M IN A MEETING OVER HERE!
EXHIBIT #2
BEANS
YOU HAVE TO SAVE OUR WORLD FROM AN APOCALYPTIC DISASTER!
WELL, I WAAAS GONNA DO A COURTESY FLUSH.
I'M NOT TALKING 'BOUT YOUR PERSONAL DIRTY BOMBS.
I'M TALKIN' END OF WORLD STUFF!
YOU'RE SQUATTIN' ON A PORTAL POTTY! I'M GONNA FLUSH YOU DOWN TO A DISTANT REALM FULL OF FANTASTICAL CREATURES WITH NO SOCIAL SKILLS!
SOUNDS LIKE A FURRY COSPLAY CONVENTION.
FLUSH
YOU MUST SEEK THE REPULSIVELY GROSS ITEM THAT WILL SAVE US AND BRING IT BACK TO ME.
WHAT'S THE GROSS ITEM?
LOOK FOR THE SACRED, USED-AND-ABUSED, WAX-INFESTED COTTON EAR SWAB OF CUTE TIPPI!
NO PROB. AGAIN, WHAT'S THE GROSS ITEM?

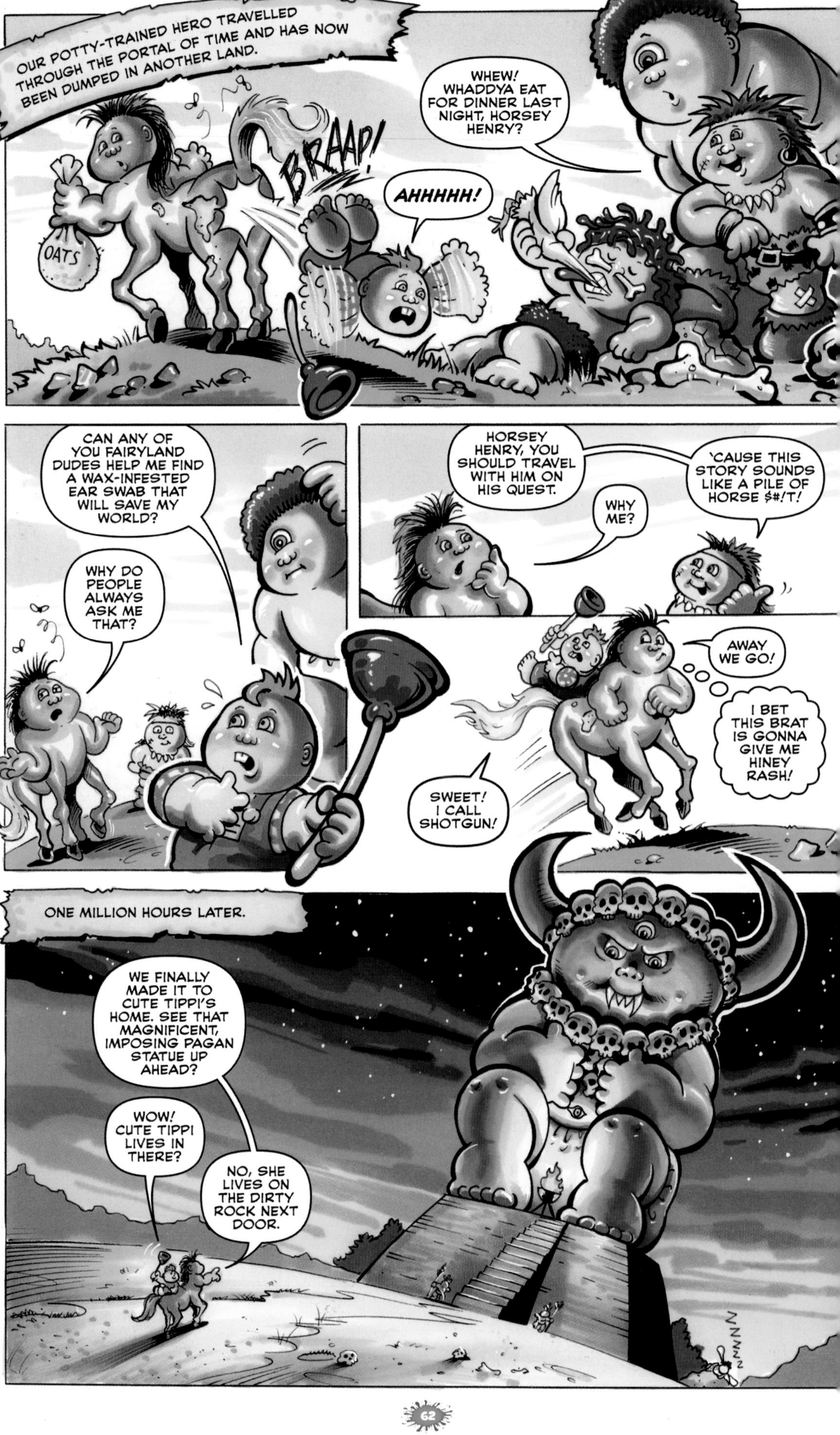
OUR POTTY-TRAINED HERO TRAVELLED THROUGH THE PORTAL OF TIME AND HAS NOW BEEN DUMPED IN ANOTHER LAND.
OATS
BRAAP!
AHHHHH!
WHEW! WHADDYA EAT FOR DINNER LAST NIGHT, HORSEY HENRY?
CAN ANY OF YOU FAIRYLAND DUDES HELP ME FIND A WAX-INFESTED EAR SWAB THAT WILL SAVE MY WORLD?
WHY DO PEOPLE ALWAYS ASK ME THAT?
HORSEY HENRY, YOU SHOULD TRAVEL WITH HIM ON HIS QUEST.
WHY ME?
'CAUSE THIS STORY SOUNDS LIKE A PILE OF HORSE $#!T!
AWAY WE GO!
I BET THIS BRAT IS GONNA GIVE ME HINEY RASH!
SWEET! I CALL SHOTGUN!
ONE MILLION HOURS LATER.
WE FINALLY MADE IT TO CUTE TIPPI'S HOME. SEE THAT MAGNIFICENT, IMPOSING PAGAN STATUE UP AHEAD?
WOW! CUTE TIPPI LIVES IN THERE?
NO, SHE LIVES ON THE DIRTY ROCK NEXT DOOR.
ZZZZ

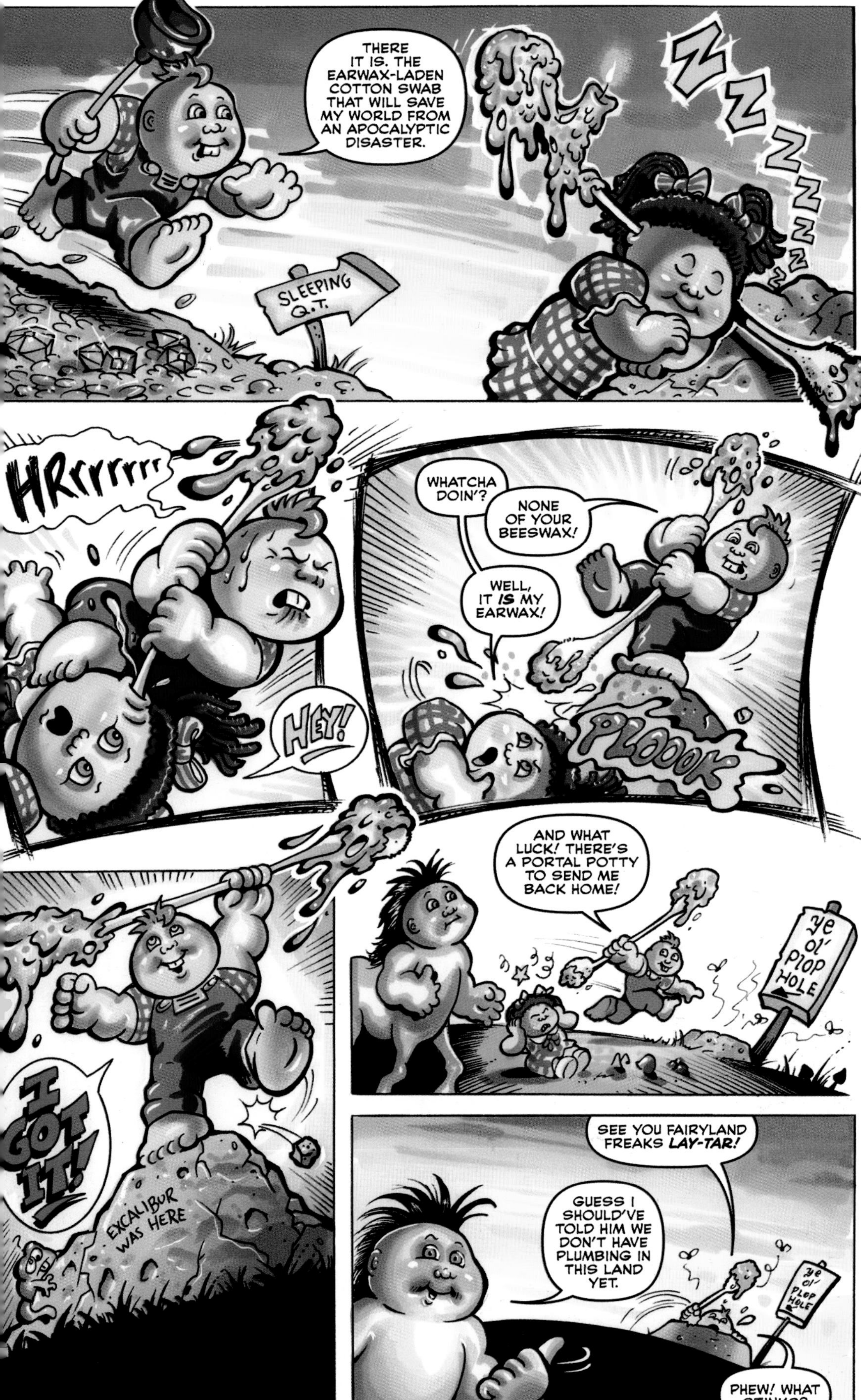

THERE IT IS. THE EARWAX-LADEN COTTON SWAB THAT WILL SAVE MY WORLD FROM AN APOCALYPTIC DISASTER.
ZZZZZZZZ
SLEEPING Q.T.
HRrrrrrr
HEY!
WHATCHA DOIN'?
NONE OF YOUR BEESWAX!
WELL, IT *IS* MY EARWAX!
PLOOOK
I GOT IT!
EXCALIBUR WAS HERE
AND WHAT LUCK! THERE'S A PORTAL POTTY TO SEND ME BACK HOME!
YE OL' PLOP HOLE
SEE YOU FAIRYLAND FREAKS *LAY-TAR!*
GUESS I SHOULD'VE TOLD HIM WE DON'T HAVE PLUMBING IN THIS LAND YET.
YE OL' PLOP HOLE
PHEW! WHAT STINKS?

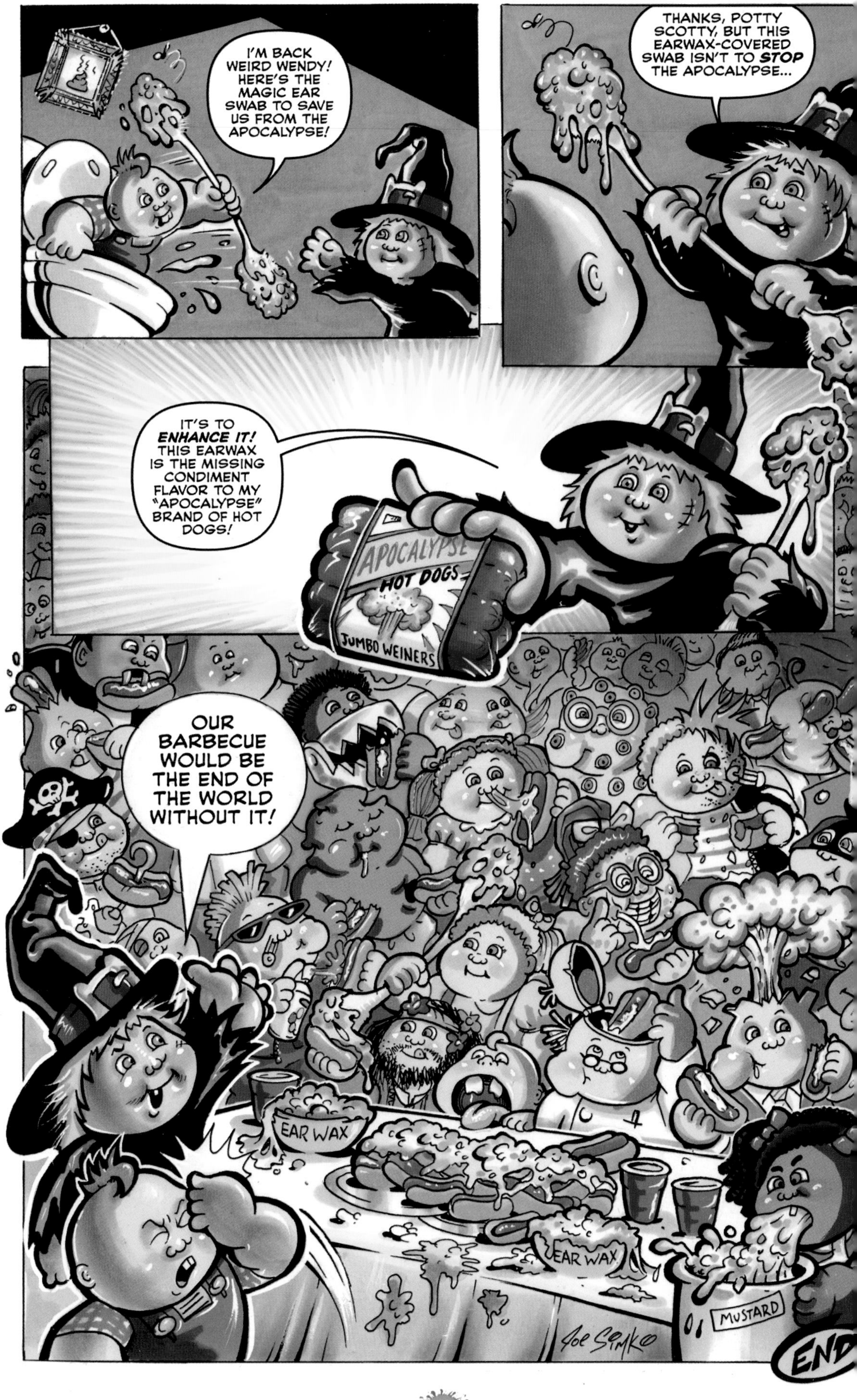
I'M BACK WEIRD WENDY! HERE'S THE MAGIC EAR SWAB TO SAVE US FROM THE APOCALYPSE!
THANKS, POTTY SCOTTY, BUT THIS EARWAX-COVERED SWAB ISN'T TO *STOP* THE APOCALYPSE...
IT'S TO *ENHANCE IT!* THIS EARWAX IS THE MISSING CONDIMENT FLAVOR TO MY "APOCALYPSE" BRAND OF HOT DOGS!
APOCALYPSE
HOT DOGS
JUMBO WEINERS
OUR BARBECUE WOULD BE THE END OF THE WORLD WITHOUT IT!
EAR WAX
EAR WAX
MUSTARD
END

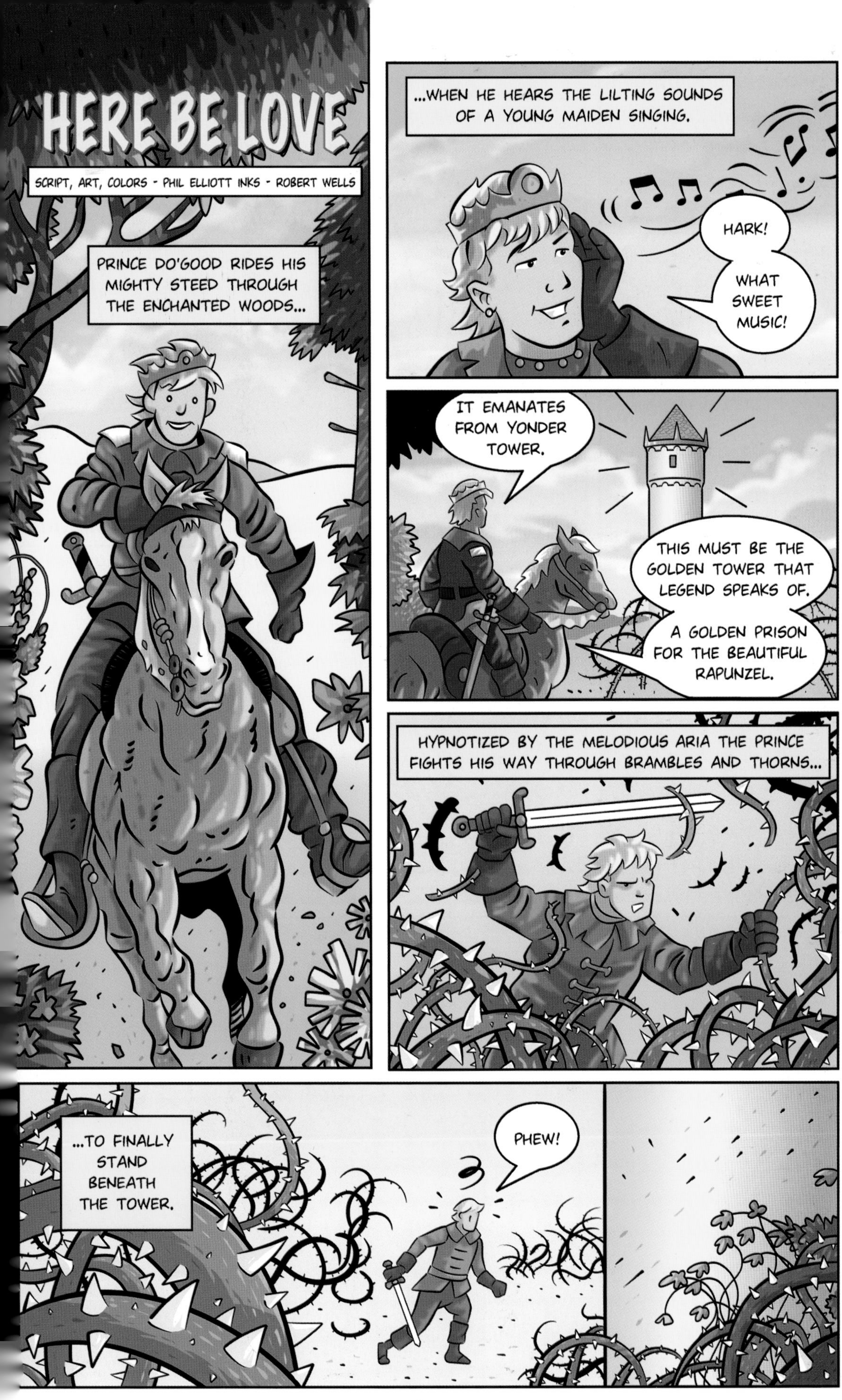
HERE BE LOVE
SCRIPT, ART, COLORS - PHIL ELLIOTT INKS - ROBERT WELLS
PRINCE DO'GOOD RIDES HIS MIGHTY STEED THROUGH THE ENCHANTED WOODS...
...WHEN HE HEARS THE LILTING SOUNDS OF A YOUNG MAIDEN SINGING.
HARK!
WHAT SWEET MUSIC!
IT EMANATES FROM YONDER TOWER.
THIS MUST BE THE GOLDEN TOWER THAT LEGEND SPEAKS OF.
A GOLDEN PRISON FOR THE BEAUTIFUL RAPUNZEL.
HYPNOTIZED BY THE MELODIOUS ARIA THE PRINCE FIGHTS HIS WAY THROUGH BRAMBLES AND THORNS...
...TO FINALLY STAND BENEATH THE TOWER.
PHEW!

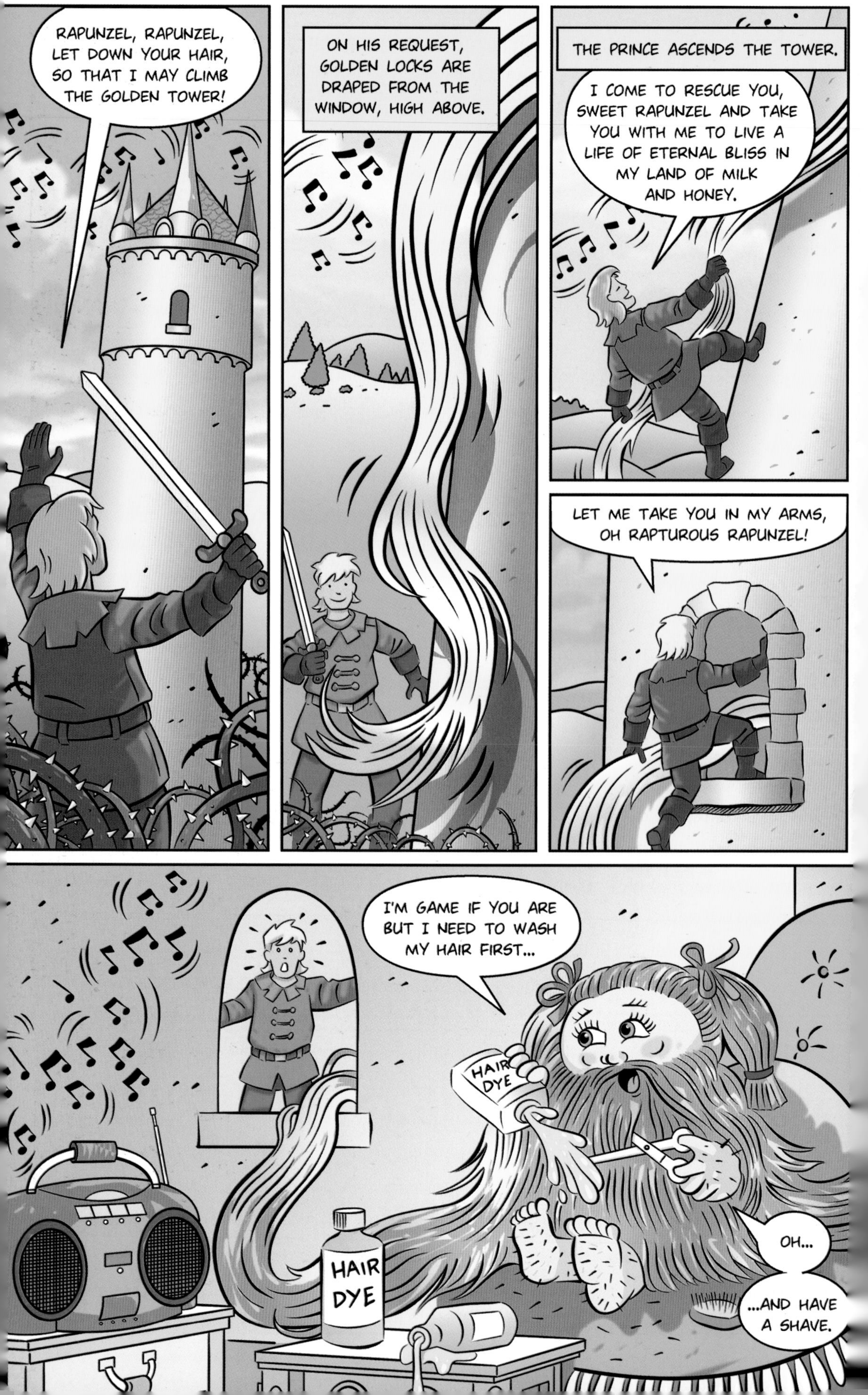
RAPUNZEL, RAPUNZEL, LET DOWN YOUR HAIR, SO THAT I MAY CLIMB THE GOLDEN TOWER!
ON HIS REQUEST, GOLDEN LOCKS ARE DRAPED FROM THE WINDOW, HIGH ABOVE.
THE PRINCE ASCENDS THE TOWER.
I COME TO RESCUE YOU, SWEET RAPUNZEL AND TAKE YOU WITH ME TO LIVE A LIFE OF ETERNAL BLISS IN MY LAND OF MILK AND HONEY.
LET ME TAKE YOU IN MY ARMS, OH RAPTUROUS RAPUNZEL!
I'M GAME IF YOU ARE BUT I NEED TO WASH MY HAIR FIRST...
HAIR DYE
OH...
...AND HAVE A SHAVE.
HAIR DYE

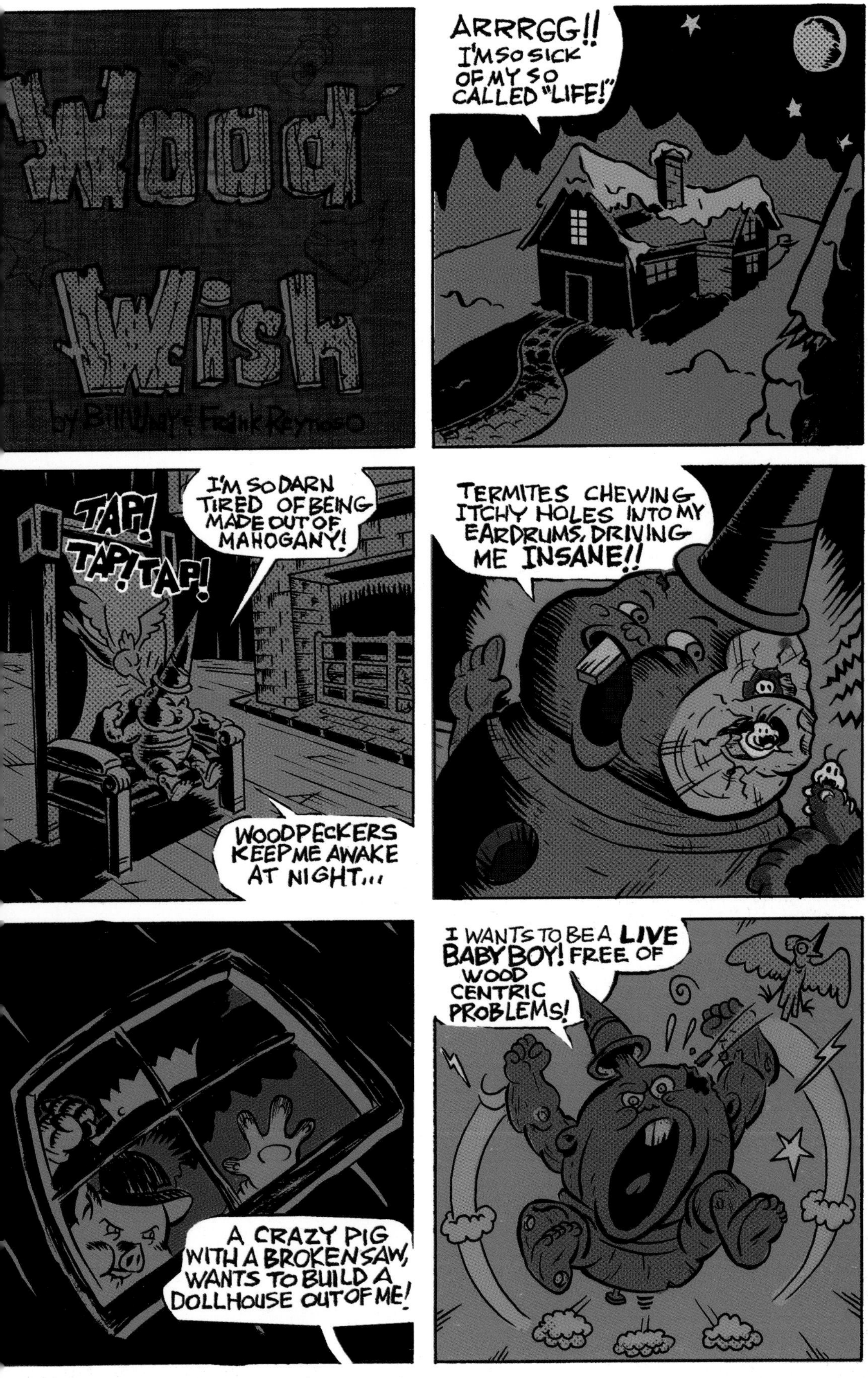
Wood Wish
by Bill Wray & Frank Reynoso
ARRRGG!! I'M SO SICK OF MY SO CALLED "LIFE!"
TAP! TAP! TAP!
I'M SO DARN TIRED OF BEING MADE OUT OF MAHOGANY!
WOODPECKERS KEEP ME AWAKE AT NIGHT...
TERMITES CHEWING ITCHY HOLES INTO MY EARDRUMS, DRIVING ME INSANE!!
A CRAZY PIG WITH A BROKEN SAW, WANTS TO BUILD A DOLLHOUSE OUT OF ME!
I WANTS TO BE A LIVE BABY BOY! FREE OF WOOD CENTRIC PROBLEMS!

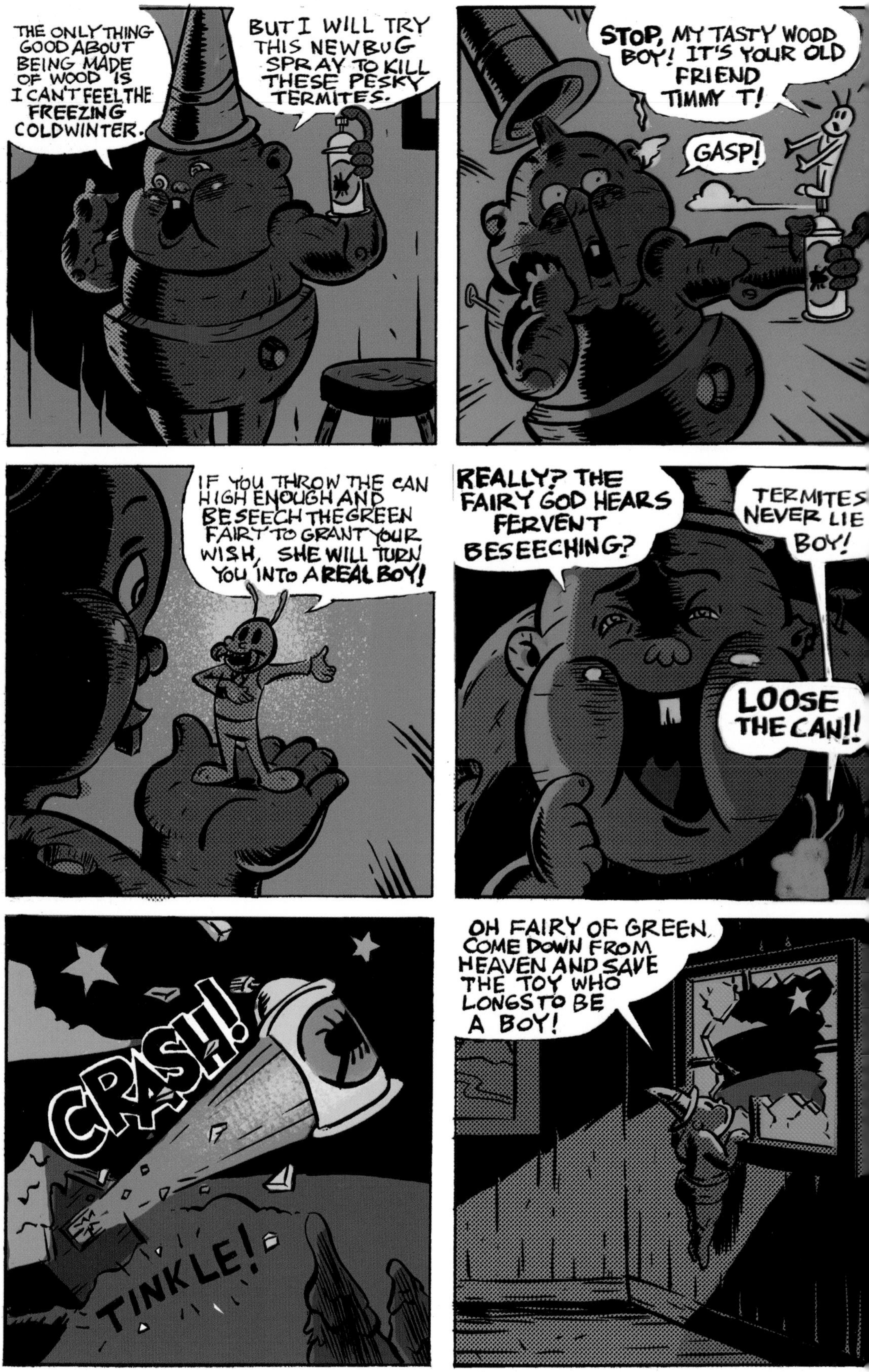
THE ONLY THING GOOD ABOUT BEING MADE OF WOOD IS I CAN'T FEEL THE FREEZING COLD WINTER.
BUT I WILL TRY THIS NEW BUG SPRAY TO KILL THESE PESKY TERMITES.
STOP, MY TASTY WOOD BOY! IT'S YOUR OLD FRIEND TIMMY T!
GASP!
IF YOU THROW THE CAN HIGH ENOUGH AND BESEECH THE GREEN FAIRY TO GRANT YOUR WISH, SHE WILL TURN YOU INTO A REAL BOY!
REALLY? THE FAIRY GOD HEARS FERVENT BESEECHING?
TERMITES NEVER LIE BOY!
LOOSE THE CAN!!
CRASH!
TINKLE!
OH FAIRY OF GREEN, COME DOWN FROM HEAVEN AND SAVE THE TOY WHO LONGS TO BE A BOY!

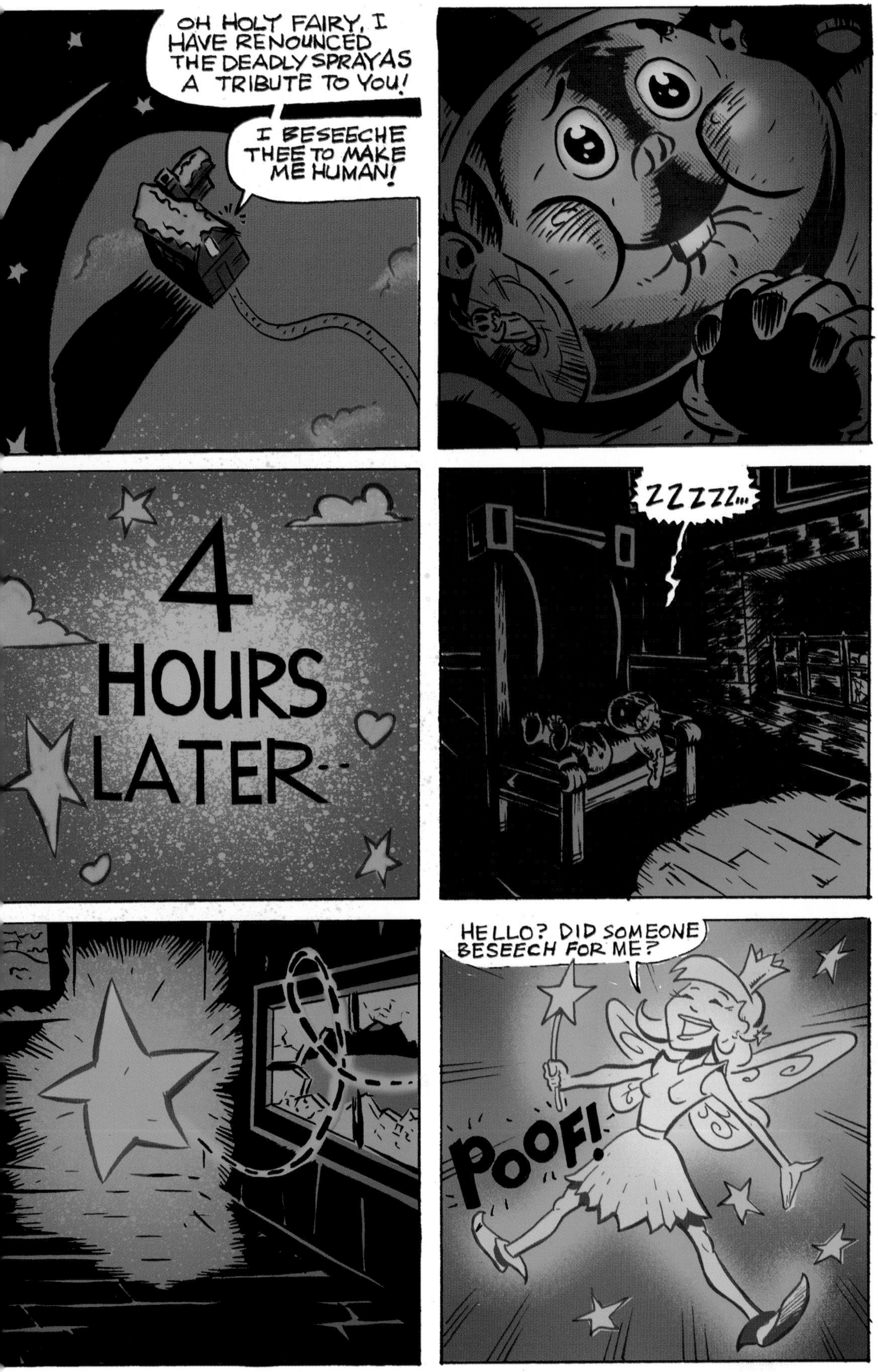
OH HOLY FAIRY, I HAVE RENOUNCED THE DEADLY SPRAY AS A TRIBUTE TO YOU!
I BESEECHE THEE TO MAKE ME HUMAN!
4 HOURS LATER--
ZZZZZ...
HELLO? DID SOMEONE BESEECH FOR ME?
POOF!

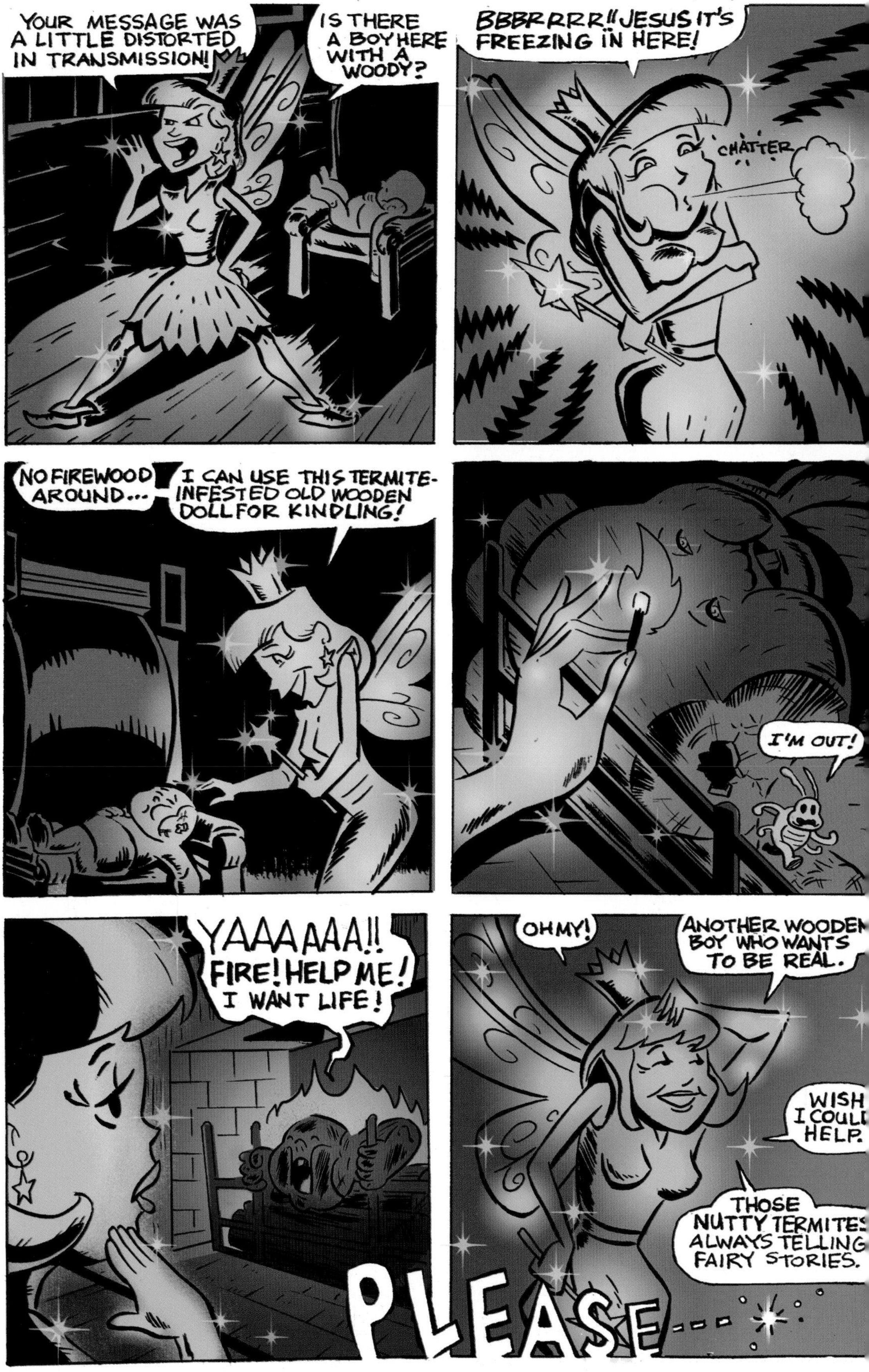
YOUR MESSAGE WAS A LITTLE DISTORTED IN TRANSMISSION!
IS THERE A BOY HERE WITH A WOODY?
BBBRRRR!! JESUS IT'S FREEZING IN HERE!
CHATTER
NO FIREWOOD AROUND...
I CAN USE THIS TERMITE-INFESTED OLD WOODEN DOLL FOR KINDLING!
I'M OUT!
YAAAAAA!! FIRE! HELP ME! I WANT LIFE!
PLEASE...
OH MY!
ANOTHER WOODEN BOY WHO WANTS TO BE REAL.
WISH I COULD HELP.
THOSE NUTTY TERMITES ALWAYS TELLING FAIRY STORIES.

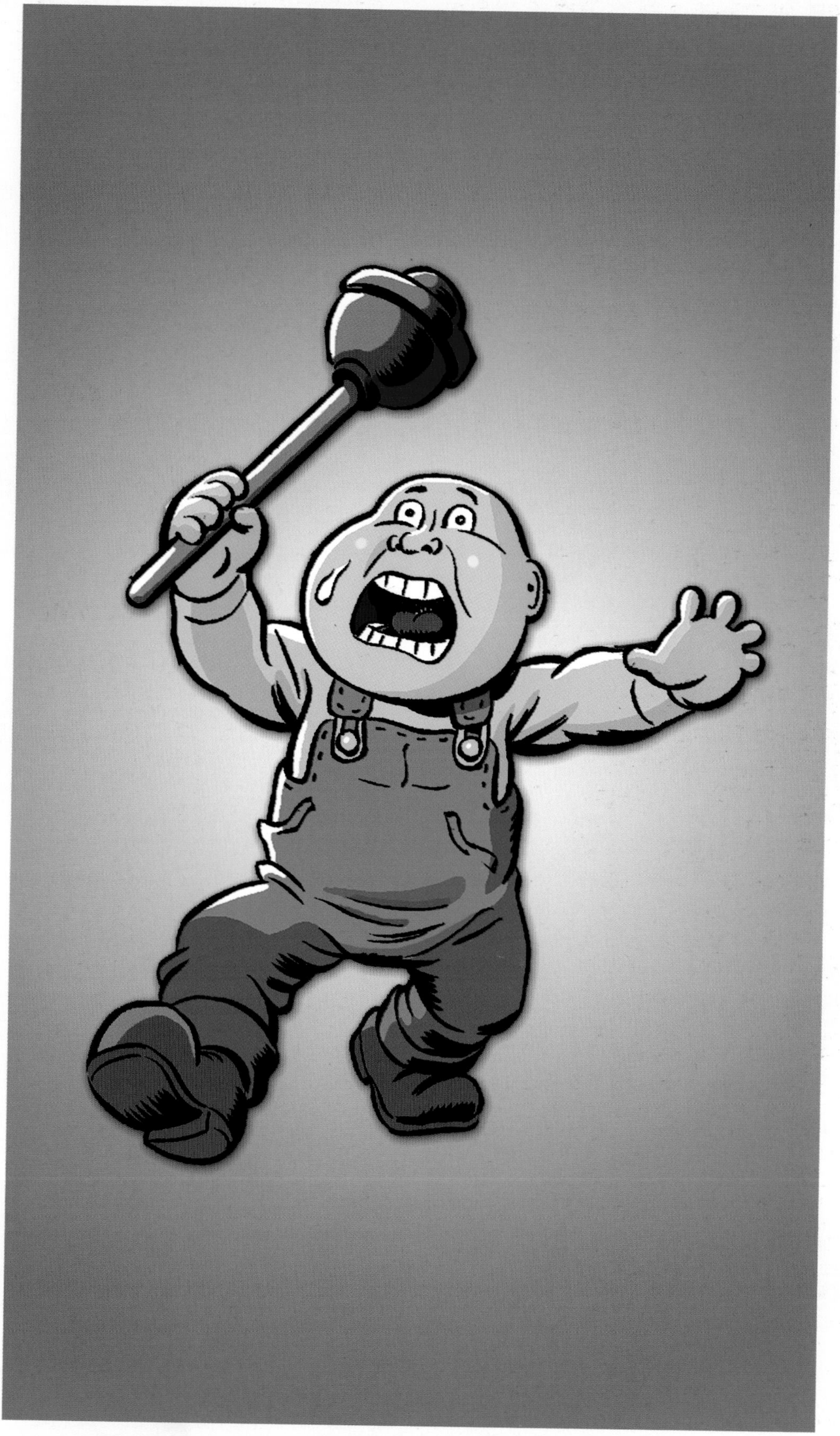

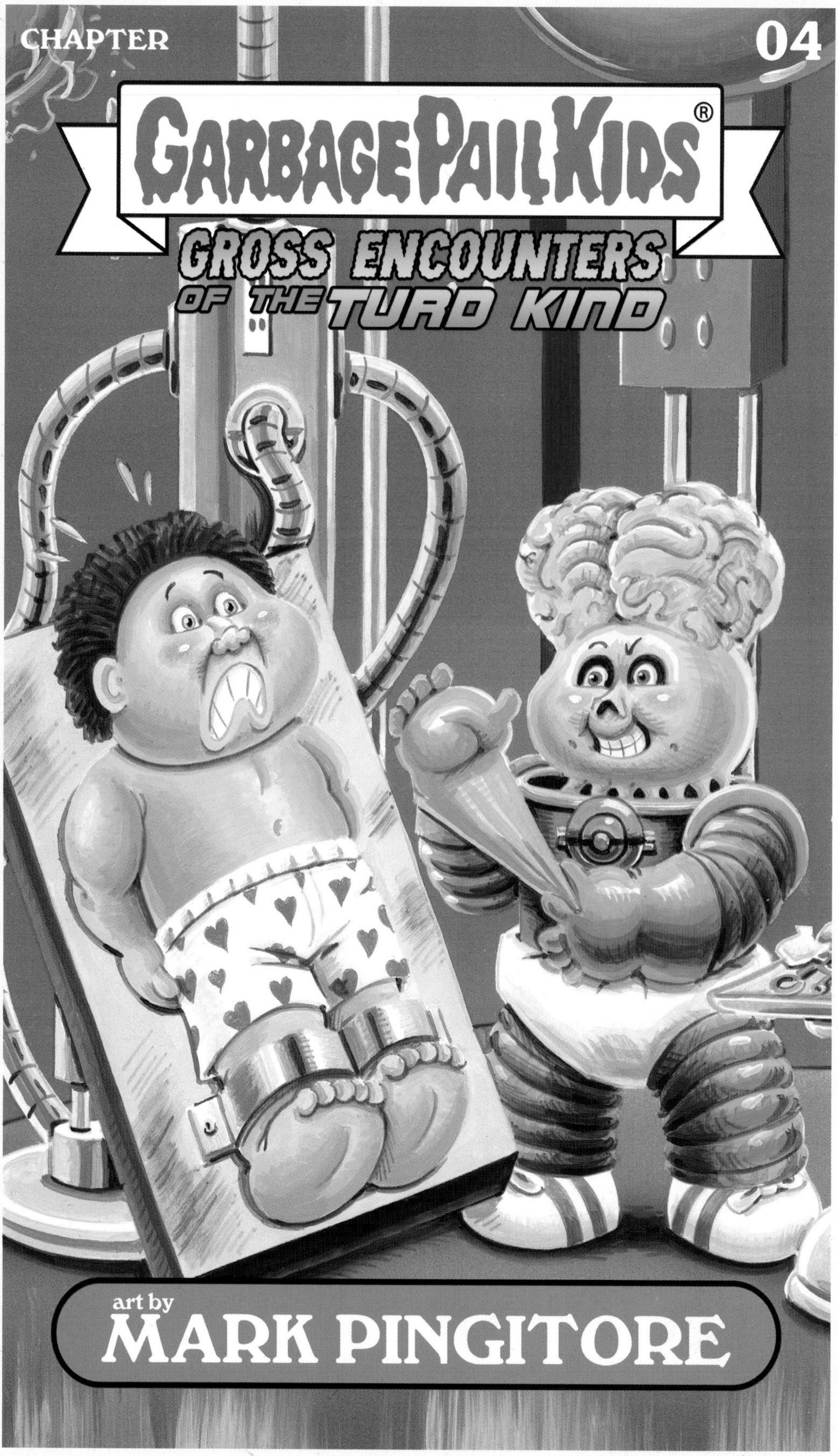
CHAPTER
04
GARBAGE PAIL KIDS®
GROSS ENCOUNTERS
OF THE TURD KIND
art by
MARK PINGITORE

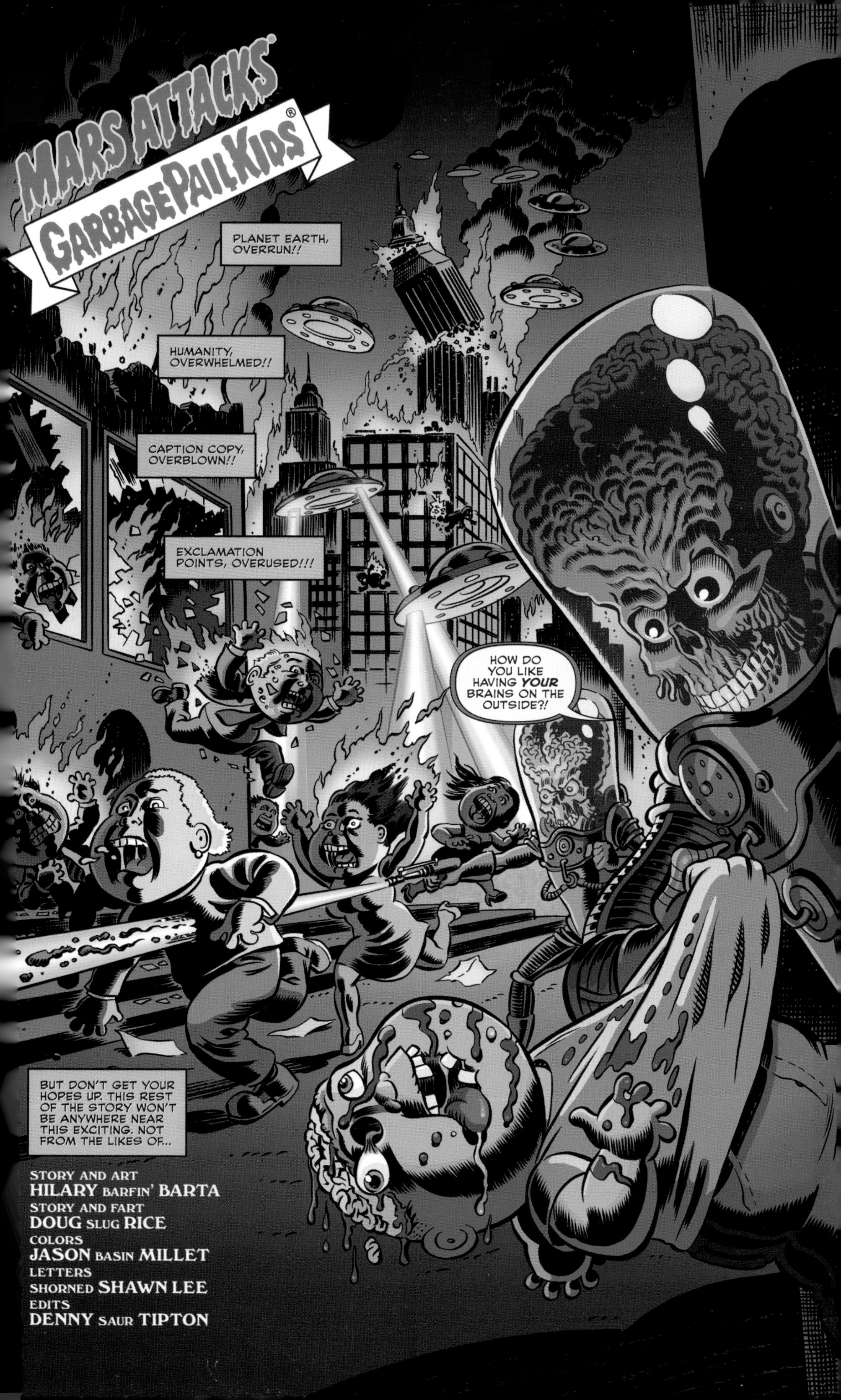

MARS ATTACKS®
GARBAGE PAIL KIDS®
PLANET EARTH, OVERRUN!!
HUMANITY, OVERWHELMED!!
CAPTION COPY, OVERBLOWN!!
EXCLAMATION POINTS, OVERUSED!!!
HOW DO YOU LIKE HAVING *YOUR* BRAINS ON THE OUTSIDE?!
BUT DON'T GET YOUR HOPES UP. THIS REST OF THE STORY WON'T BE ANYWHERE NEAR THIS EXCITING. NOT FROM THE LIKES OF...
STORY AND ART
HILARY BARFIN' BARTA
STORY AND FART
DOUG SLUG RICE
COLORS
JASON BASIN MILLET
LETTERS
SHORNED SHAWN LEE
EDITS
DENNY SAUR TIPTON

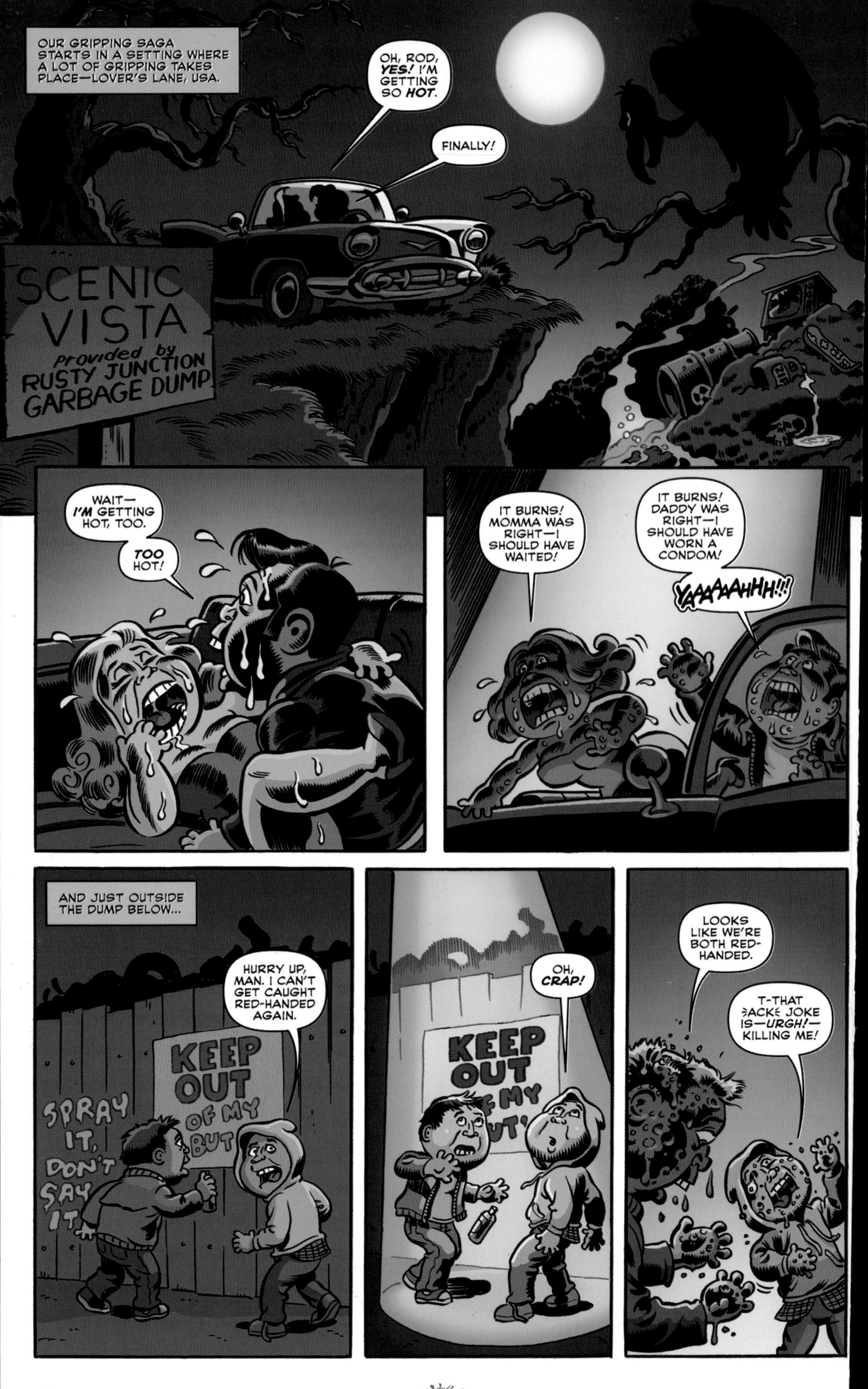
OUR GRIPPING SAGA STARTS IN A SETTING WHERE A LOT OF GRIPPING TAKES PLACE—LOVER'S LANE, USA.
OH, ROD, YES! I'M GETTING SO HOT.
FINALLY!
SCENIC VISTA provided by RUSTY JUNCTION GARBAGE DUMP
WAIT— I'M GETTING HOT, TOO.
TOO HOT!
IT BURNS! MOMMA WAS RIGHT—I SHOULD HAVE WAITED!
IT BURNS! DADDY WAS RIGHT—I SHOULD HAVE WORN A CONDOM!
YAAAAAHHH!!!
AND JUST OUTSIDE THE DUMP BELOW...
HURRY UP, MAN. I CAN'T GET CAUGHT RED-HANDED AGAIN.
KEEP OUT OF MY BUT
SPRAY IT, DON'T SAY IT
OH, CRAP!
LOOKS LIKE WE'RE BOTH RED-HANDED.
T-THAT ACK JOKE IS—URGH!— KILLING ME!

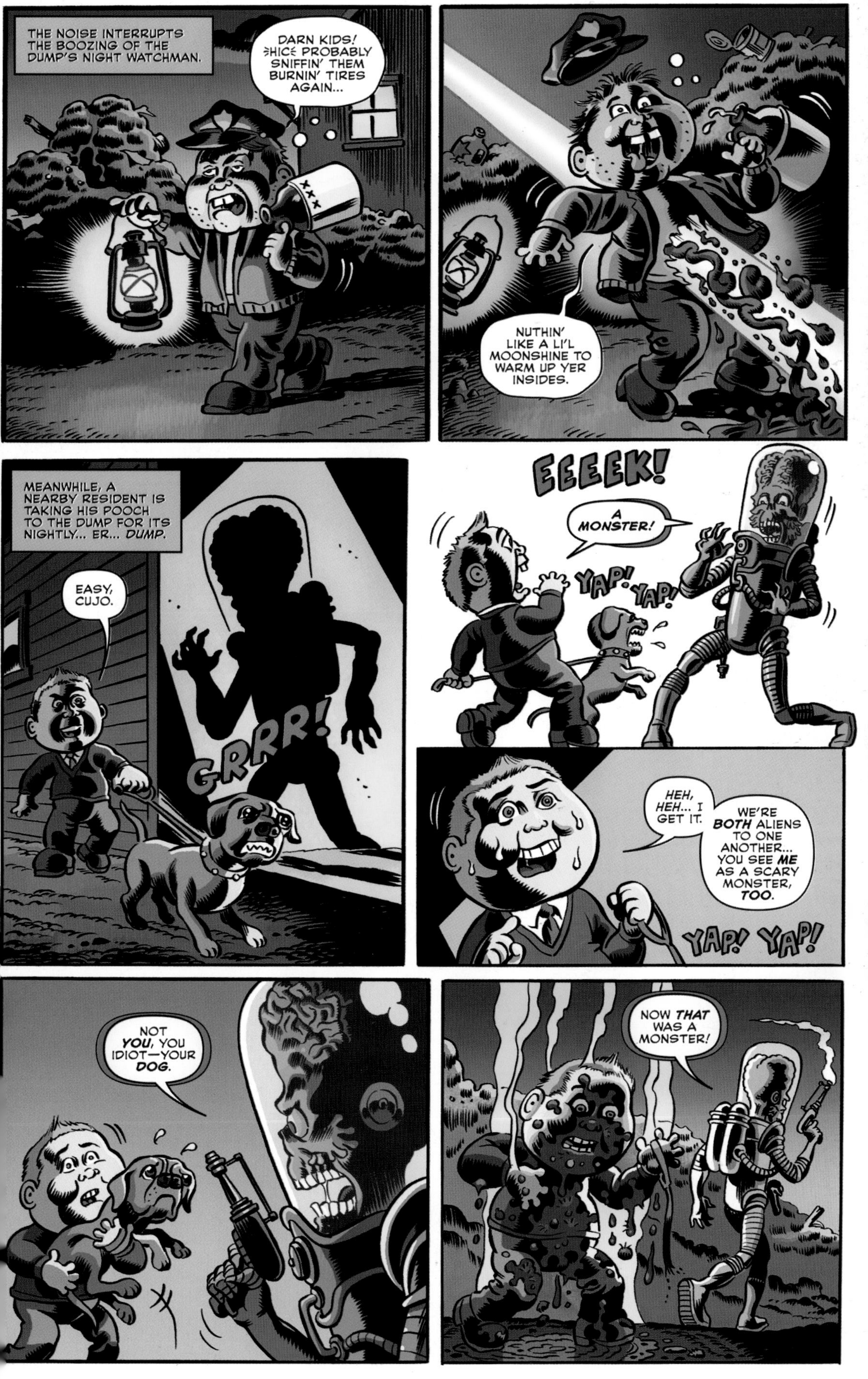

THE NOISE INTERRUPTS THE BOOZING OF THE DUMP'S NIGHT WATCHMAN.
DARN KIDS! *HIC* PROBABLY SNIFFIN' THEM BURNIN' TIRES AGAIN...
XXX
NUTHIN' LIKE A LI'L MOONSHINE TO WARM UP YER INSIDES.
MEANWHILE, A NEARBY RESIDENT IS TAKING HIS POOCH TO THE DUMP FOR ITS NIGHTLY... ER... *DUMP*.
EASY, CUJO.
GRRR!
EEEEK!
A *MONSTER!*
YAP! YAP!
HEH, HEH... I GET IT.
WE'RE *BOTH* ALIENS TO ONE ANOTHER... YOU SEE *ME* AS A SCARY MONSTER, *TOO*.
YAP! YAP!
NOT *YOU*, YOU IDIOT—YOUR *DOG*.
NOW *THAT* WAS A MONSTER!

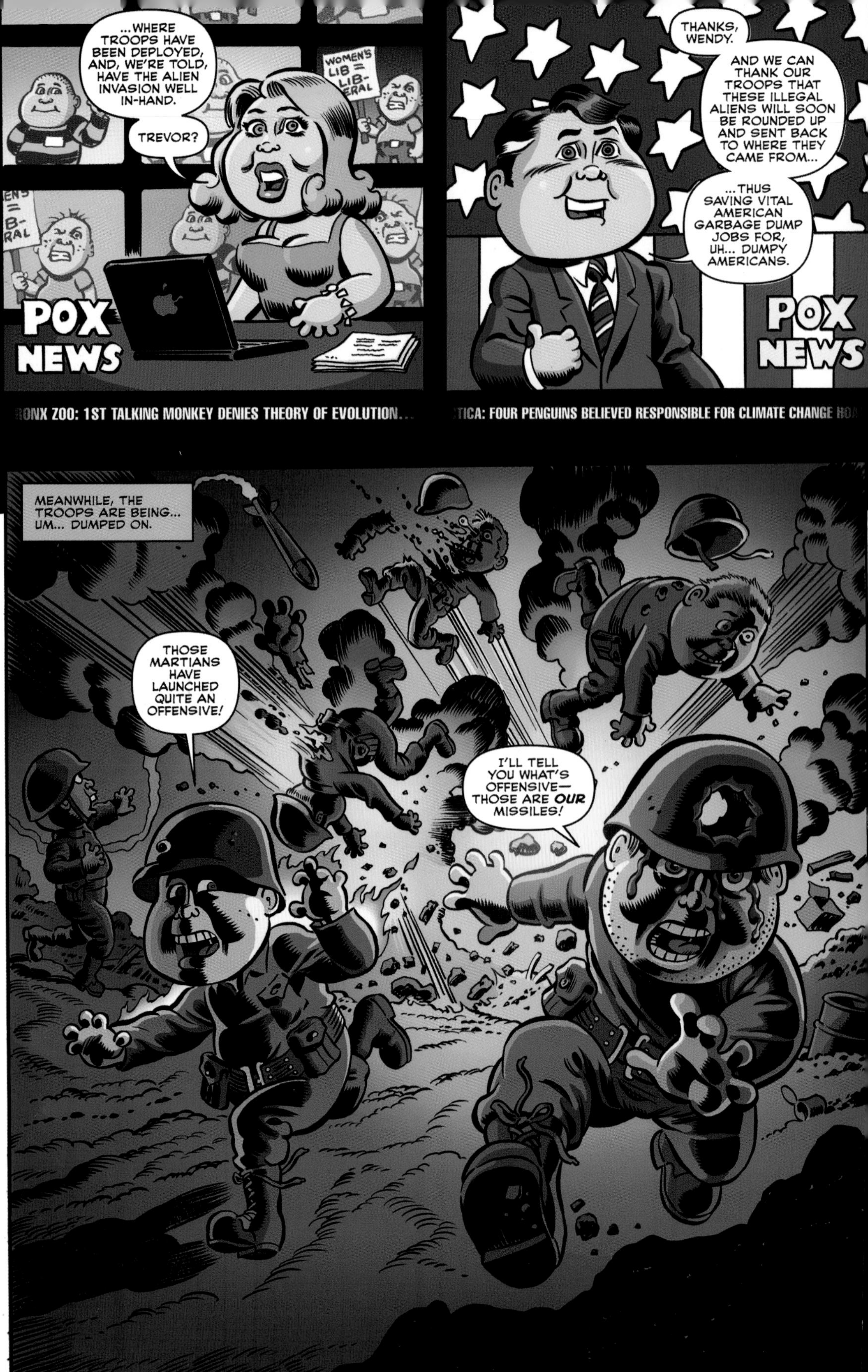
...WHERE TROOPS HAVE BEEN DEPLOYED, AND, WE'RE TOLD, HAVE THE ALIEN INVASION WELL IN-HAND.
TREVOR?
WOMEN'S LIB = LIB-ERAL
POX NEWS
THANKS, WENDY.
AND WE CAN THANK OUR TROOPS THAT THESE ILLEGAL ALIENS WILL SOON BE ROUNDED UP AND SENT BACK TO WHERE THEY CAME FROM...
...THUS SAVING VITAL AMERICAN GARBAGE DUMP JOBS FOR, UH... DUMPY AMERICANS.
POX NEWS
ONX ZOO: 1ST TALKING MONKEY DENIES THEORY OF EVOLUTION...
TICA: FOUR PENGUINS BELIEVED RESPONSIBLE FOR CLIMATE CHANGE
MEANWHILE, THE TROOPS ARE BEING... UM... DUMPED ON.
THOSE MARTIANS HAVE LAUNCHED QUITE AN OFFENSIVE!
I'LL TELL YOU WHAT'S OFFENSIVE— THOSE ARE *OUR* MISSILES!

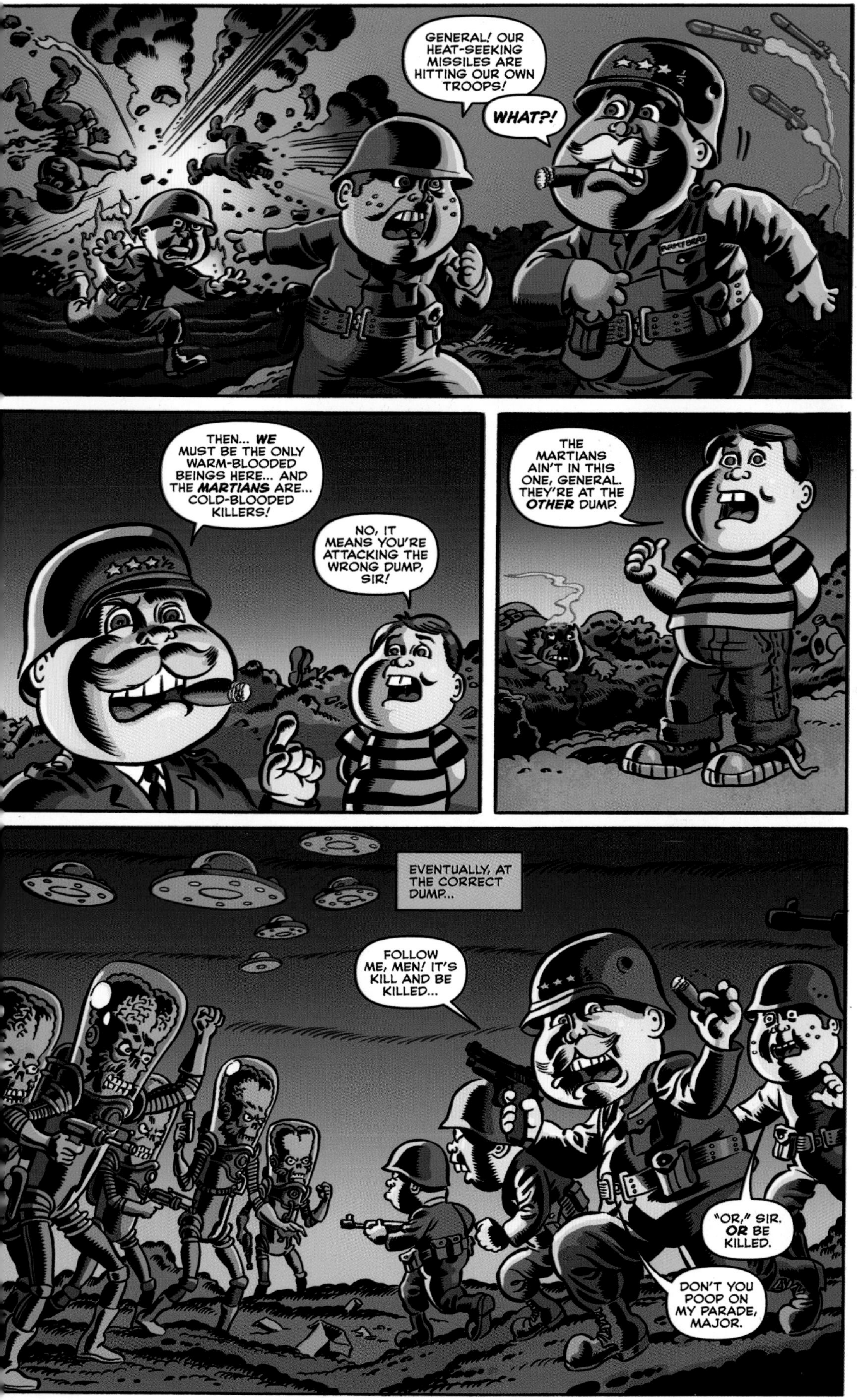
GENERAL! OUR HEAT-SEEKING MISSILES ARE HITTING OUR OWN TROOPS!
WHAT?!
THEN... WE MUST BE THE ONLY WARM-BLOODED BEINGS HERE... AND THE MARTIANS ARE... COLD-BLOODED KILLERS!
NO, IT MEANS YOU'RE ATTACKING THE WRONG DUMP, SIR!
THE MARTIANS AIN'T IN THIS ONE, GENERAL. THEY'RE AT THE OTHER DUMP.
EVENTUALLY, AT THE CORRECT DUMP...
FOLLOW ME, MEN! IT'S KILL AND BE KILLED...
"OR," SIR. OR BE KILLED.
DON'T YOU POOP ON MY PARADE, MAJOR.

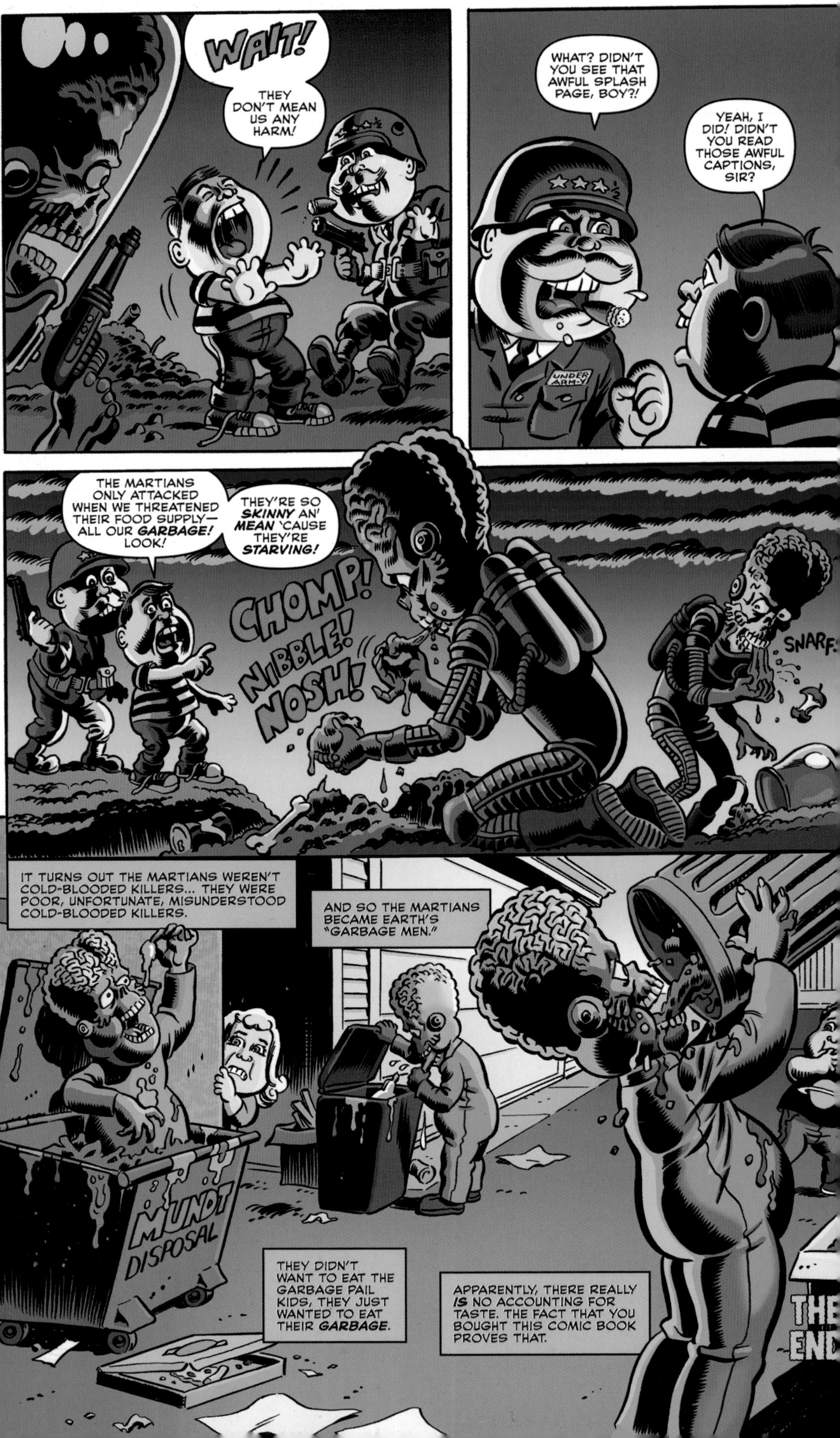

WAIT!
THEY DON'T MEAN US ANY HARM!
WHAT? DIDN'T YOU SEE THAT AWFUL SPLASH PAGE, BOY?!
YEAH, I DID! DIDN'T YOU READ THOSE AWFUL CAPTIONS, SIR?
UNDER ARM-Y
THE MARTIANS ONLY ATTACKED WHEN WE THREATENED THEIR FOOD SUPPLY— ALL OUR GARBAGE! LOOK!
THEY'RE SO SKINNY AN' MEAN 'CAUSE THEY'RE STARVING!
CHOMP!
NIBBLE!
NOSH!
SNARF!
IT TURNS OUT THE MARTIANS WEREN'T COLD-BLOODED KILLERS... THEY WERE POOR, UNFORTUNATE, MISUNDERSTOOD COLD-BLOODED KILLERS.
AND SO THE MARTIANS BECAME EARTH'S "GARBAGE MEN."
MUNDT DISPOSAL
THEY DIDN'T WANT TO EAT THE GARBAGE PAIL KIDS, THEY JUST WANTED TO EAT THEIR GARBAGE.
APPARENTLY, THERE REALLY IS NO ACCOUNTING FOR TASTE. THE FACT THAT YOU BOUGHT THIS COMIC BOOK PROVES THAT.

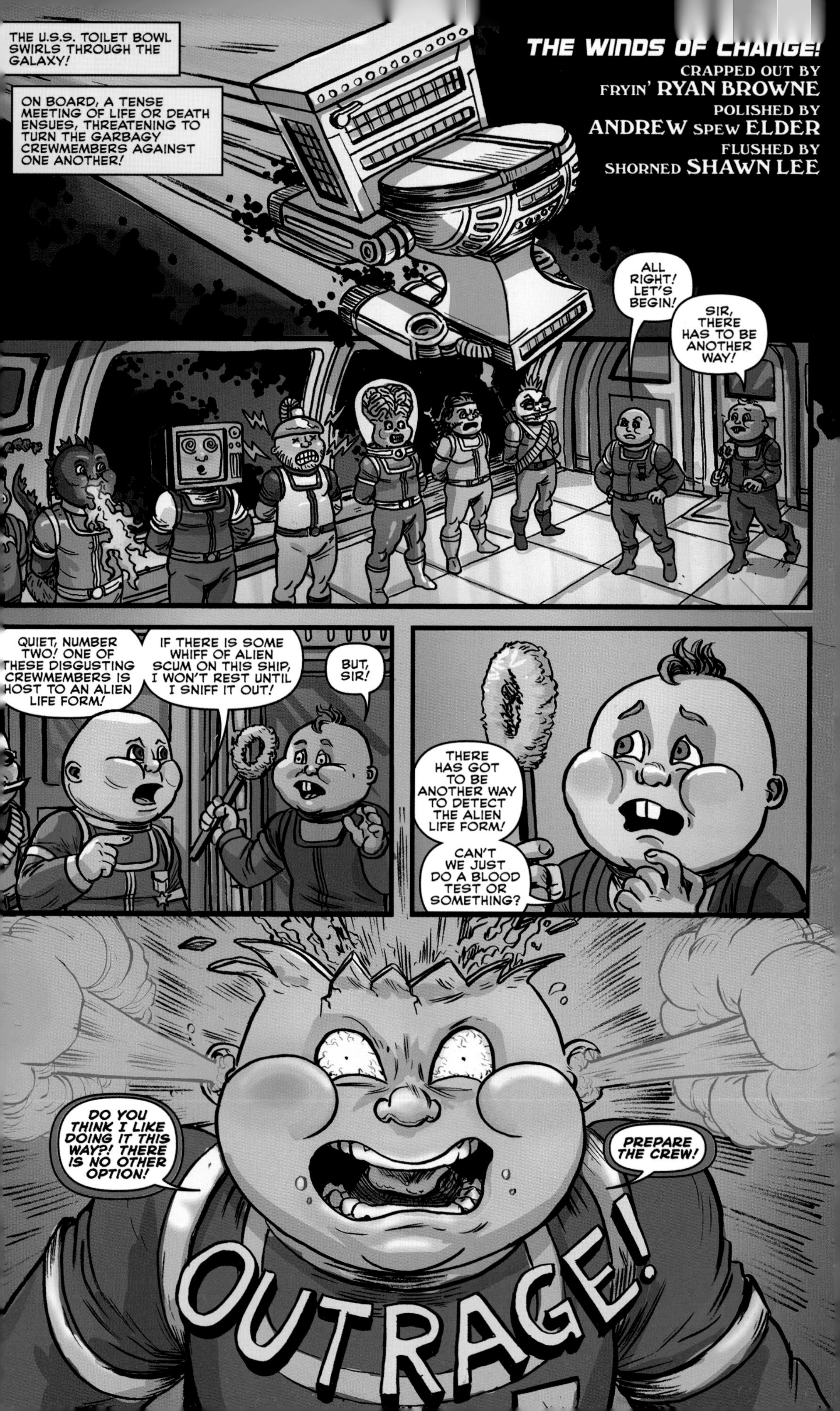
THE U.S.S. TOILET BOWL SWIRLS THROUGH THE GALAXY!
ON BOARD, A TENSE MEETING OF LIFE OR DEATH ENSUES, THREATENING TO TURN THE GARBAGY CREWMEMBERS AGAINST ONE ANOTHER!
THE WINDS OF CHANGE!
CRAPPED OUT BY FRYIN' RYAN BROWNE
POLISHED BY ANDREW SPEW ELDER
FLUSHED BY SHORNED SHAWN LEE
ALL RIGHT! LET'S BEGIN!
SIR, THERE HAS TO BE ANOTHER WAY!
QUIET, NUMBER TWO! ONE OF THESE DISGUSTING CREWMEMBERS IS HOST TO AN ALIEN LIFE FORM!
IF THERE IS SOME WHIFF OF ALIEN SCUM ON THIS SHIP, I WON'T REST UNTIL I SNIFF IT OUT!
BUT, SIR!
THERE HAS GOT TO BE ANOTHER WAY TO DETECT THE ALIEN LIFE FORM!
CAN'T WE JUST DO A BLOOD TEST OR SOMETHING?
DO YOU THINK I LIKE DOING IT THIS WAY?! THERE IS NO OTHER OPTION!
PREPARE THE CREW!
OUTRAGE!

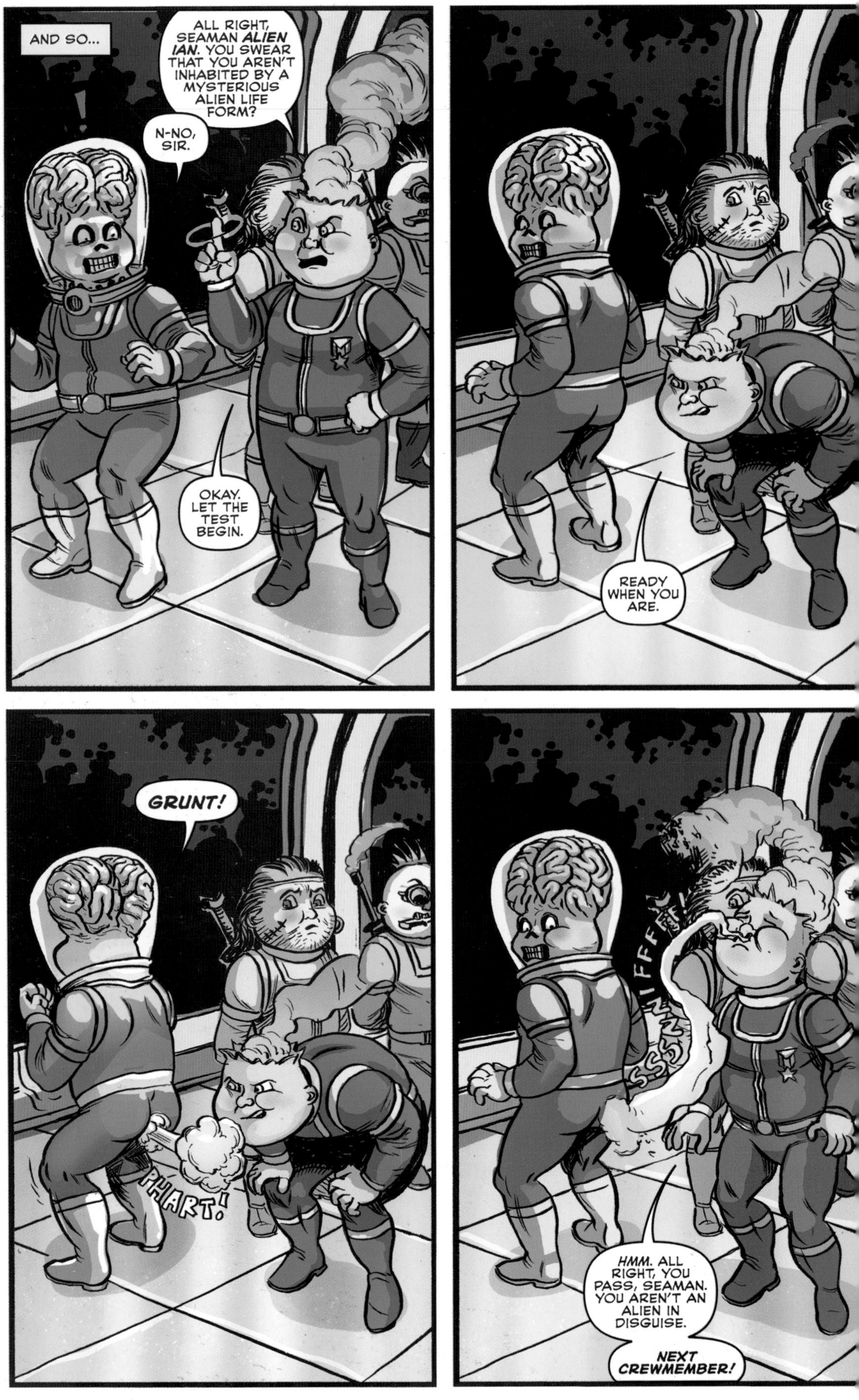
AND SO...
ALL RIGHT, SEAMAN ALIEN IAN. YOU SWEAR THAT YOU AREN'T INHABITED BY A MYSTERIOUS ALIEN LIFE FORM?
N-NO, SIR.
OKAY. LET THE TEST BEGIN.
READY WHEN YOU ARE.
GRUNT!
PHART!
SSSNIFFF
HMM. ALL RIGHT, YOU PASS, SEAMAN. YOU AREN'T AN ALIEN IN DISGUISE.
NEXT CREWMEMBER!

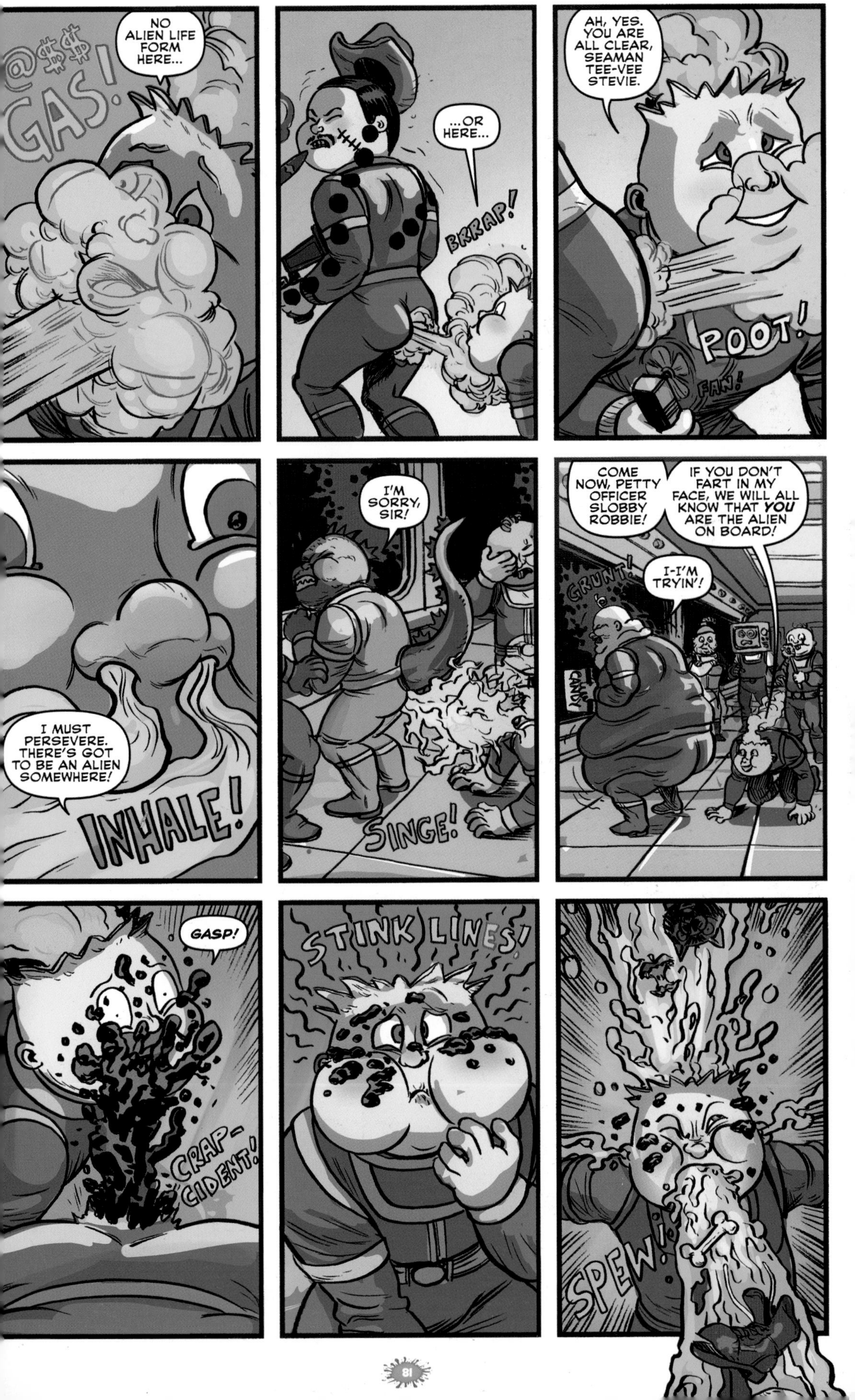
@$$$ GAS!
NO ALIEN LIFE FORM HERE...
...OR HERE...
BRRAP!
AH, YES. YOU ARE ALL CLEAR, SEAMAN TEE-VEE STEVIE.
POOT!
FAN!
I MUST PERSEVERE. THERE'S GOT TO BE AN ALIEN SOMEWHERE!
INHALE!
I'M SORRY, SIR!
SINGE!
COME NOW, PETTY OFFICER SLOBBY ROBBIE!
IF YOU DON'T FART IN MY FACE, WE WILL ALL KNOW THAT YOU ARE THE ALIEN ON BOARD!
GRUNT!
I-I'M TRYIN'!
CANDY
GASP!
CRAP-CIDENT!
STINK LINES!
SPEW!

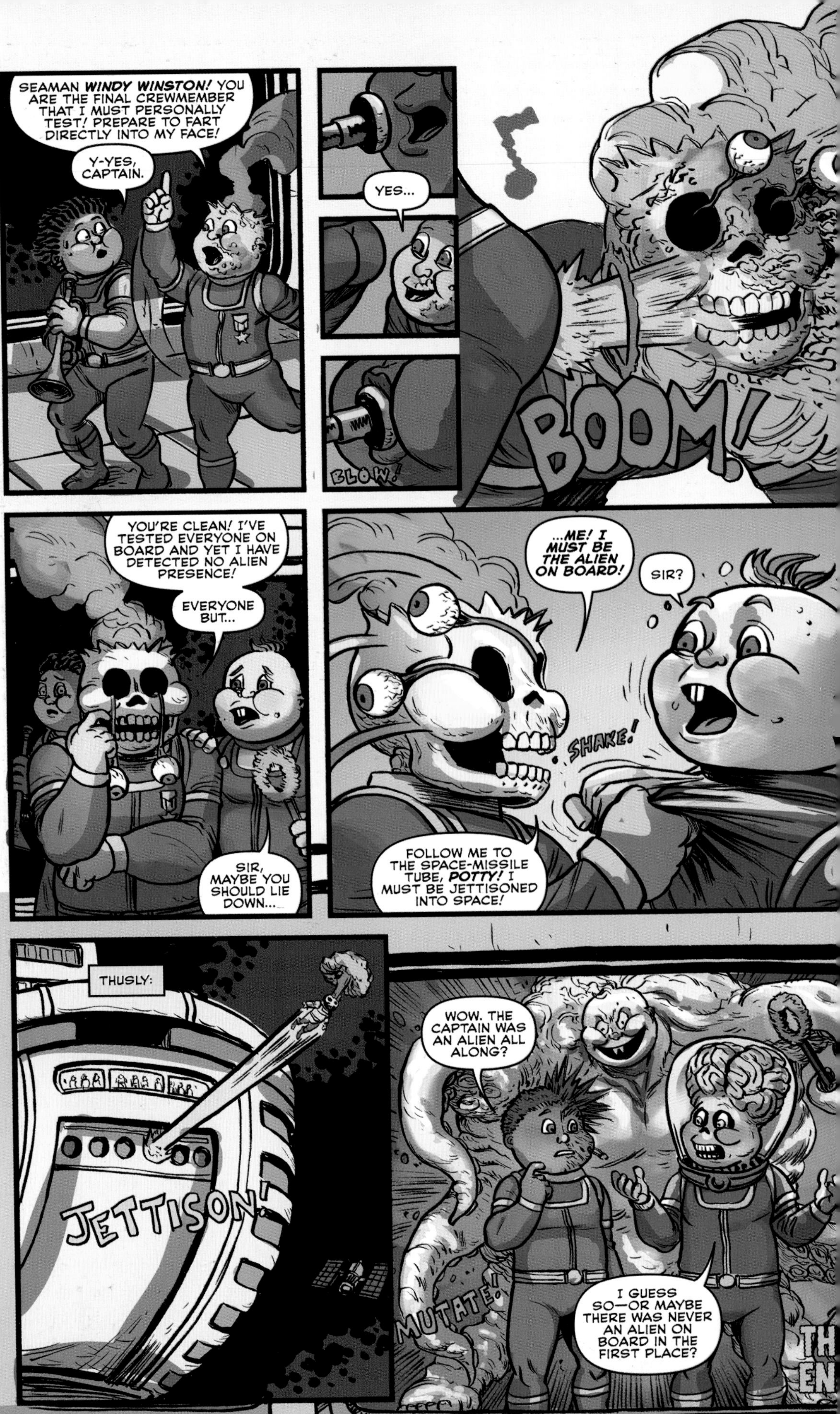
SEAMAN WINDY WINSTON! YOU ARE THE FINAL CREWMEMBER THAT I MUST PERSONALLY TEST! PREPARE TO FART DIRECTLY INTO MY FACE!
Y-YES, CAPTAIN.
YES...
BLOW!
BOOM!
YOU'RE CLEAN! I'VE TESTED EVERYONE ON BOARD AND YET I HAVE DETECTED NO ALIEN PRESENCE!
EVERYONE BUT...
SIR, MAYBE YOU SHOULD LIE DOWN...
...ME! I MUST BE THE ALIEN ON BOARD!
SIR?
SHAKE!
FOLLOW ME TO THE SPACE-MISSILE TUBE, POTTY! I MUST BE JETTISONED INTO SPACE!
THUSLY:
JETTISON!
WOW. THE CAPTAIN WAS AN ALIEN ALL ALONG?
MUTATE!
I GUESS SO—OR MAYBE THERE WAS NEVER AN ALIEN ON BOARD IN THE FIRST PLACE?

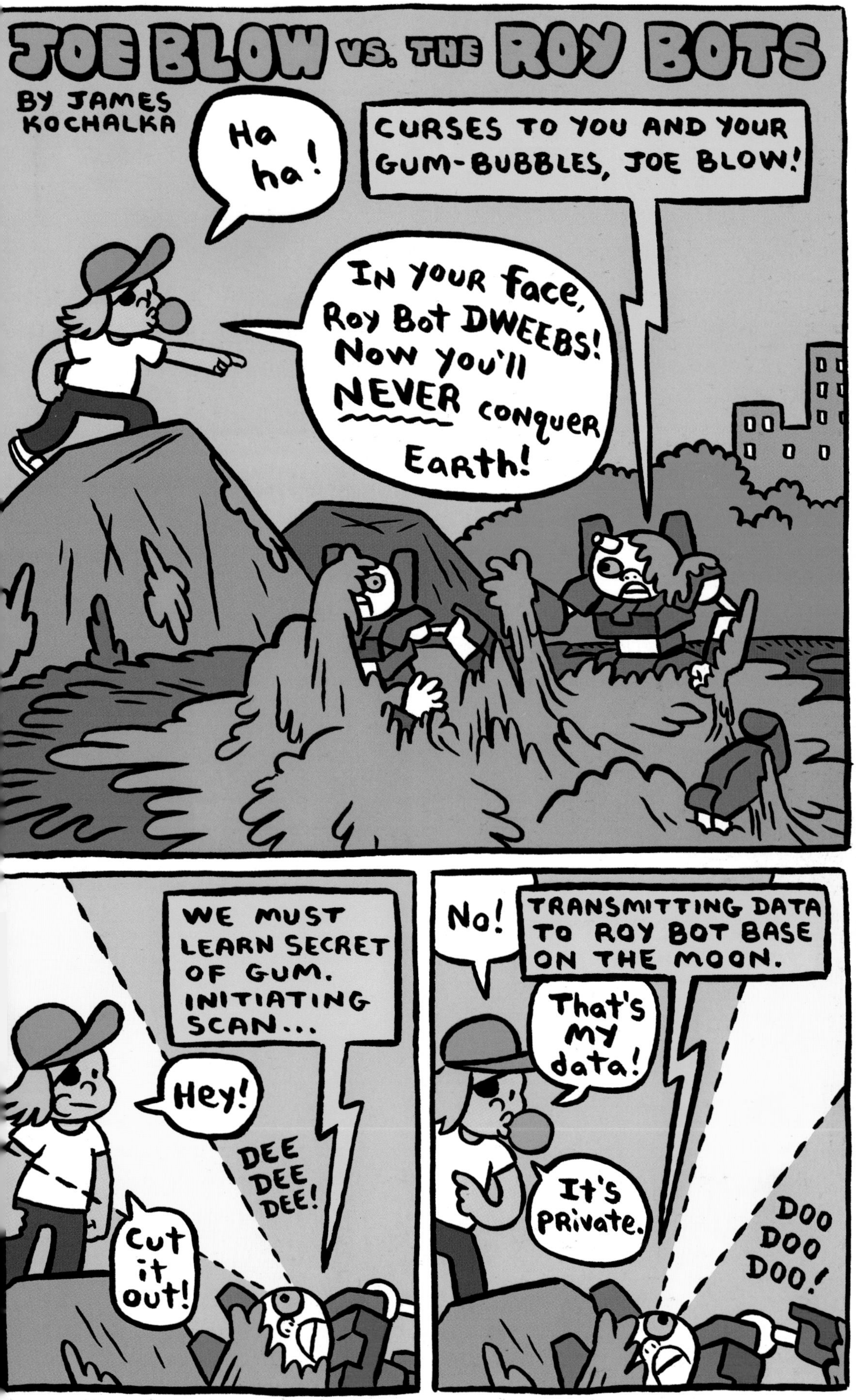
JOE BLOW VS. THE ROY BOTS
BY JAMES KOCHALKA
Ha ha!
CURSES TO YOU AND YOUR GUM-BUBBLES, JOE BLOW!
In your face, Roy Bot DWEEBS! Now you'll NEVER conquer Earth!
WE MUST LEARN SECRET OF GUM. INITIATING SCAN...
Hey!
DEE DEE DEE!
Cut it out!
No!
TRANSMITTING DATA TO ROY BOT BASE ON THE MOON.
That's my data!
It's private.
DOO DOO DOO!

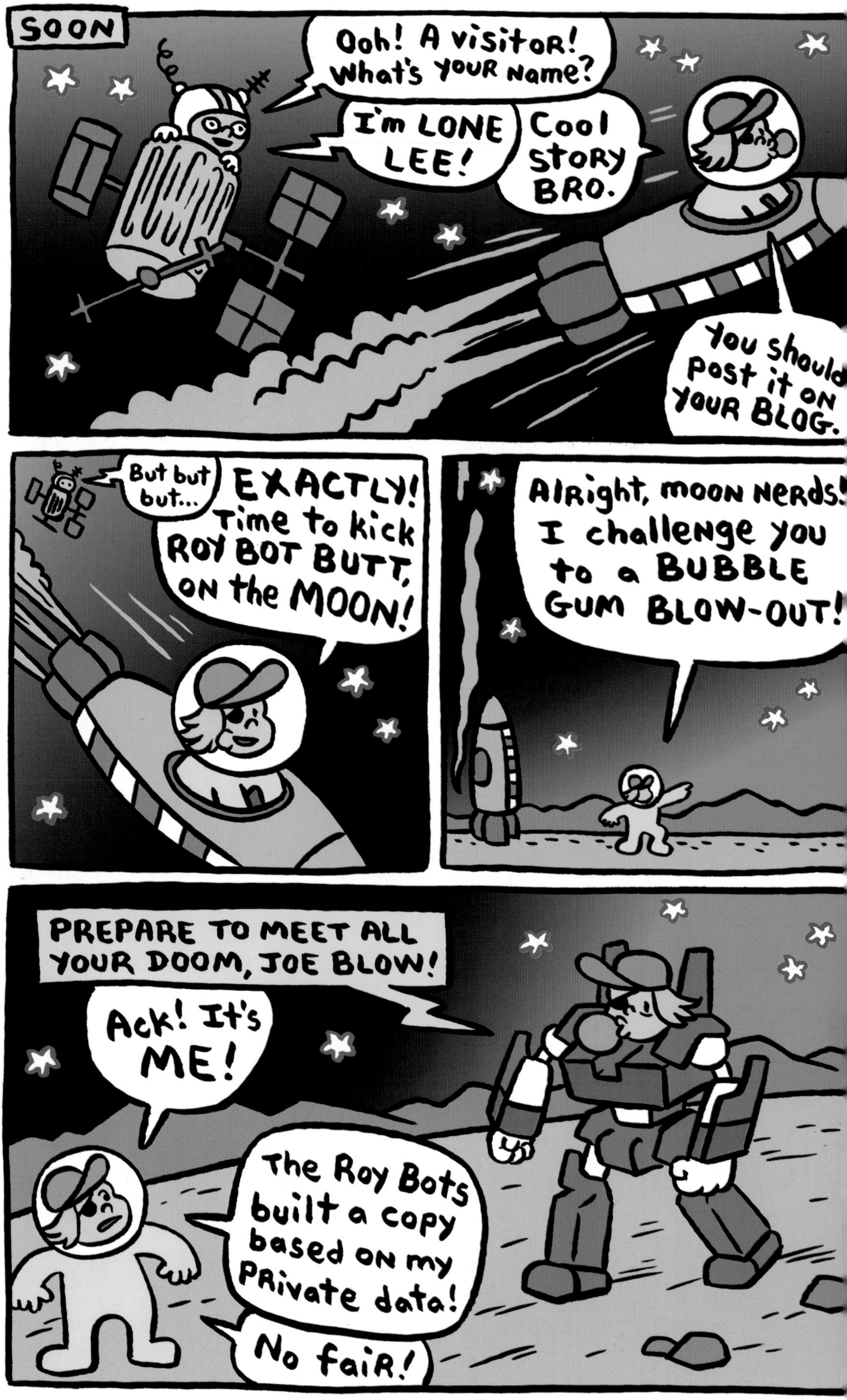
SOON
Ooh! A visitor! What's your name?
I'm LONE LEE!
Cool story BRO.
You should post it on your BLOG.
But but but...
EXACTLY! Time to kick ROY BOT BUTT, on the MOON!
Alright, moon nerds! I challenge you to a BUBBLE GUM BLOW-OUT!
PREPARE TO MEET ALL YOUR DOOM, JOE BLOW!
Ack! It's ME!
The Roy Bots built a copy based on my private data!
No fair!

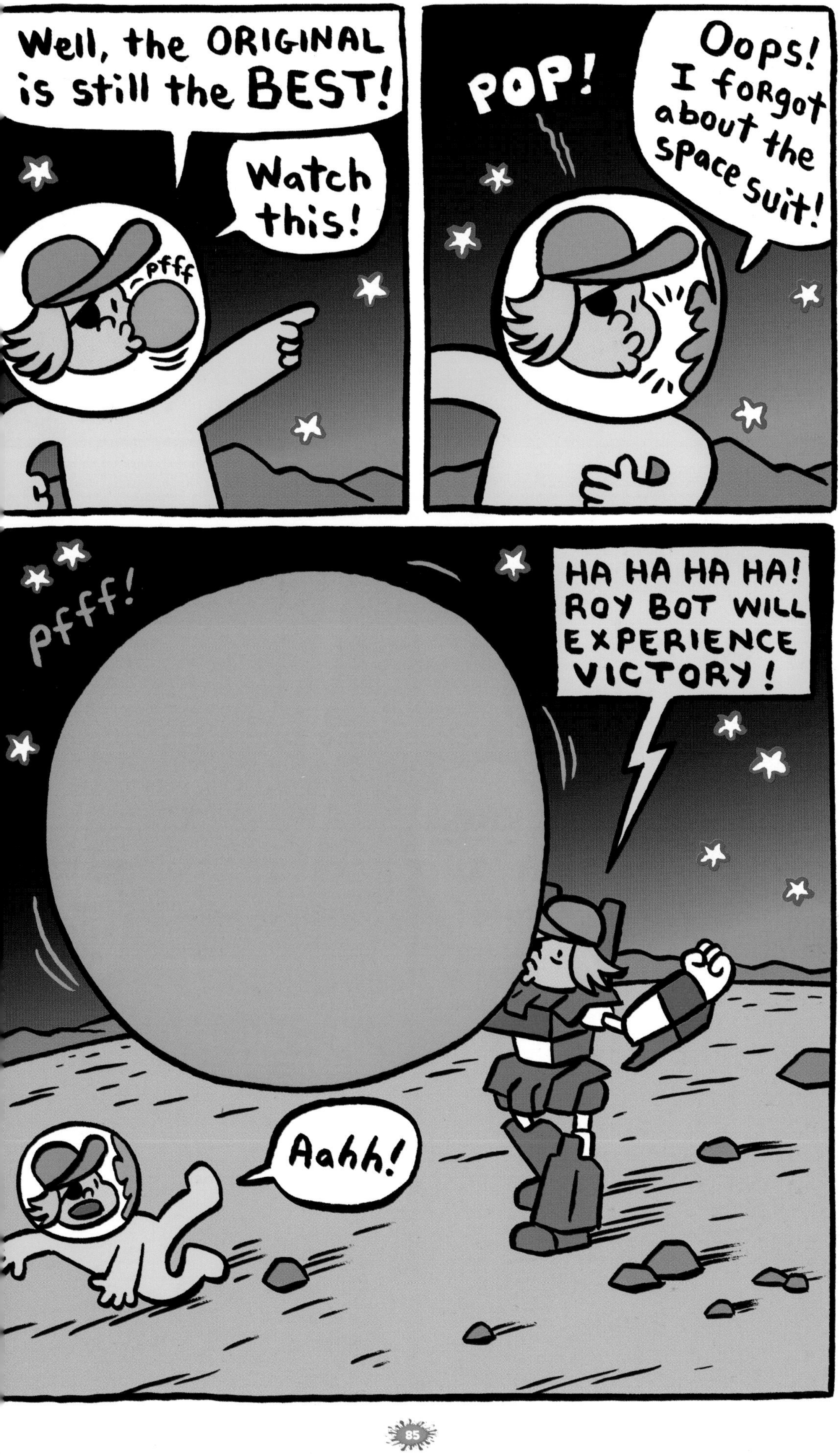
Well, the ORIGINAL is still the BEST!
Watch this!
pfff
POP!
Oops! I forgot about the space suit!
pfff!
HA HA HA HA! ROY BOT WILL EXPERIENCE VICTORY!
Aahh!

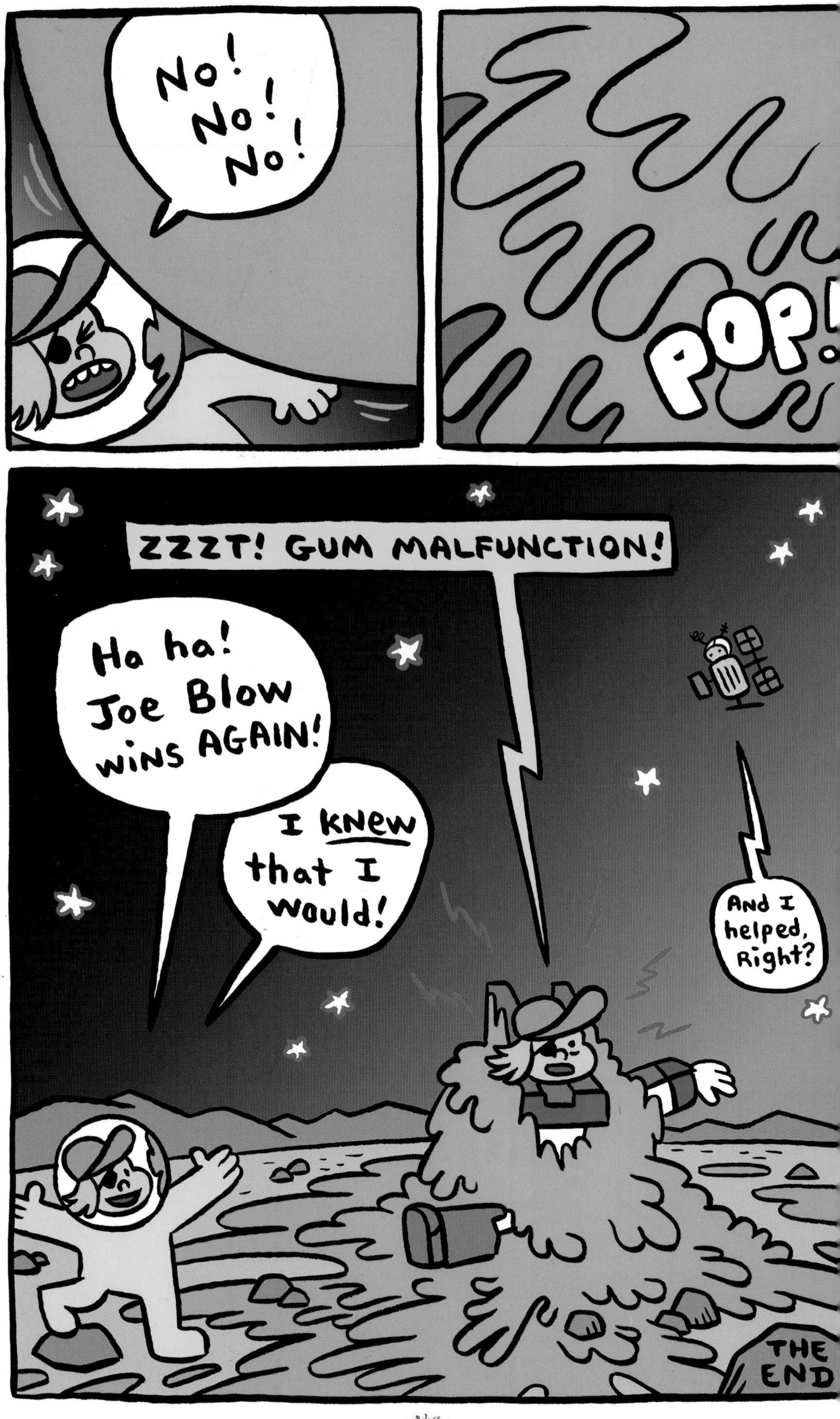
No! No! No!
POP!
ZZZT! GUM MALFUNCTION!
Ha ha! Joe Blow wins AGAIN!
I KNEW that I would!
And I helped, Right?
THE END

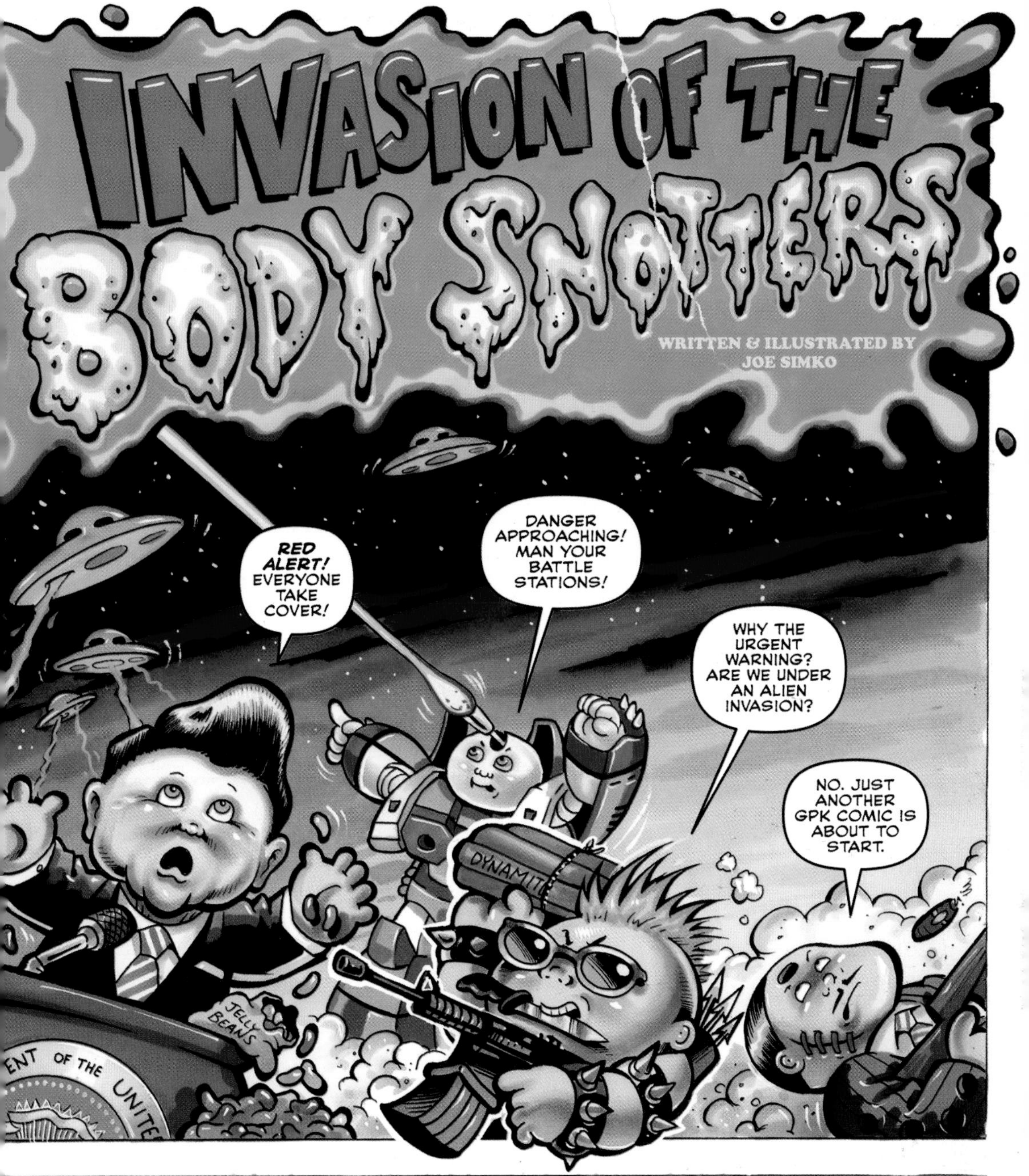
INVASION OF THE BODY SNOTTERS
WRITTEN & ILLUSTRATED BY JOE SIMKO
RED ALERT! EVERYONE TAKE COVER!
DANGER APPROACHING! MAN YOUR BATTLE STATIONS!
WHY THE URGENT WARNING? ARE WE UNDER AN ALIEN INVASION?
NO. JUST ANOTHER GPK COMIC IS ABOUT TO START.
JELLY BEANS

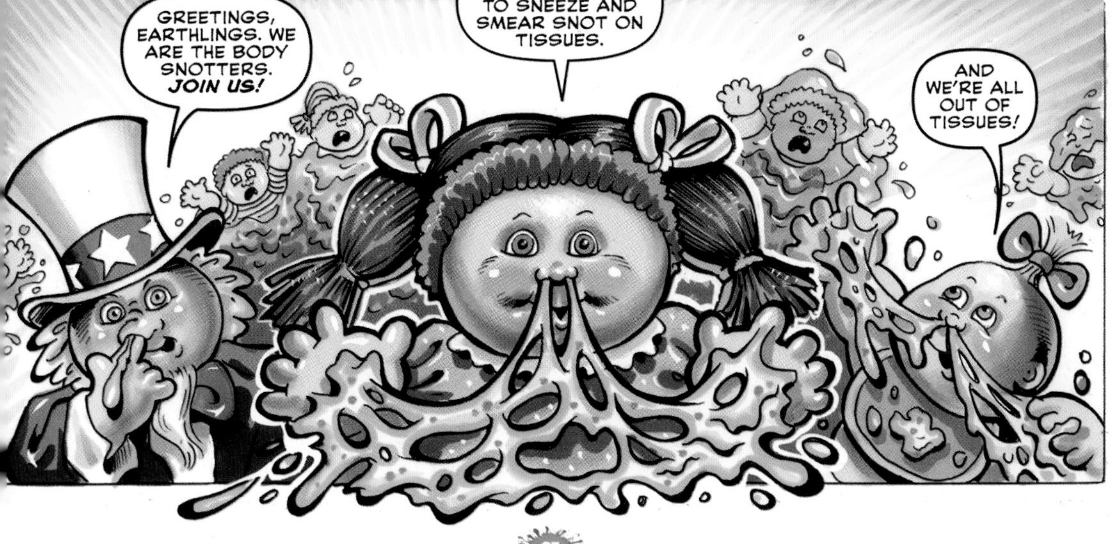
GREETINGS, EARTHLINGS. WE ARE THE BODY SNOTTERS. JOIN US!
WE'VE COME HERE TO SNEEZE AND SMEAR SNOT ON TISSUES.
AND WE'RE ALL OUT OF TISSUES!

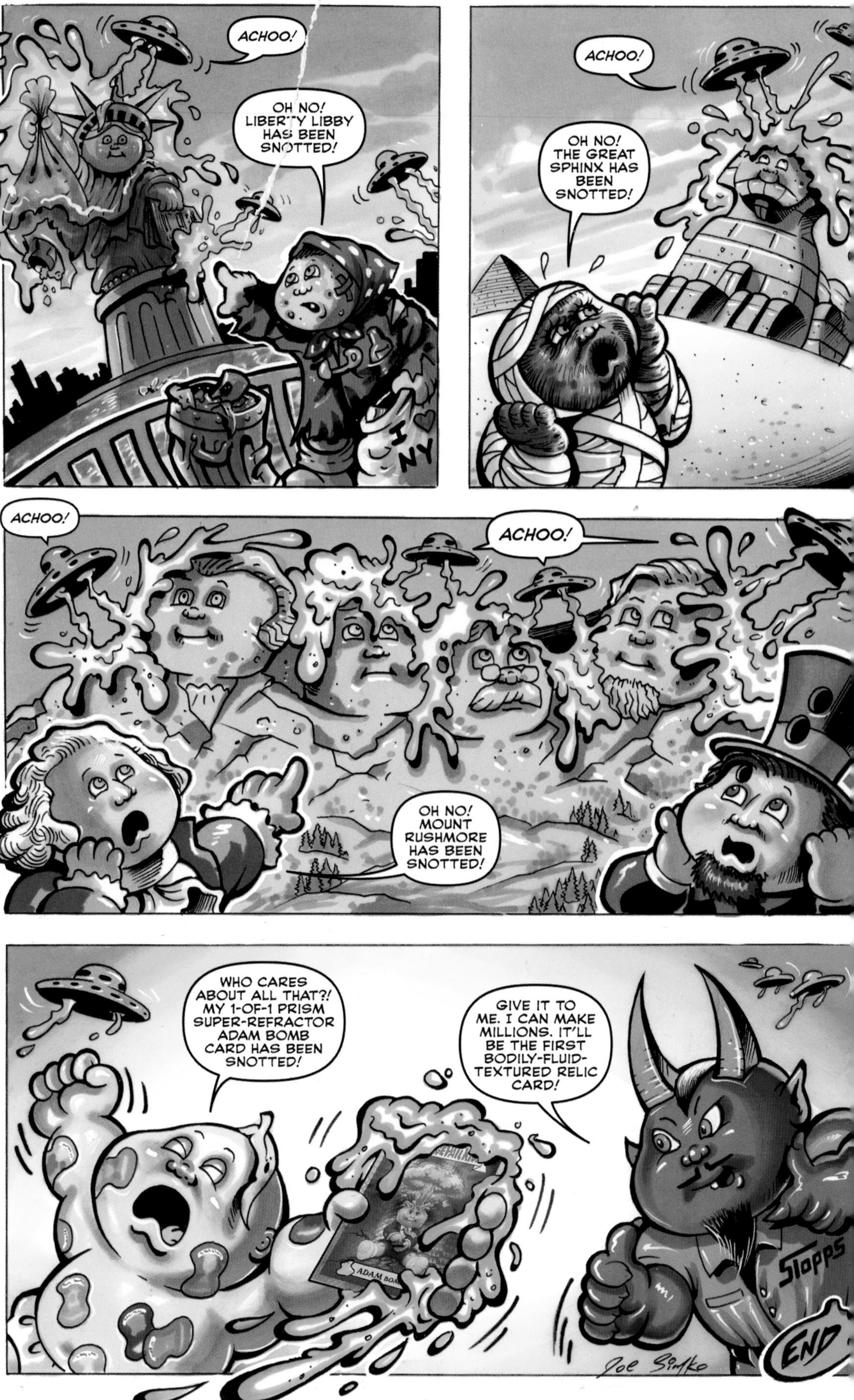
ACHOO!
OH NO! LIBERTY LIBBY HAS BEEN SNOTTED!
I ♥ NY
ACHOO!
OH NO! THE GREAT SPHINX HAS BEEN SNOTTED!
ACHOO!
ACHOO!
OH NO! MOUNT RUSHMORE HAS BEEN SNOTTED!
WHO CARES ABOUT ALL THAT?! MY 1-OF-1 PRISM SUPER-REFRACTOR ADAM BOMB CARD HAS BEEN SNOTTED!
GIVE IT TO ME. I CAN MAKE MILLIONS. IT'LL BE THE FIRST BODILY-FLUID-TEXTURED RELIC CARD!
Stopps
END
Joe Simko

THE STELLAR ADVENTURES OF INTER STELLA

with her pal, RUSTY BOLTS

HROARK! THE SMELL OF THIS PLANET MAKES ME WANT TO **HURL!**

PLAUGH! ME TOO -- AND THAT TAKES **SOME** DOING!

DISASTER! WOE! STELLA AND RUSTY ARE SURROUNDED BY GRUBBY WEE BEASTIES, MAROONED WITH **NO ROCKET FUEL**... AND **NO HOPE OF ESCAPE!** BUT HOW DID SUCH A DIRE SITUATION COME TO PASS? WHAT BROUGHT OUR HEROES TO THE **FOUL, BRACKISH BACK-WATER** THAT IS...

THE BROWN PLANET

BY JOLLY **ROGER** LANGRIDGE
COLORS BY **ANDREW** SPEW ELDER

OUR STORY BEGINS A FEW HOURS EARLIER AS STELLA AND RUSTY RETURN FROM A TRADE MISSION TO THE **BEANSTAR**...

JUST TWO MORE PARSECS UNTIL WE REACH THE WARP GATE -- THEN IT'S **STRAIGHT HOME!**

THANK GROTT! ONE MORE TIN OF **BEANS** AND I SWEAR I'LL **CHUCK** RIGHT IN MY HELMET.

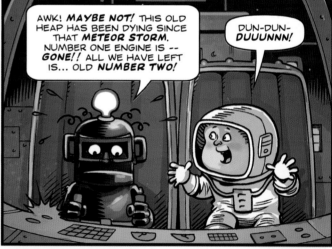

AWK! **MAYBE NOT!** THIS OLD HEAP HAS BEEN DYING SINCE THAT **METEOR STORM.** NUMBER ONE ENGINE IS -- **GONE!!** ALL WE HAVE LEFT IS... OLD **NUMBER TWO!**

DUN-DUN-DUUUNNN!

DON'T DO THAT.

SORRY.

89

JUST ONE CHANCE -- WE CAN TRY AND LAND ON THE *NEAREST PLANET* AND GET *HELP!*

NEAREST PLANET...? NOT -- *CITRUS VI,* THE *ORANGE PLANET?*

NOPE.

YOU MEAN -- *SNOTTICUS MAJOR,* THE *GREEN PLANET?*

NOT EVEN CLOSE.

I MEAN *KAKAVARIUS... THE BROWN PLANET!*

SPLORCHH!

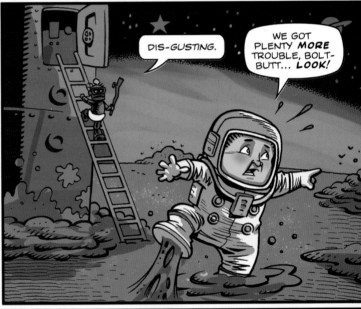

DIS-GUSTING.

WE GOT PLENTY *MORE* TROUBLE, BOLT-BUTT... *LOOK!*

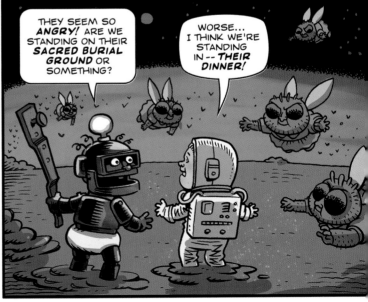

THEY SEEM SO *ANGRY!* ARE WE STANDING ON THEIR *SACRED BURIAL GROUND* OR SOMETHING?

WORSE... I THINK WE'RE STANDING IN -- *THEIR DINNER!*

OKAY, RUSTY -- GET 'EM!!
YEAH! I -- WHAT? ME?
BASIC CAPTAIN-ROBOT DYNAMIC... YOU'RE THERE TO DO THE DIRTY WORK.
AWK! DIRTY IS RIGHT! I KNEW I SHOULDA BECOME A TOASTER LIKE MAMA SAID!
WHAT ARE YOU DOING, STELLA?
SPLORT
SPLUDGE
SPLORCH
IMPORTANT CAPTAIN STUFF -- NAMELY, LOOKING UP THE PROTOCOL FOR THIS SITUATION. IT SEEMS TO BE EITHER HONORABLE SUICIDE OR --
HEY! WAIT A MINUTE! "ESCAPE CAPSULE?"
AARGH
OOF
EEK
CAPTAIN'S MANUAL
DID YOU JUST SAY WHAT I THINK I THOUGHT YOU SAID YOU THOUGHT?
I... HAVE NO IDEA WHAT YOU JUST SAID. BUT YES! THERE'S AN ESCAPE CAPSULE -- AND IT RUNS ON METHANE!
DO WE HAVE ANY METHANE?
NOT ON BOARD -- BUT GIVE ME FIVE MINUTES AND I CAN HOOK US UP TO AN INEXHAUSTIBLE SUPPLY!
YOU CAN? GEE! IT'S TOO BAD YOU HAVE TO STAY HERE AND FIGHT THE --
AH.
CAPTAIN'S MANUAL
CAPTAIN'S MANUAL
HIT 'EM IN THE FLAGELLUM -- THAT'S WHERE IT REALLY HURTS!
EEK
OOF
ORK
ECK
AARGH
GETTING... WEARY... HOPE RUSTY.. GETS IT SORTED OUT... SOON...
NO USE... I'M GONNA --
YAWP!

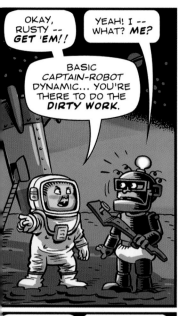

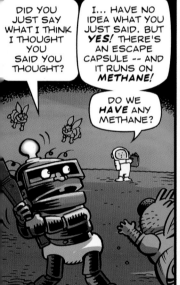

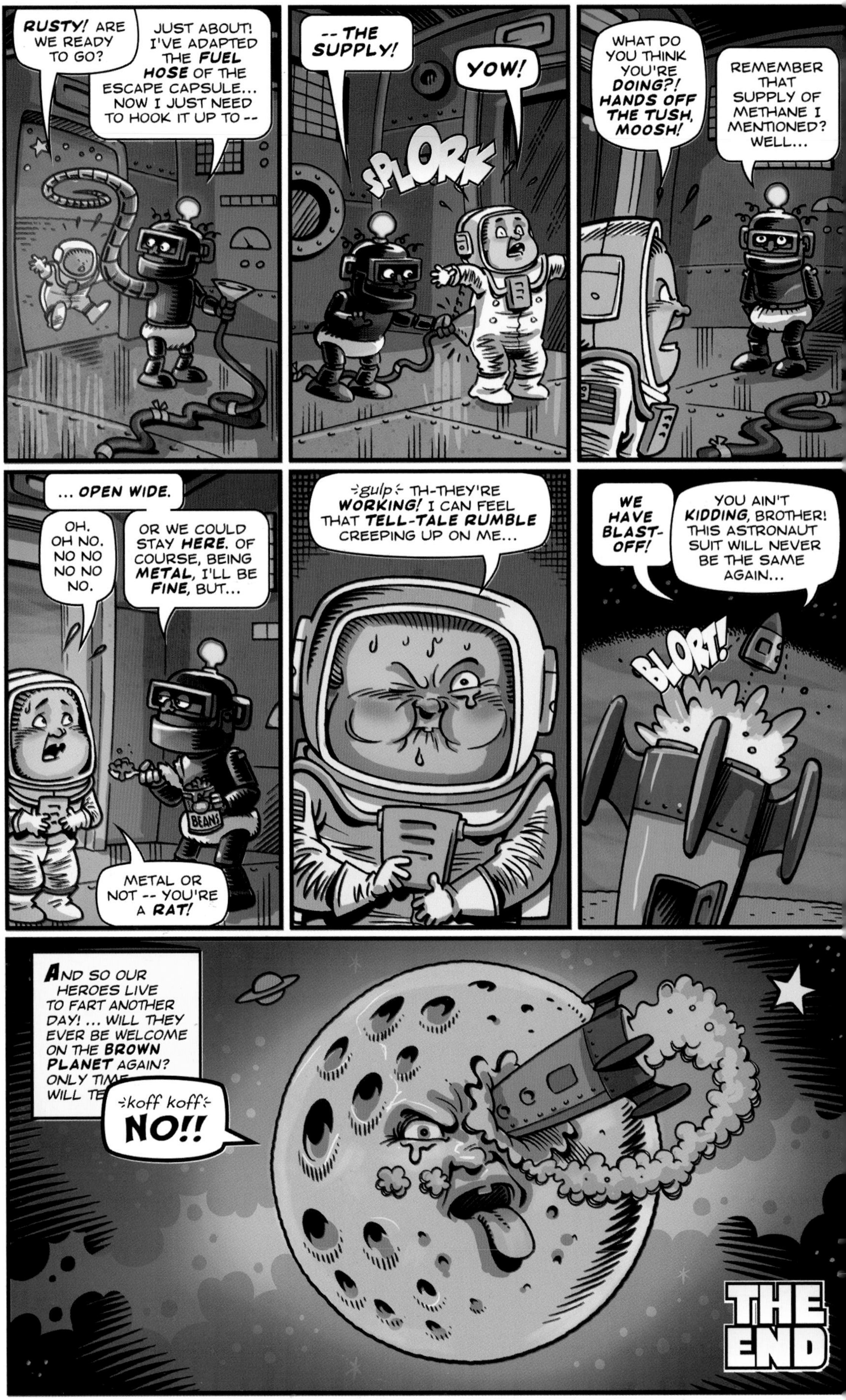

RUSTY! ARE WE READY TO GO?
JUST ABOUT! I'VE ADAPTED THE FUEL HOSE OF THE ESCAPE CAPSULE... NOW I JUST NEED TO HOOK IT UP TO --
-- THE SUPPLY!
YOW!
SPLORK
WHAT DO YOU THINK YOU'RE DOING?! HANDS OFF THE TUSH, MOOSH!
REMEMBER THAT SUPPLY OF METHANE I MENTIONED? WELL...
... OPEN WIDE.
OH. OH NO. NO NO NO NO NO.
OR WE COULD STAY HERE. OF COURSE, BEING METAL, I'LL BE FINE, BUT...
BEANS
METAL OR NOT -- YOU'RE A RAT!
gulp TH-THEY'RE WORKING! I CAN FEEL THAT TELL-TALE RUMBLE CREEPING UP ON ME...
WE HAVE BLAST-OFF!
YOU AIN'T KIDDING, BROTHER! THIS ASTRONAUT SUIT WILL NEVER BE THE SAME AGAIN...
BLORT!
AND SO OUR HEROES LIVE TO FART ANOTHER DAY! ... WILL THEY EVER BE WELCOME ON THE BROWN PLANET AGAIN? ONLY TIME WILL TE
koff koff NO!!
THE END

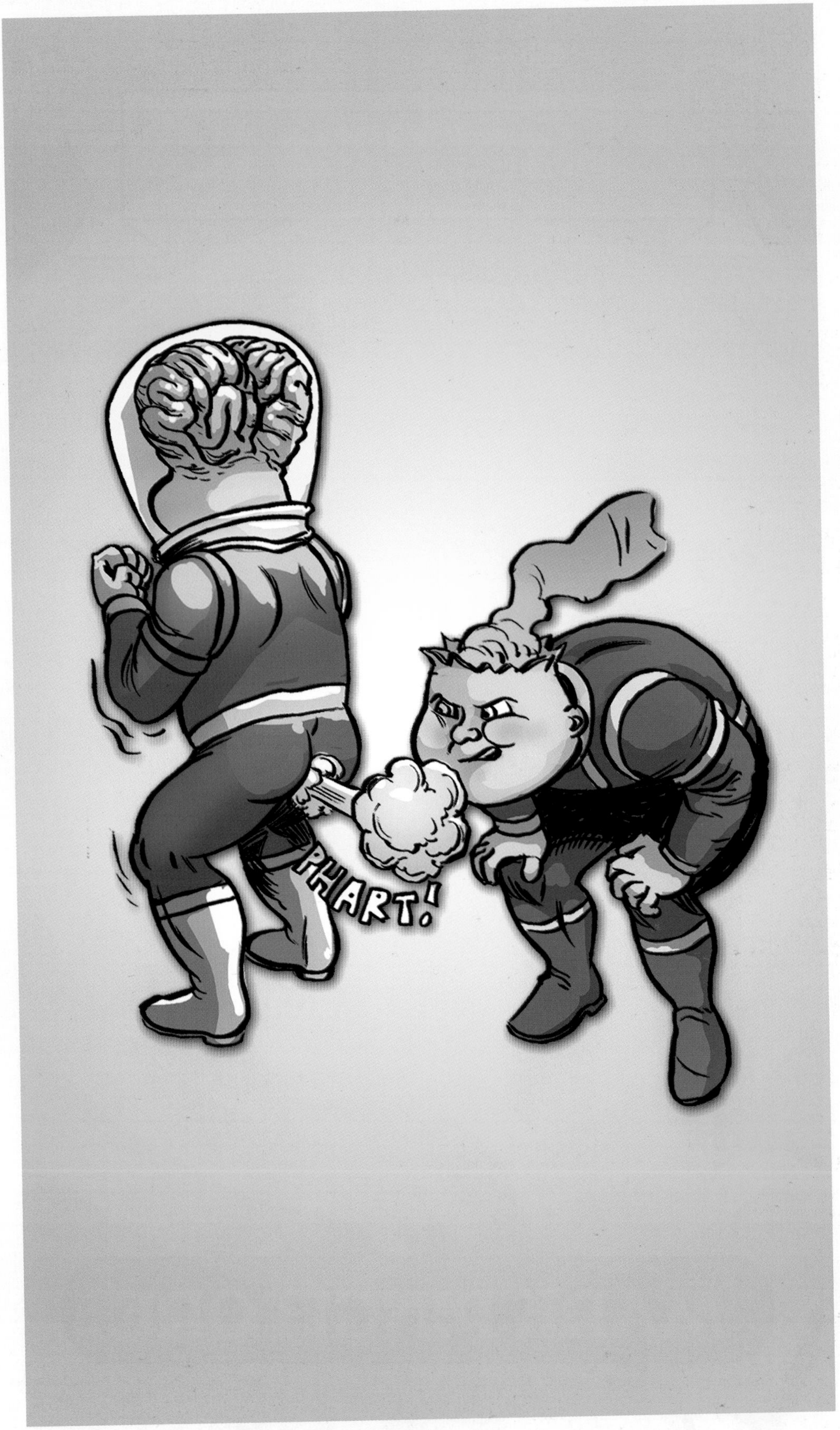
PHART!

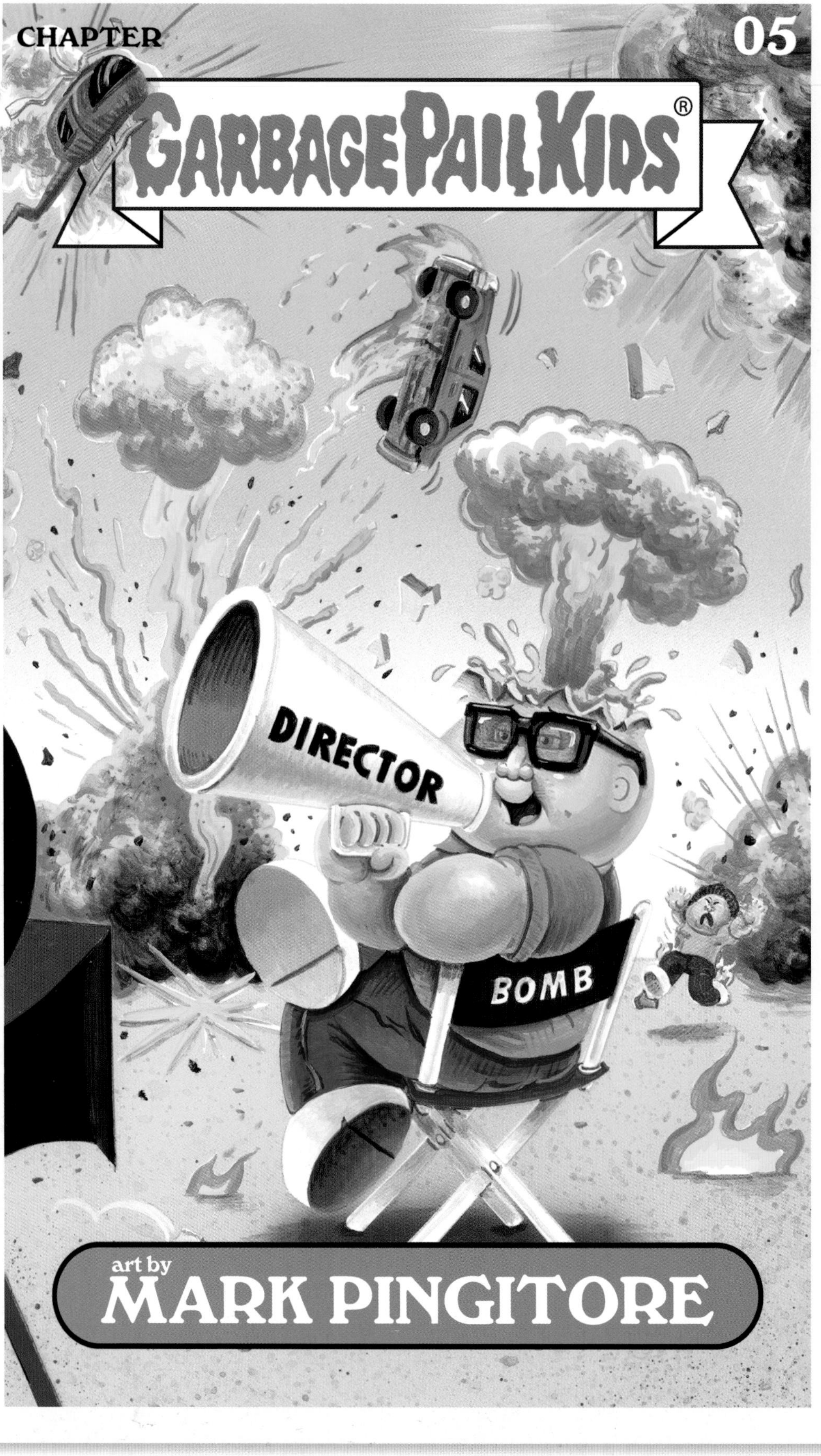
CHAPTER
05
GARBAGE PAIL KIDS®
DIRECTOR
BOMB
art by
MARK PINGITORE

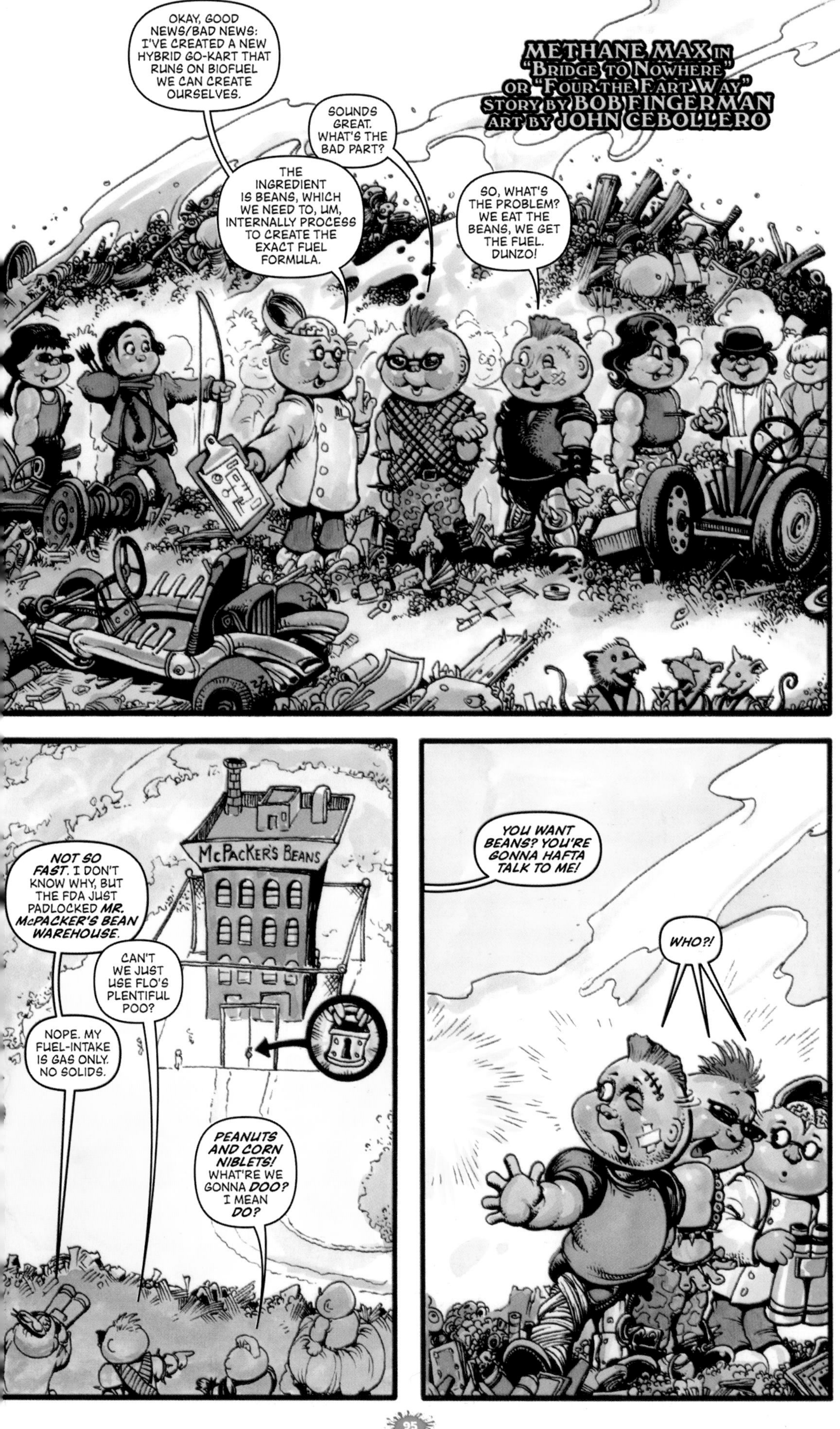
METHANE MAX IN "BRIDGE TO NOWHERE" OR "FOUR THE FART WAY"
STORY BY BOB FINGERMAN
ART BY JOHN CEBOLLERO
OKAY, GOOD NEWS/BAD NEWS: I'VE CREATED A NEW HYBRID GO-KART THAT RUNS ON BIOFUEL WE CAN CREATE OURSELVES.
SOUNDS GREAT. WHAT'S THE BAD PART?
THE INGREDIENT IS BEANS, WHICH WE NEED TO, UM, INTERNALLY PROCESS TO CREATE THE EXACT FUEL FORMULA.
SO, WHAT'S THE PROBLEM? WE EAT THE BEANS, WE GET THE FUEL. DUNZO!
McPACKER'S BEANS
NOT SO FAST. I DON'T KNOW WHY, BUT THE FDA JUST PADLOCKED MR. McPACKER'S BEAN WAREHOUSE.
CAN'T WE JUST USE FLO'S PLENTIFUL POO?
NOPE. MY FUEL-INTAKE IS GAS ONLY. NO SOLIDS.
PEANUTS AND CORN NIBLETS! WHAT'RE WE GONNA DOO? I MEAN DO?
YOU WANT BEANS? YOU'RE GONNA HAFTA TALK TO ME!
WHO?!

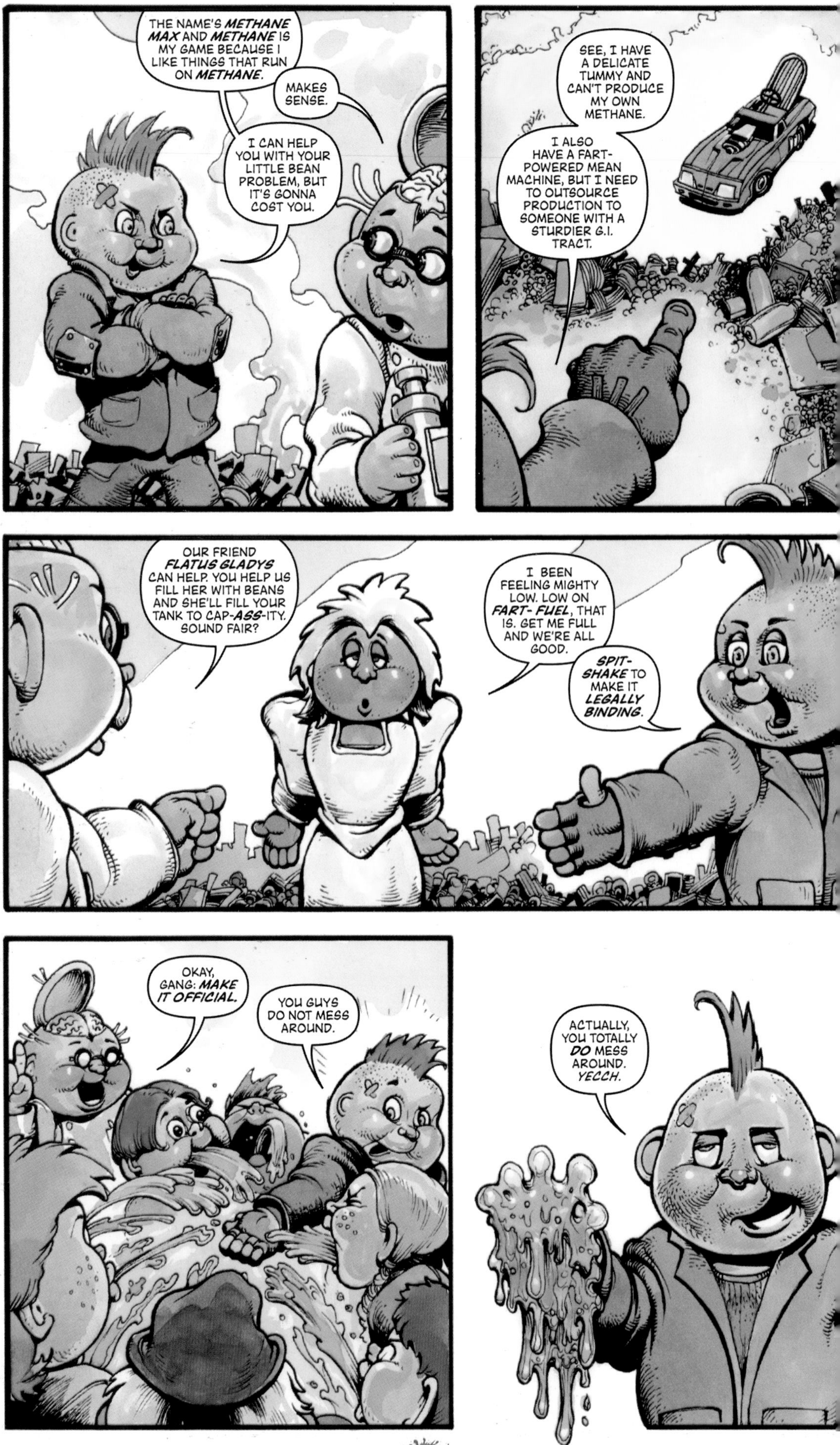
THE NAME'S METHANE MAX AND METHANE IS MY GAME BECAUSE I LIKE THINGS THAT RUN ON METHANE.
MAKES SENSE.
I CAN HELP YOU WITH YOUR LITTLE BEAN PROBLEM, BUT IT'S GONNA COST YOU.
SEE, I HAVE A DELICATE TUMMY AND CAN'T PRODUCE MY OWN METHANE.
I ALSO HAVE A FART-POWERED MEAN MACHINE, BUT I NEED TO OUTSOURCE PRODUCTION TO SOMEONE WITH A STURDIER G.I. TRACT.
OUR FRIEND FLATUS GLADYS CAN HELP. YOU HELP US FILL HER WITH BEANS AND SHE'LL FILL YOUR TANK TO CAP-ASS-ITY. SOUND FAIR?
I BEEN FEELING MIGHTY LOW. LOW ON FART-FUEL, THAT IS. GET ME FULL AND WE'RE ALL GOOD.
SPIT-SHAKE TO MAKE IT LEGALLY BINDING.
OKAY, GANG: MAKE IT OFFICIAL.
YOU GUYS DO NOT MESS AROUND.
ACTUALLY, YOU TOTALLY DO MESS AROUND. YECCH.

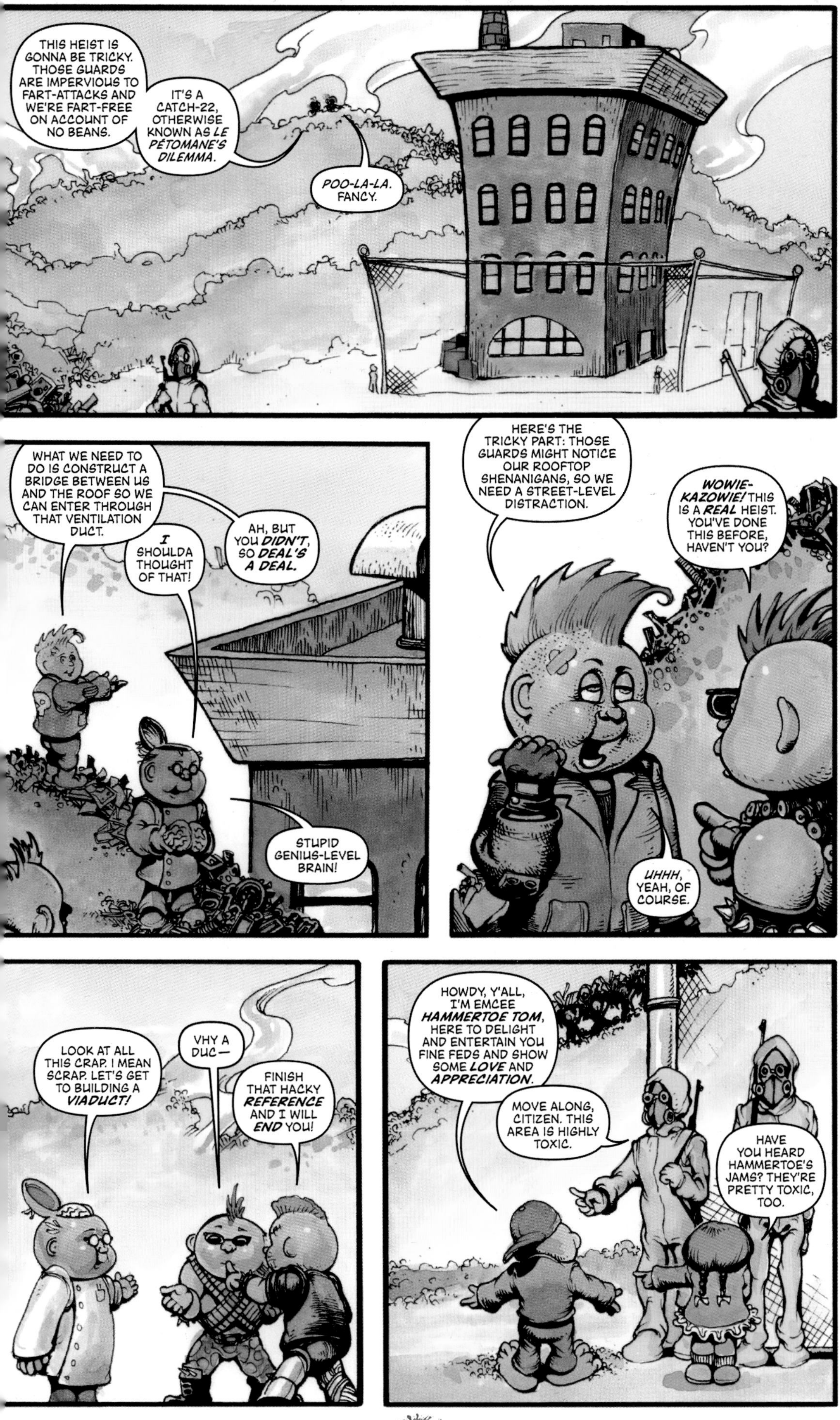

THIS HEIST IS GONNA BE TRICKY. THOSE GUARDS ARE IMPERVIOUS TO FART-ATTACKS AND WE'RE FART-FREE ON ACCOUNT OF NO BEANS.
IT'S A CATCH-22, OTHERWISE KNOWN AS *LE PÉTOMANE'S DILEMMA*.
POO-LA-LA. FANCY.
WHAT WE NEED TO DO IS CONSTRUCT A BRIDGE BETWEEN US AND THE ROOF SO WE CAN ENTER THROUGH THAT VENTILATION DUCT.
I SHOULDA THOUGHT OF THAT!
AH, BUT YOU ***DIDN'T***, SO ***DEAL'S A DEAL.***
STUPID GENIUS-LEVEL BRAIN!
HERE'S THE TRICKY PART: THOSE GUARDS MIGHT NOTICE OUR ROOFTOP SHENANIGANS, SO WE NEED A STREET-LEVEL DISTRACTION.
WOWIE-KAZOWIE! THIS IS A ***REAL*** HEIST. YOU'VE DONE THIS BEFORE, HAVEN'T YOU?
UHHH, YEAH, OF COURSE.
LOOK AT ALL THIS CRAP. I MEAN SCRAP. LET'S GET TO BUILDING A ***VIADUCT!***
VHY A DUC—
FINISH THAT HACKY ***REFERENCE*** AND I WILL ***END*** YOU!
HOWDY, Y'ALL, I'M EMCEE ***HAMMERTOE TOM***, HERE TO DELIGHT AND ENTERTAIN YOU FINE FEDS AND SHOW SOME ***LOVE*** AND ***APPRECIATION***.
MOVE ALONG, CITIZEN. THIS AREA IS HIGHLY TOXIC.
HAVE YOU HEARD HAMMERTOE'S JAMS? THEY'RE PRETTY TOXIC, TOO.

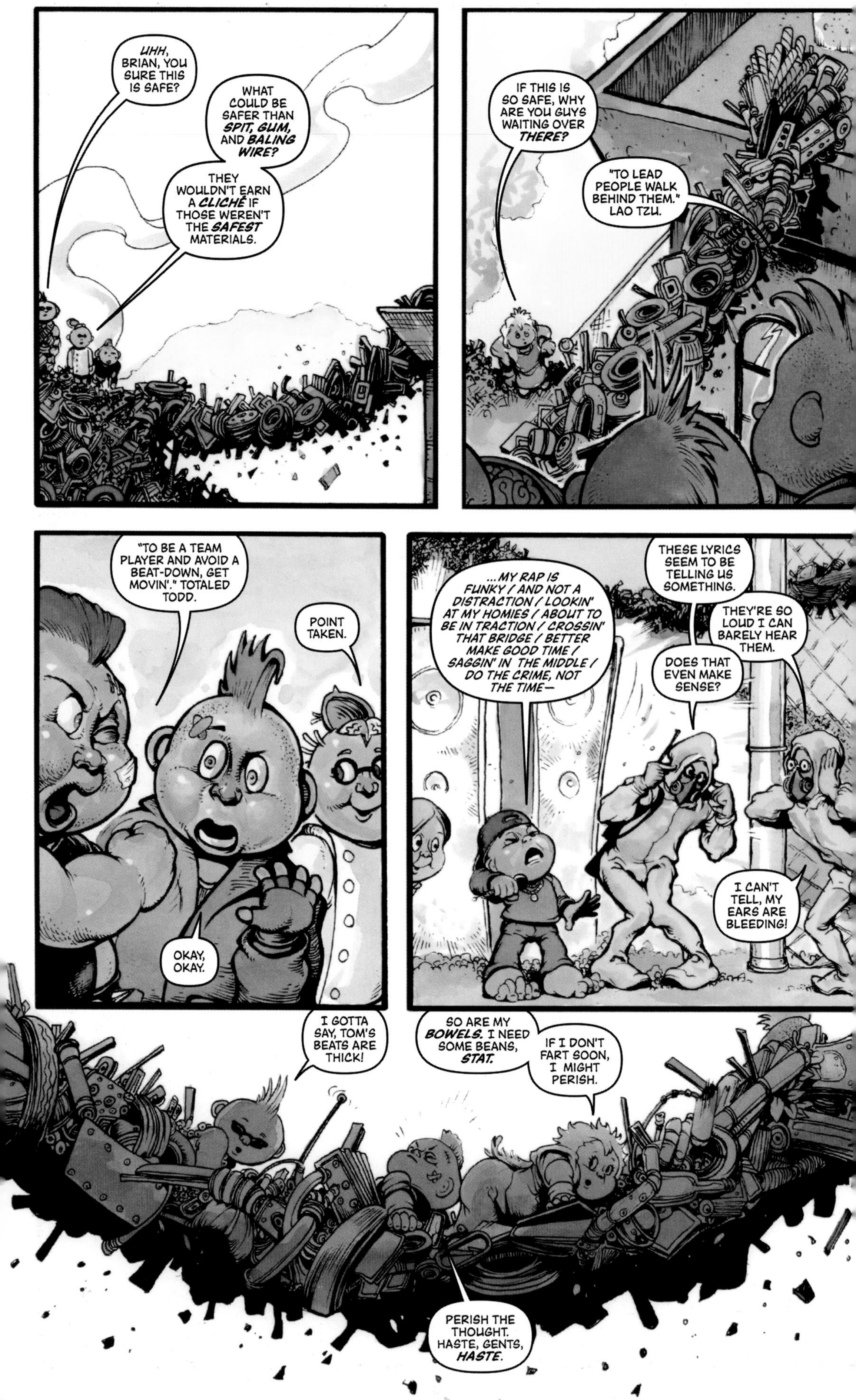
UHH, BRIAN, YOU SURE THIS IS SAFE?
WHAT COULD BE SAFER THAN SPIT, GUM, AND BALING WIRE?
THEY WOULDN'T EARN A CLICHÉ IF THOSE WEREN'T THE SAFEST MATERIALS.
IF THIS IS SO SAFE, WHY ARE YOU GUYS WAITING OVER THERE?
"TO LEAD PEOPLE WALK BEHIND THEM." LAO TZU.
"TO BE A TEAM PLAYER AND AVOID A BEAT-DOWN, GET MOVIN'." TOTALED TODD.
POINT TAKEN.
OKAY, OKAY.
...MY RAP IS FUNKY / AND NOT A DISTRACTION / LOOKIN' AT MY HOMIES / ABOUT TO BE IN TRACTION / CROSSIN' THAT BRIDGE / BETTER MAKE GOOD TIME / SAGGIN' IN THE MIDDLE / DO THE CRIME, NOT THE TIME—
THESE LYRICS SEEM TO BE TELLING US SOMETHING.
THEY'RE SO LOUD I CAN BARELY HEAR THEM.
DOES THAT EVEN MAKE SENSE?
I CAN'T TELL, MY EARS ARE BLEEDING!
I GOTTA SAY, TOM'S BEATS ARE THICK!
SO ARE MY BOWELS. I NEED SOME BEANS, STAT.
IF I DON'T FART SOON, I MIGHT PERISH.
PERISH THE THOUGHT. HASTE, GENTS, HASTE.

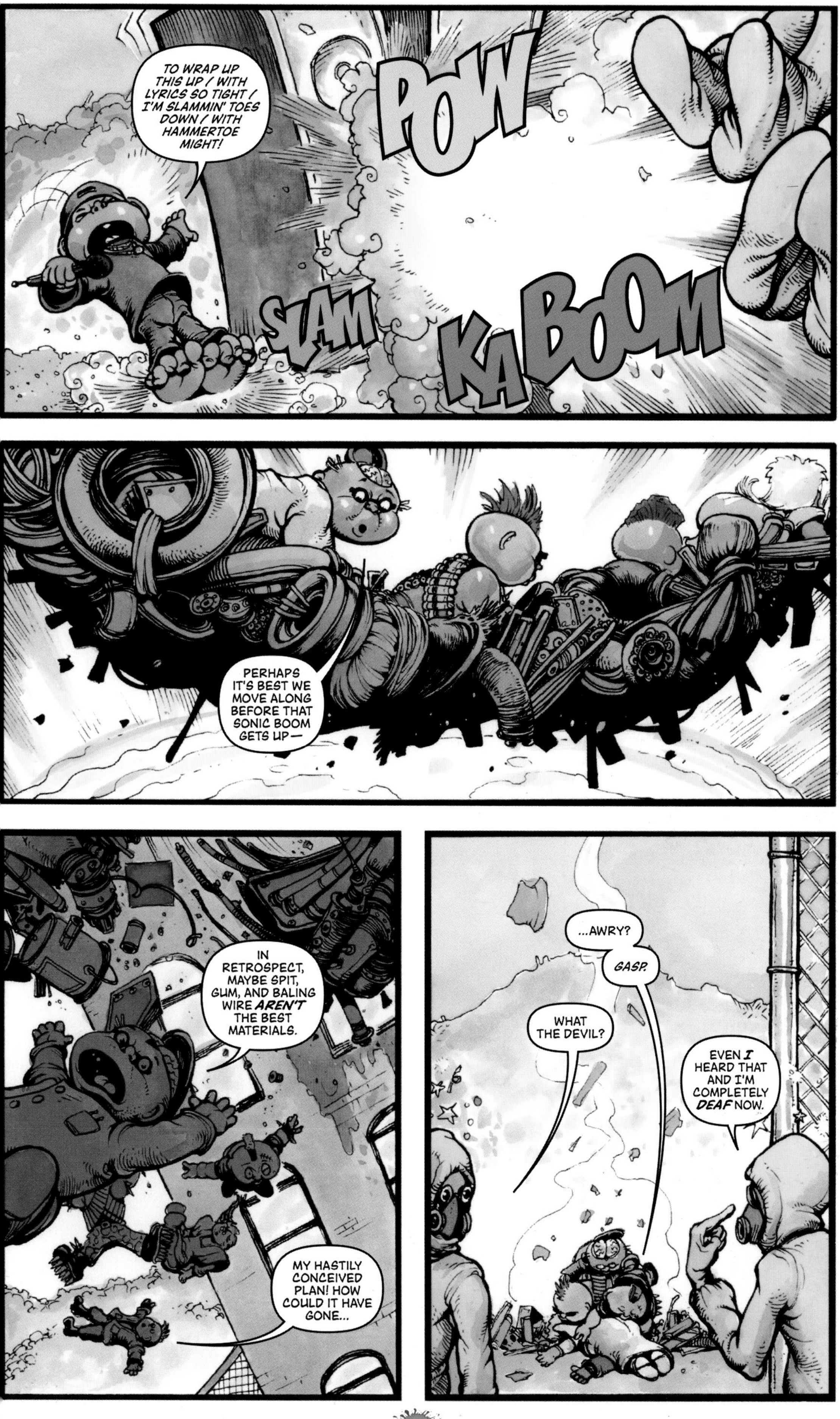
TO WRAP UP THIS UP / WITH LYRICS SO TIGHT / I'M SLAMMIN' TOES DOWN / WITH HAMMERTOE MIGHT!
POW
SLAM
KA BOOM
PERHAPS IT'S BEST WE MOVE ALONG BEFORE THAT SONIC BOOM GETS UP—
IN RETROSPECT, MAYBE SPIT, GUM, AND BALING WIRE AREN'T THE BEST MATERIALS.
MY HASTILY CONCEIVED PLAN! HOW COULD IT HAVE GONE...
...AWRY?
GASP.
WHAT THE DEVIL?
EVEN I HEARD THAT AND I'M COMPLETELY DEAF NOW.

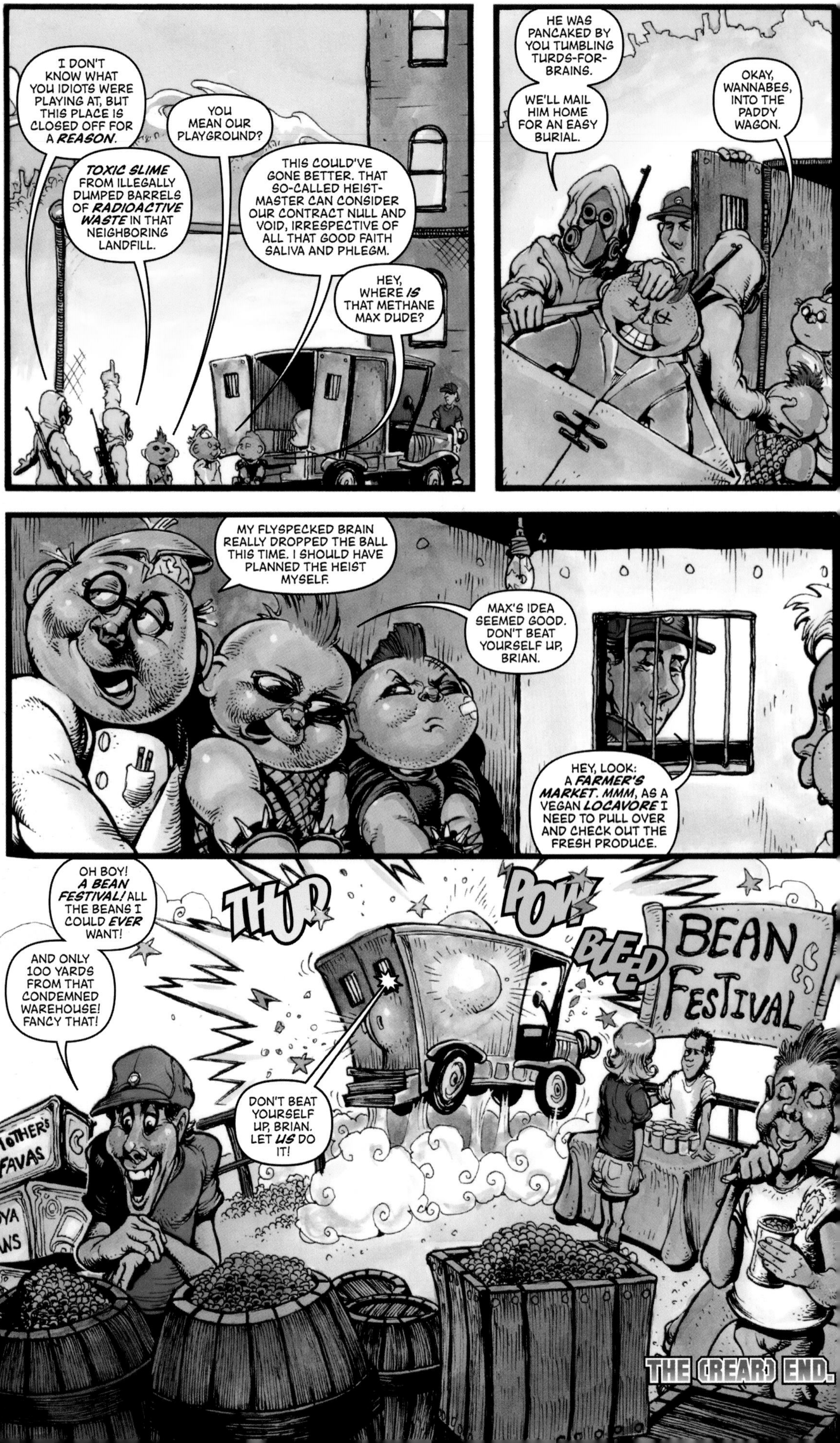
I DON'T KNOW WHAT YOU IDIOTS WERE PLAYING AT, BUT THIS PLACE IS CLOSED OFF FOR A *REASON*.
TOXIC SLIME FROM ILLEGALLY DUMPED BARRELS OF *RADIOACTIVE WASTE* IN THAT NEIGHBORING LANDFILL.
YOU MEAN OUR PLAYGROUND?
THIS COULD'VE GONE BETTER. THAT SO-CALLED HEIST-MASTER CAN CONSIDER OUR CONTRACT NULL AND VOID, IRRESPECTIVE OF ALL THAT GOOD FAITH SALIVA AND PHLEGM.
HEY, WHERE *IS* THAT METHANE MAX DUDE?
HE WAS PANCAKED BY YOU TUMBLING TURDS-FOR-BRAINS.
WE'LL MAIL HIM HOME FOR AN EASY BURIAL.
OKAY, WANNABES, INTO THE PADDY WAGON.
MY FLYSPECKED BRAIN REALLY DROPPED THE BALL THIS TIME. I SHOULD HAVE PLANNED THE HEIST MYSELF.
MAX'S IDEA SEEMED GOOD. DON'T BEAT YOURSELF UP, BRIAN.
HEY, LOOK: A *FARMER'S MARKET*. *MMM*, AS A VEGAN *LOCAVORE* I NEED TO PULL OVER AND CHECK OUT THE FRESH PRODUCE.
OH BOY! *A BEAN FESTIVAL!* ALL THE BEANS I COULD *EVER* WANT!
AND ONLY 100 YARDS FROM THAT CONDEMNED WAREHOUSE! FANCY THAT!
THUP
POW
BLEED
BEAN FESTIVAL
DON'T BEAT YOURSELF UP, BRIAN. LET *US* DO IT!
MOTHER'S FAVAS
HOWYA BEANS
THE (REAR) END.

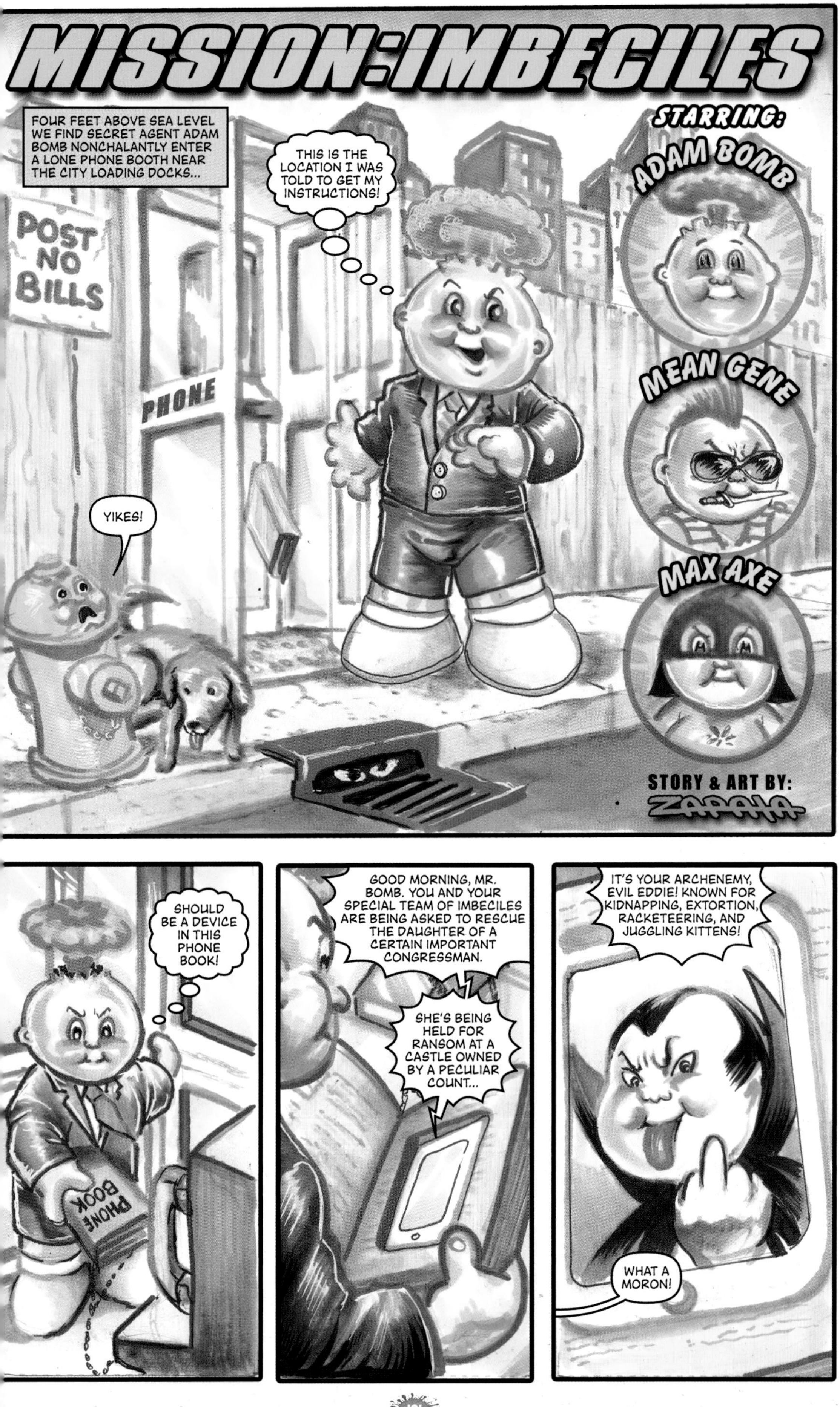
MISSION: IMBECILES
FOUR FEET ABOVE SEA LEVEL WE FIND SECRET AGENT ADAM BOMB NONCHALANTLY ENTER A LONE PHONE BOOTH NEAR THE CITY LOADING DOCKS...
STARRING:
ADAM BOMB
MEAN GENE
MAX AXE
POST NO BILLS
PHONE
THIS IS THE LOCATION I WAS TOLD TO GET MY INSTRUCTIONS!
YIKES!
STORY & ART BY:
SHOULD BE A DEVICE IN THIS PHONE BOOK!
PHONE BOOK
GOOD MORNING, MR. BOMB. YOU AND YOUR SPECIAL TEAM OF IMBECILES ARE BEING ASKED TO RESCUE THE DAUGHTER OF A CERTAIN IMPORTANT CONGRESSMAN.
SHE'S BEING HELD FOR RANSOM AT A CASTLE OWNED BY A PECULIAR COUNT...
IT'S YOUR ARCHENEMY, EVIL EDDIE! KNOWN FOR KIDNAPPING, EXTORTION, RACKETEERING, AND JUGGLING KITTENS!
WHAT A MORON!

THIS IS EDDIE'S BODYGUARD, *GREASER GREG.* HE'S MEAN AND RUTHLESS!

THIS IS EDDIE'S GIRLFRIEND WEIRD WENDY. SHE'S WEIRD AND TOOTHLESS!

THE TWO WILL MAKE SURE NO ONE WILL GET IN EDDIE'S WAY!

YOUR MISSION, IF YOU CHOOSE EXCEPT IT, IS TO PENETRATE THE CASTLE, RESCUE THE CONGRESSMAN'S DAUGHTER, AND TERMINATE EDDIE!

IF YOU FAIL OR ARE CAUGHT, OUR OFFICE WILL DISAVOW THIS COMIC STORY EVER HAPPENED.

THIS RECORDING WILL FART IN 5 SECONDS. GOOD LUCK, ADAM.

THAT REEKS!

MUST ASSEMBLE THE IMBECILE TEAM AND HEAD OVER TO EVIL EDDIE'S CASTLE TO PUT AN END TO THIS MADNESS!

YOU REALLY DID IT DIS TIME, ADAM. HOW DID VEE END UP IN DIS MESS?!

STOP YOUR LOUD YAPPING, MY AUSTRIAN FRIEND, OR WE'RE ALL GONNA DIE.

DON'T MESS AROUND AND START QUOTING LINES FROM *PREDATOR.*

LET'S ME BACK HE AFTER W FINISH O MISSION

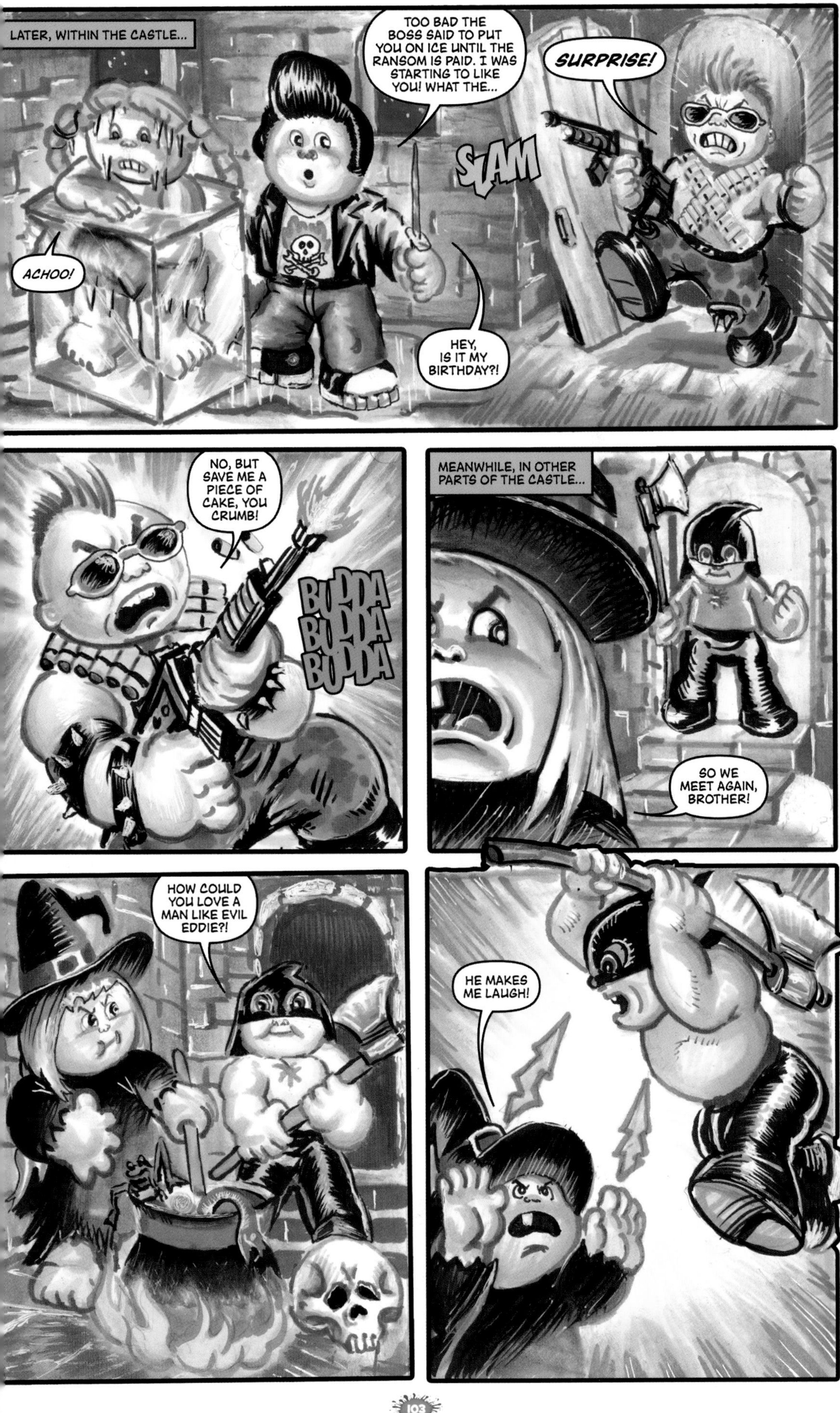

LATER, WITHIN THE CASTLE...
ACHOO!
TOO BAD THE BOSS SAID TO PUT YOU ON ICE UNTIL THE RANSOM IS PAID. I WAS STARTING TO LIKE YOU! WHAT THE...
SLAM
SURPRISE!
HEY, IS IT MY BIRTHDAY?!
NO, BUT SAVE ME A PIECE OF CAKE, YOU CRUMB!
BUDDA BUDDA BUDDA
MEANWHILE, IN OTHER PARTS OF THE CASTLE...
SO WE MEET AGAIN, BROTHER!
HOW COULD YOU LOVE A MAN LIKE EVIL EDDIE?!
HE MAKES ME LAUGH!

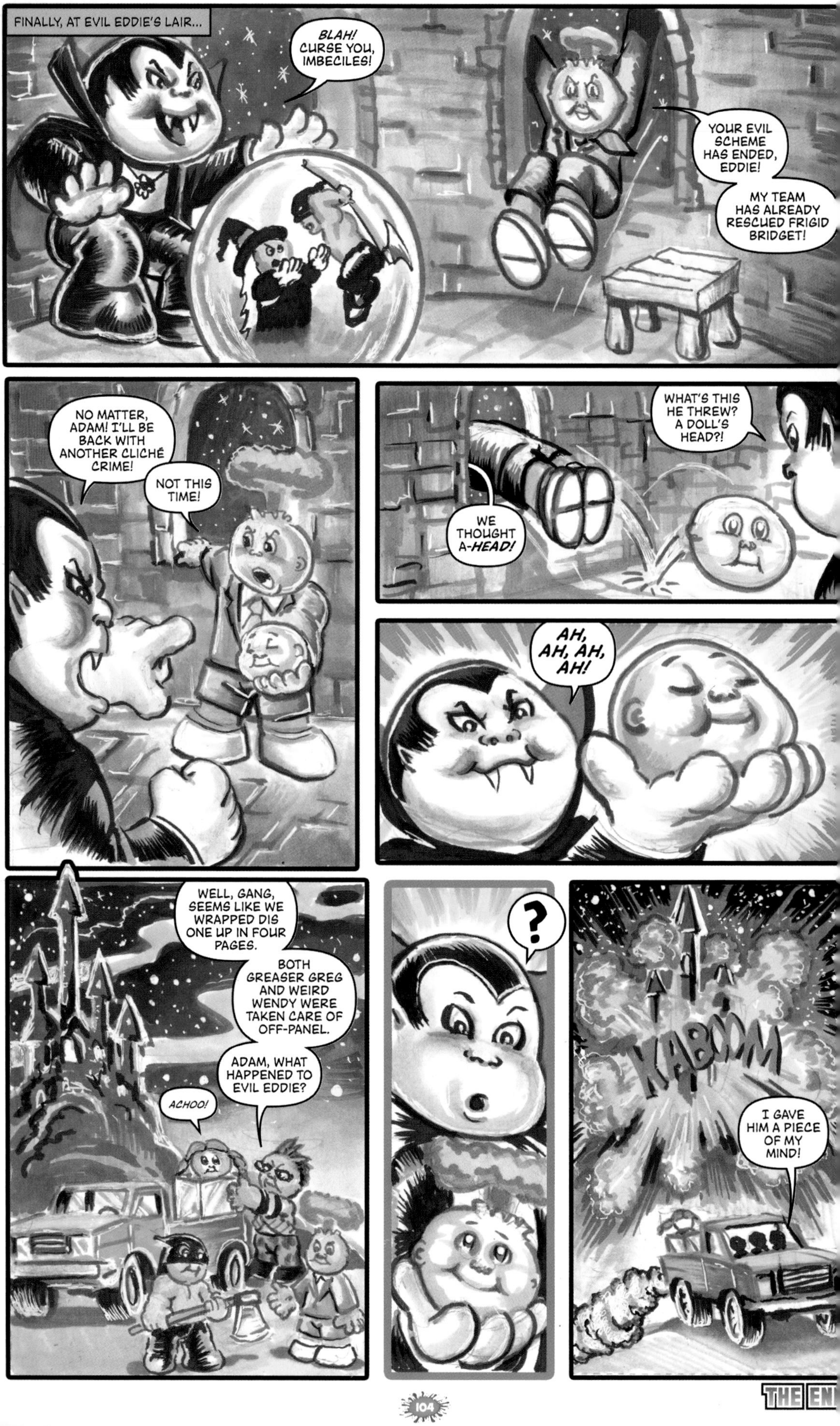
FINALLY, AT EVIL EDDIE'S LAIR...
BLAH! CURSE YOU, IMBECILES!
YOUR EVIL SCHEME HAS ENDED, EDDIE!
MY TEAM HAS ALREADY RESCUED FRIGID BRIDGET!
NO MATTER, ADAM! I'LL BE BACK WITH ANOTHER CLICHÉ CRIME!
NOT THIS TIME!
WHAT'S THIS HE THREW? A DOLL'S HEAD?!
WE THOUGHT A-HEAD!
AH, AH, AH, AH!
WELL, GANG, SEEMS LIKE WE WRAPPED DIS ONE UP IN FOUR PAGES.
BOTH GREASER GREG AND WEIRD WENDY WERE TAKEN CARE OF OFF-PANEL.
ADAM, WHAT HAPPENED TO EVIL EDDIE?
ACHOO!
?
KABOOM
I GAVE HIM A PIECE OF MY MIND!
THE EN

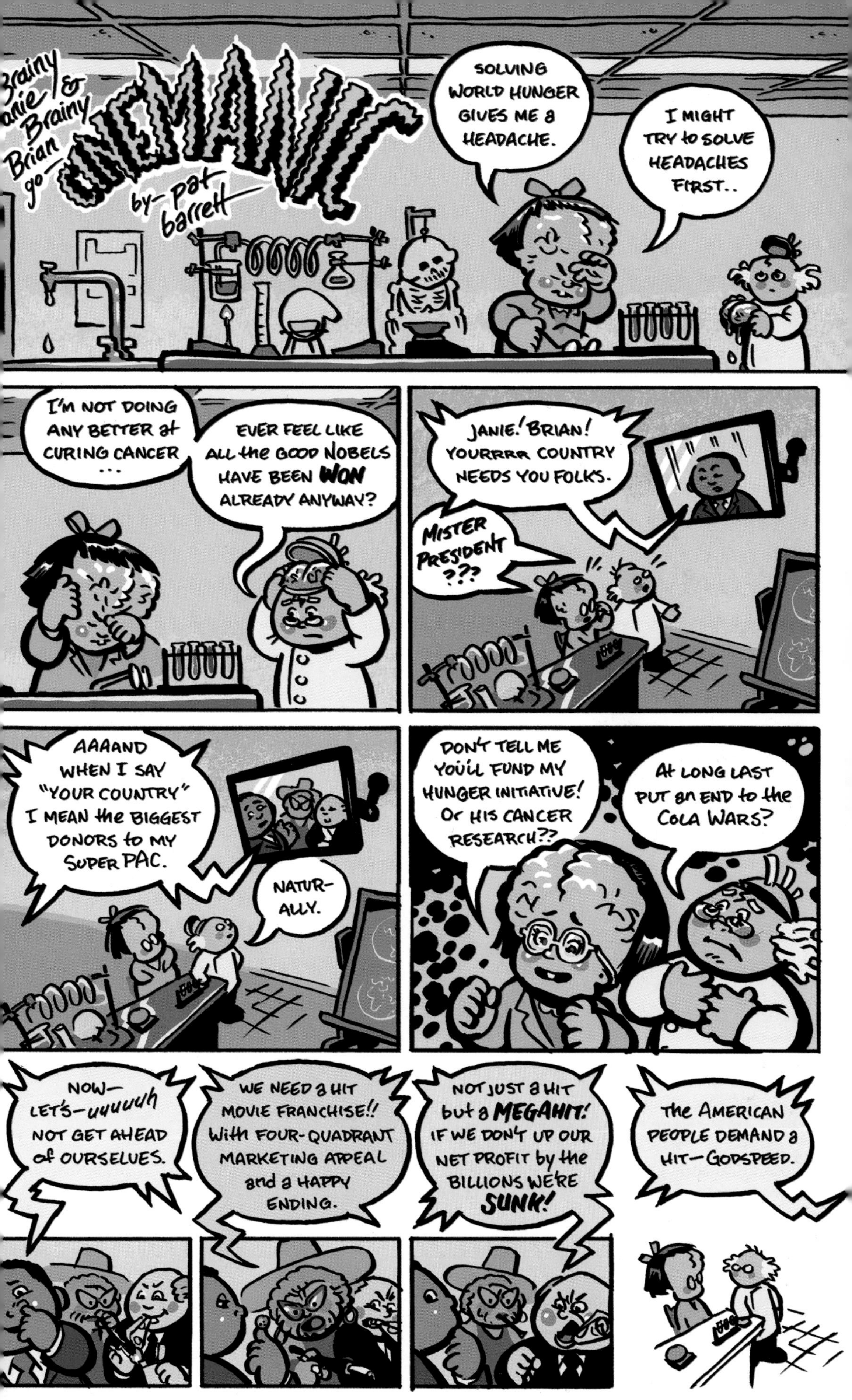

Brainy Janie & Brainy Brian go—CINEMANIC
by— pat barrett
SOLVING WORLD HUNGER GIVES ME A HEADACHE.
I MIGHT TRY to SOLVE HEADACHES FIRST..
I'M NOT DOING ANY BETTER at CURING CANCER...
EVER FEEL LIKE ALL the GOOD NOBELS HAVE BEEN WON ALREADY ANYWAY?
JANIE! BRIAN! YOURRRR COUNTRY NEEDS YOU FOLKS.
MISTER PRESIDENT???
AAAAND WHEN I SAY "YOUR COUNTRY" I MEAN the BIGGEST DONORS to MY SUPER PAC.
NATUR-ALLY.
DON'T TELL ME YOU'LL FUND MY HUNGER INITIATIVE! Or HIS CANCER RESEARCH??
At LONG LAST PUT an END to the COLA WARS?
NOW— LET'S—uuuuh NOT GET AHEAD of OURSELVES.
WE NEED a HIT MOVIE FRANCHISE!! With FOUR-QUADRANT MARKETING APPEAL and a HAPPY ENDING.
NOT JUST a HIT but a MEGAHIT! IF WE DON'T UP OUR NET PROFIT by the BILLIONS WE'RE SUNK!
The AMERICAN PEOPLE DEMAND a HIT—GODSPEED.

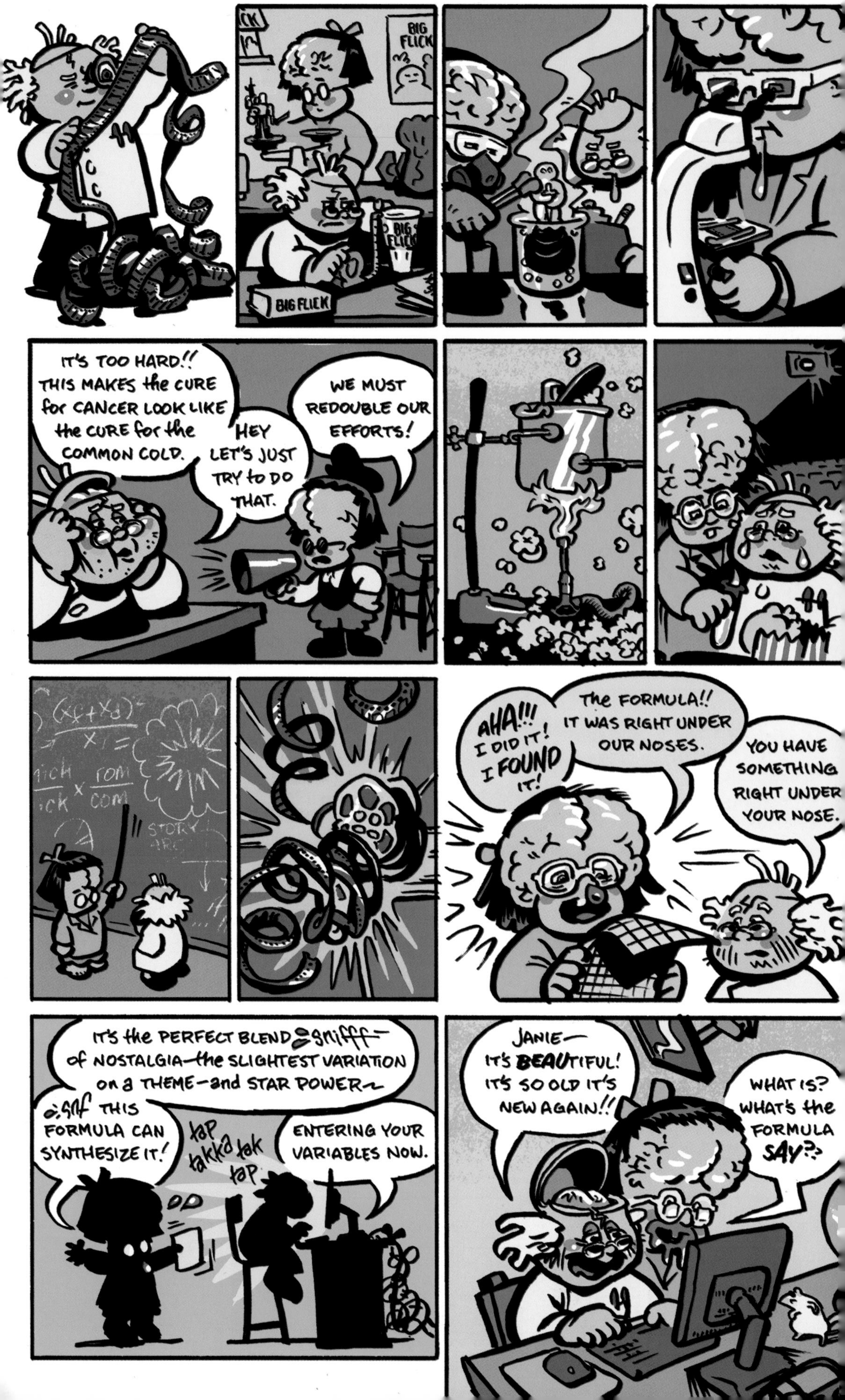

BIG FLICK
BIG FLICK
BIG FLICK
IT'S TOO HARD!! THIS MAKES the CURE for CANCER LOOK LIKE the CURE for the COMMON COLD.
HEY LET'S JUST TRY to DO THAT.
WE MUST REDOUBLE OUR EFFORTS!
STORY ARC
AHA!!! I DID IT! I FOUND IT!
The FORMULA!! IT WAS RIGHT UNDER OUR NOSES.
YOU HAVE SOMETHING RIGHT UNDER YOUR NOSE.
IT'S the PERFECT BLEND sniff of NOSTALGIA the SLIGHTEST VARIATION on a THEME and STAR POWER
snf THIS FORMULA CAN SYNTHESIZE IT!
tap takka tak tap
ENTERING YOUR VARIABLES NOW.
JANIE— IT'S BEAUTIFUL! IT'S SO OLD IT'S NEW AGAIN!!
WHAT IS? WHAT'S the FORMULA SAY?

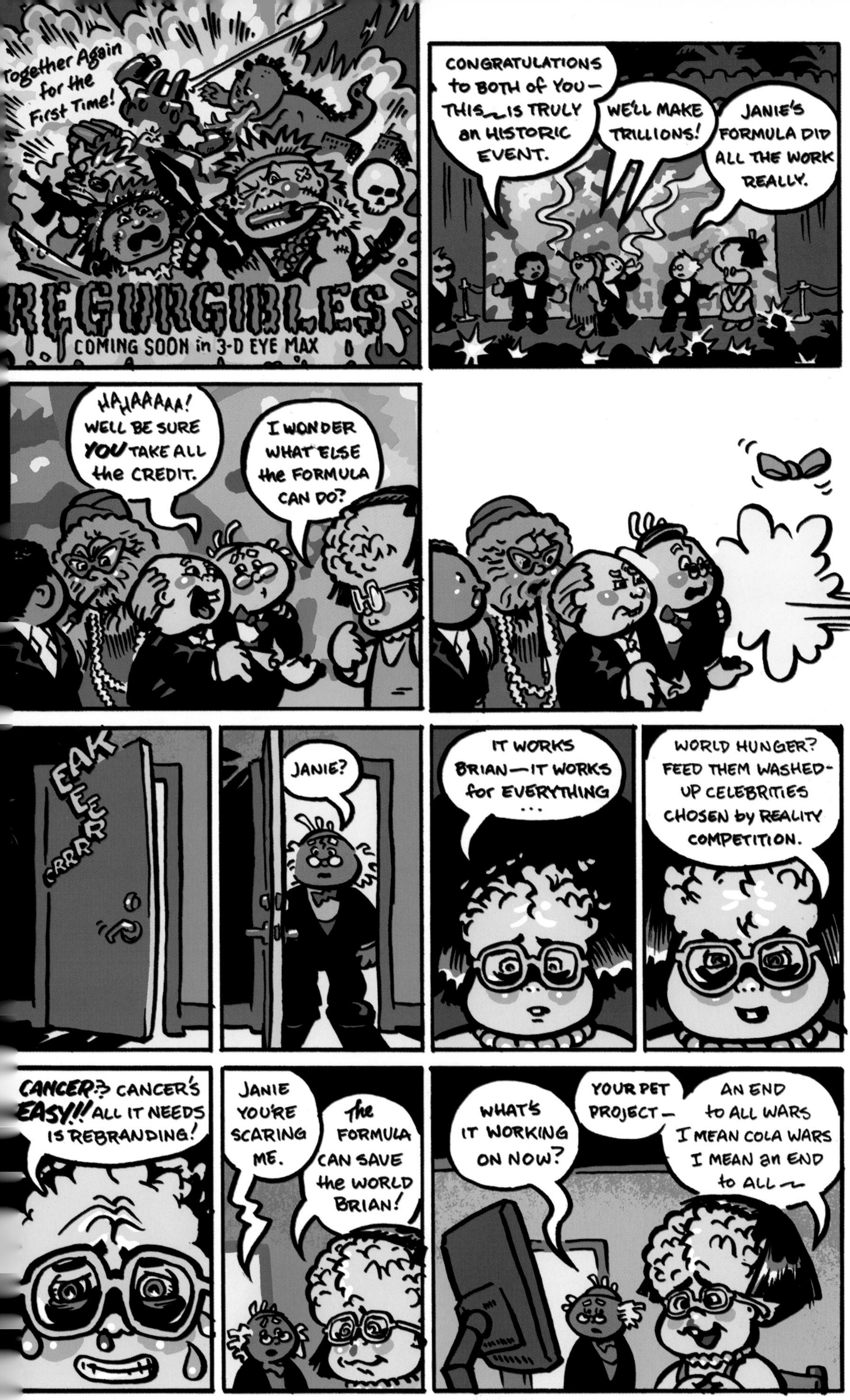

Together Again for the First Time!
REGURGIBLES
COMING SOON in 3-D EYE MAX
CONGRATULATIONS to BOTH of YOU— THIS~ IS TRULY an HISTORIC EVENT.
WE'LL MAKE TRILLIONS!
JANIE'S FORMULA DID ALL THE WORK REALLY.
HAHAAAAA! WELL BE SURE YOU TAKE ALL the CREDIT.
I WONDER WHAT ELSE the FORMULA CAN DO?
EEEAK CRRRR
JANIE?
IT WORKS BRIAN—IT WORKS for EVERYTHING ...
WORLD HUNGER? FEED THEM WASHED-UP CELEBRITIES CHOSEN by REALITY COMPETITION.
CANCER?? CANCER'S EASY!! ALL IT NEEDS IS REBRANDING!
JANIE YOU'RE SCARING ME.
the FORMULA CAN SAVE the WORLD BRIAN!
WHAT'S IT WORKING ON NOW?
YOUR PET PROJECT—
AN END to ALL WARS I MEAN COLA WARS I MEAN an END to ALL~

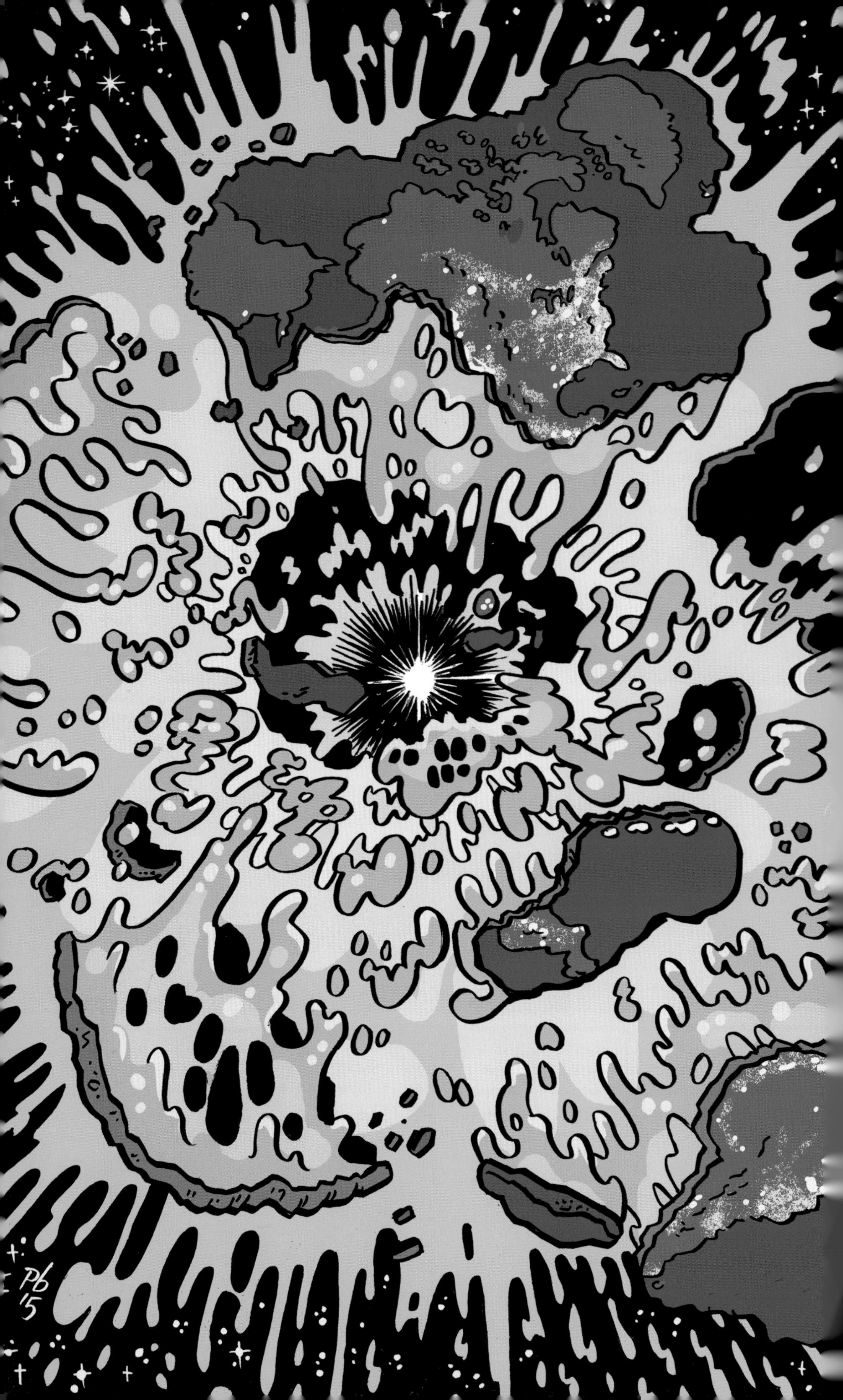

ADVERTISEMENT BY BRIAN WINKELER AND ERIC SANDHOP

OSCAR LA VISTA IN "TURDINATOR:EXODYS"

I'D LIKE TO SOLVE THE PUZZLE, PAT. "PASTA LA VISTA, BABY!"
I ♥ FIBER
POSSIBLE RESPONSE:
· WHY DON'T YOU CALL
· THANKS, OBAMA
* NUTS TO YOU
· MATLOCK!
ANALYSIS: MATCH
NUTS TO YOU.
MINE SAUERBRATEN IS CAUSING JUDGMENT DAY IN MINE TUMMY. I MUST FIND ZE JOHN.
GURGLE
COME WITH ME IF YOU WANT TO NUMBER THREE!
I AM BURIED UNDER ZE WEIGHT OF MY HUBRIS AND HOARDER TENDENCIES.
THEN USE THIS DeepEnds BEFORE YOUR SYSTEM BLOWS!
SPLURT
POP SPLASH
SQUAEEEK
PLOP
PLOP
HONK
IT'S NOT A TOOMAAAH!
I'M GETTING TOO OLD FOR THIS
HEY, THAT'S MY LINE!
DeepEnds
YOUR BOWELS CAN EXPLODE IN EVERY LOAD OF DEEP-ENDS!

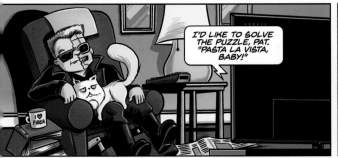

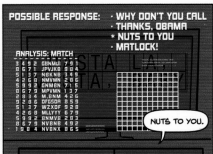

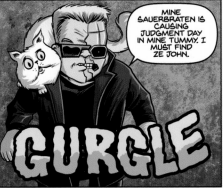

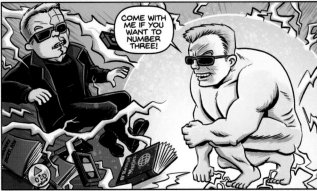

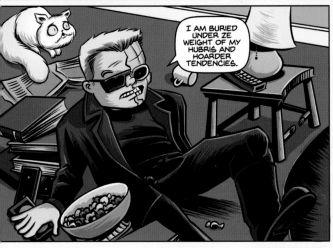

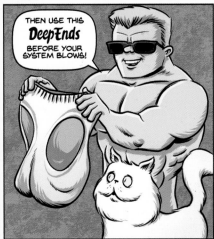

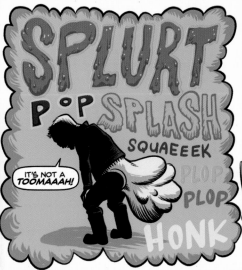

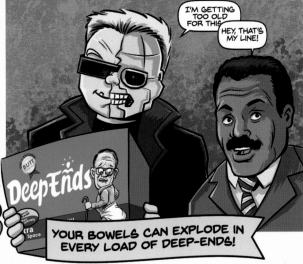

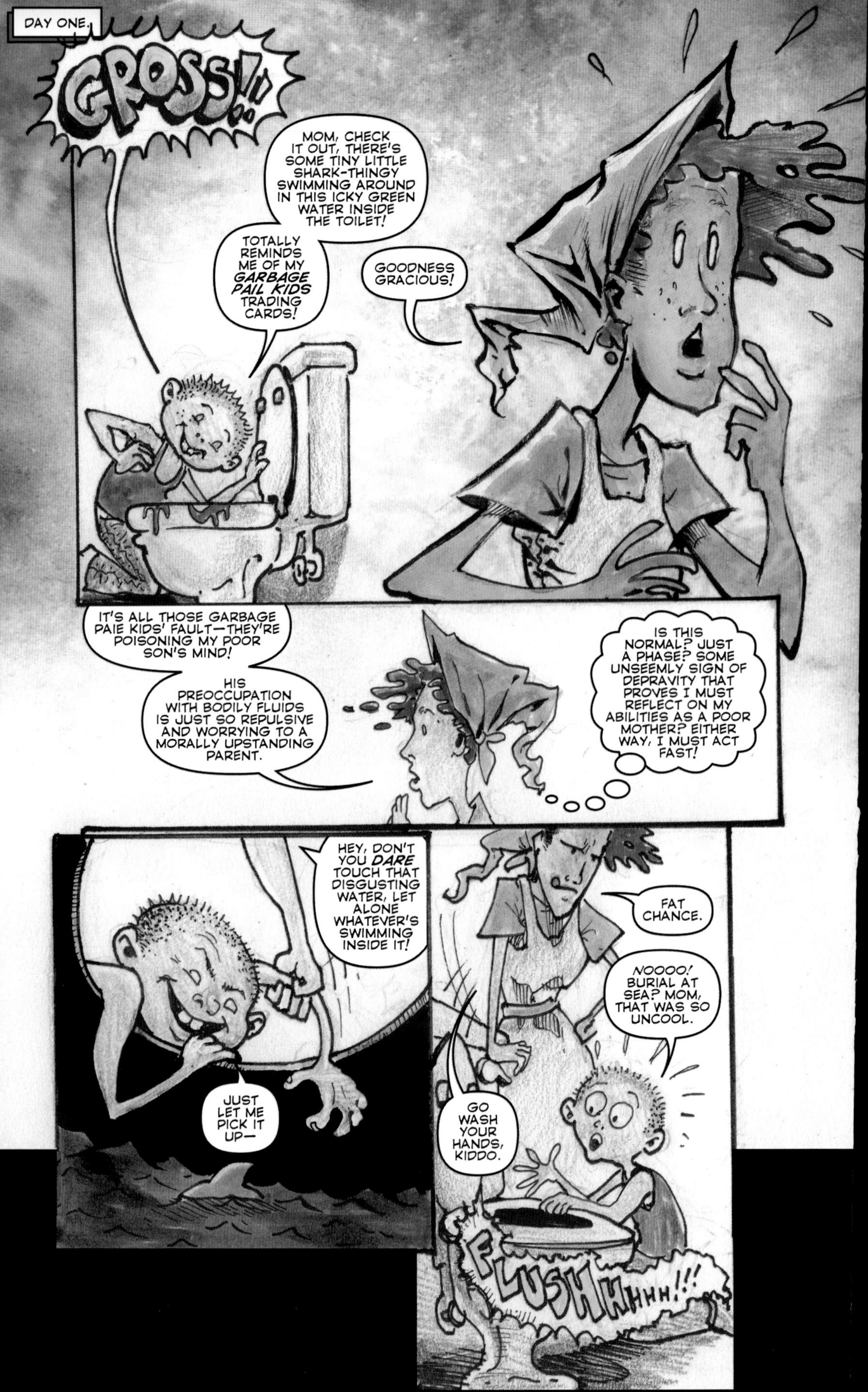
DAY ONE.
GROSS!!!
MOM, CHECK IT OUT, THERE'S SOME TINY LITTLE SHARK-THINGY SWIMMING AROUND IN THIS ICKY GREEN WATER INSIDE THE TOILET!
TOTALLY REMINDS ME OF MY ***GARBAGE PAIL KIDS*** TRADING CARDS!
GOODNESS GRACIOUS!
IT'S ALL THOSE GARBAGE PAIE KIDS' FAULT—THEY'RE POISONING MY POOR SON'S MIND!
HIS PREOCCUPATION WITH BODILY FLUIDS IS JUST SO REPULSIVE AND WORRYING TO A MORALLY UPSTANDING PARENT.
IS THIS NORMAL? JUST A PHASE? SOME UNSEEMLY SIGN OF DEPRAVITY THAT PROVES I MUST REFLECT ON MY ABILITIES AS A POOR MOTHER? EITHER WAY, I MUST ACT FAST!
HEY, DON'T YOU ***DARE*** TOUCH THAT DISGUSTING WATER, LET ALONE WHATEVER'S SWIMMING INSIDE IT!
JUST LET ME PICK IT UP—
FAT CHANCE.
NOOOO! BURIAL AT SEA? MOM, THAT WAS SO UNCOOL.
GO WASH YOUR HANDS, KIDDO.
FLUSHHHHH!!!

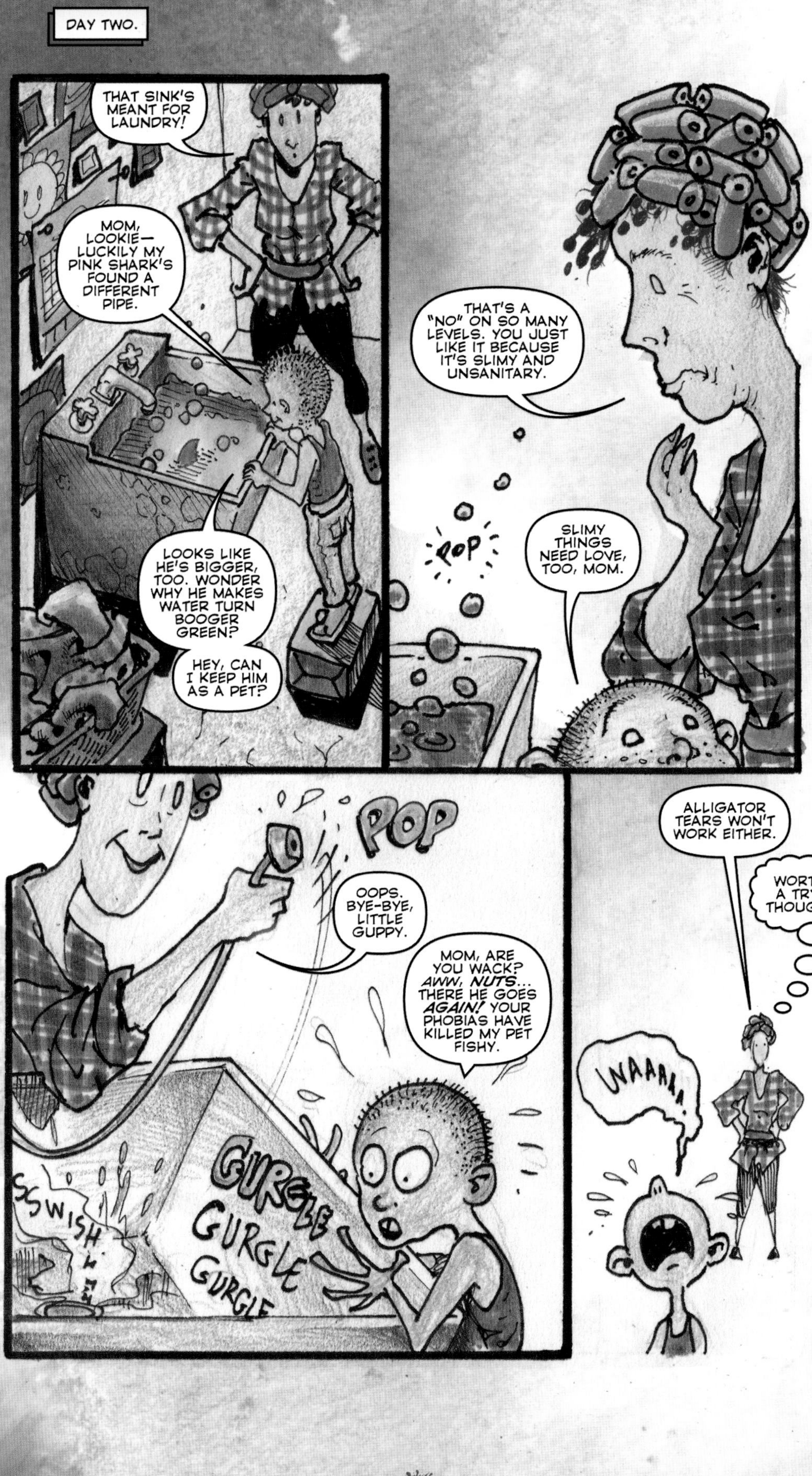
DAY TWO.
THAT SINK'S MEANT FOR LAUNDRY!
MOM, LOOKIE— LUCKILY MY PINK SHARK'S FOUND A DIFFERENT PIPE.
LOOKS LIKE HE'S BIGGER, TOO. WONDER WHY HE MAKES WATER TURN BOOGER GREEN?
HEY, CAN I KEEP HIM AS A PET?
THAT'S A "NO" ON SO MANY LEVELS. YOU JUST LIKE IT BECAUSE IT'S SLIMY AND UNSANITARY.
POP
SLIMY THINGS NEED LOVE, TOO, MOM.
POP
OOPS. BYE-BYE, LITTLE GUPPY.
MOM, ARE YOU WACK? *AWW, **NUTS**...* THERE HE GOES ***AGAIN!*** YOUR PHOBIAS HAVE KILLED MY PET FISHY.
SSWISH
GURGLE GURGLE GURGLE
ALLIGATOR TEARS WON'T WORK EITHER.
WORTH A TRY, THOUGH.
UNAAAA

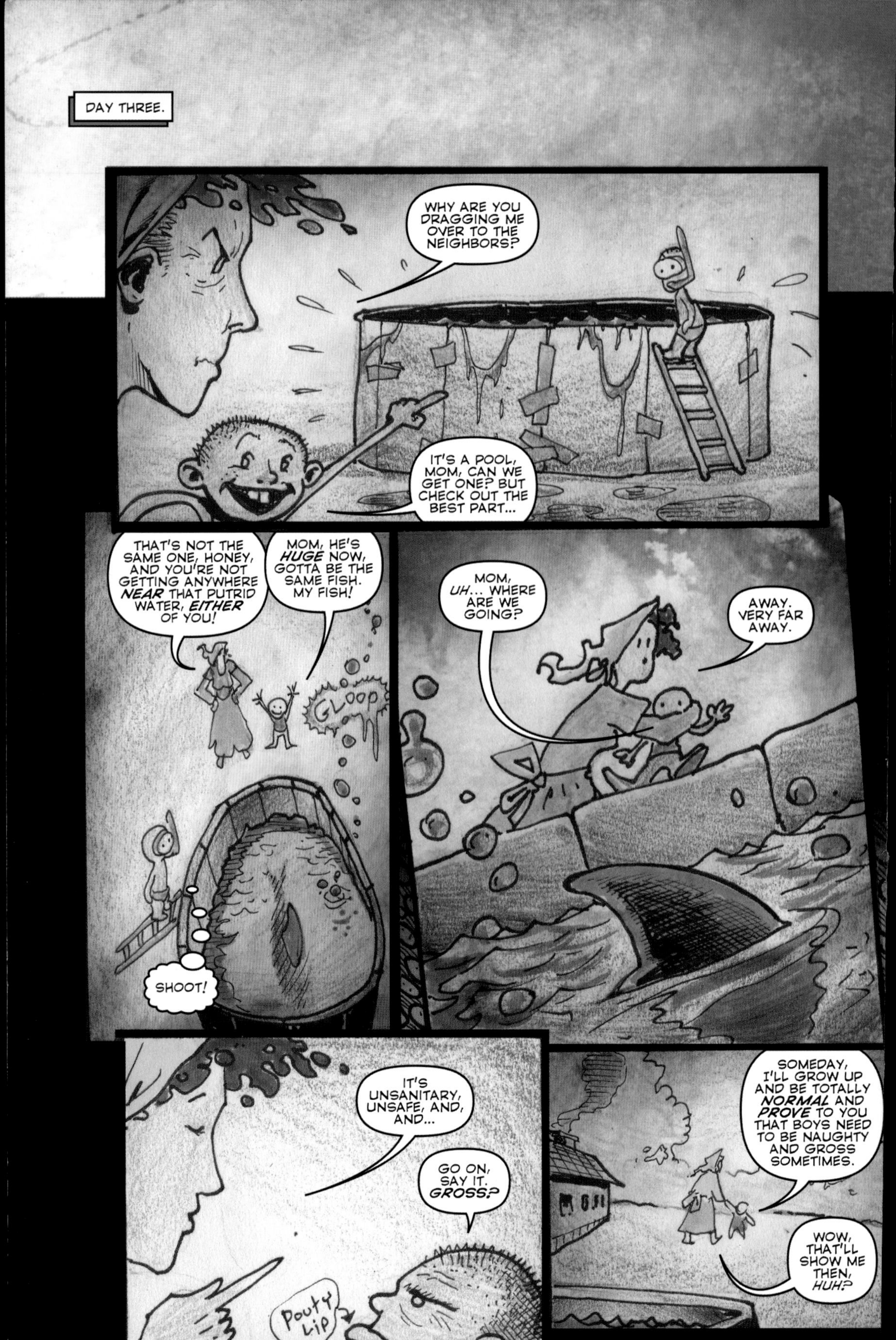
DAY THREE.
WHY ARE YOU DRAGGING ME OVER TO THE NEIGHBORS?
IT'S A POOL, MOM, CAN WE GET ONE? BUT CHECK OUT THE BEST PART...
THAT'S NOT THE SAME ONE, HONEY, AND YOU'RE NOT GETTING ANYWHERE NEAR THAT PUTRID WATER, EITHER OF YOU!
MOM, HE'S HUGE NOW, GOTTA BE THE SAME FISH. MY FISH!
GLOOP
SHOOT!
MOM, UH... WHERE ARE WE GOING?
AWAY. VERY FAR AWAY.
IT'S UNSANITARY, UNSAFE, AND, AND...
GO ON, SAY IT. GROSS?
Pouty Lip
SOMEDAY, I'LL GROW UP AND BE TOTALLY NORMAL AND PROVE TO YOU THAT BOYS NEED TO BE NAUGHTY AND GROSS SOMETIMES.
WOW, THAT'LL SHOW ME THEN, HUH?

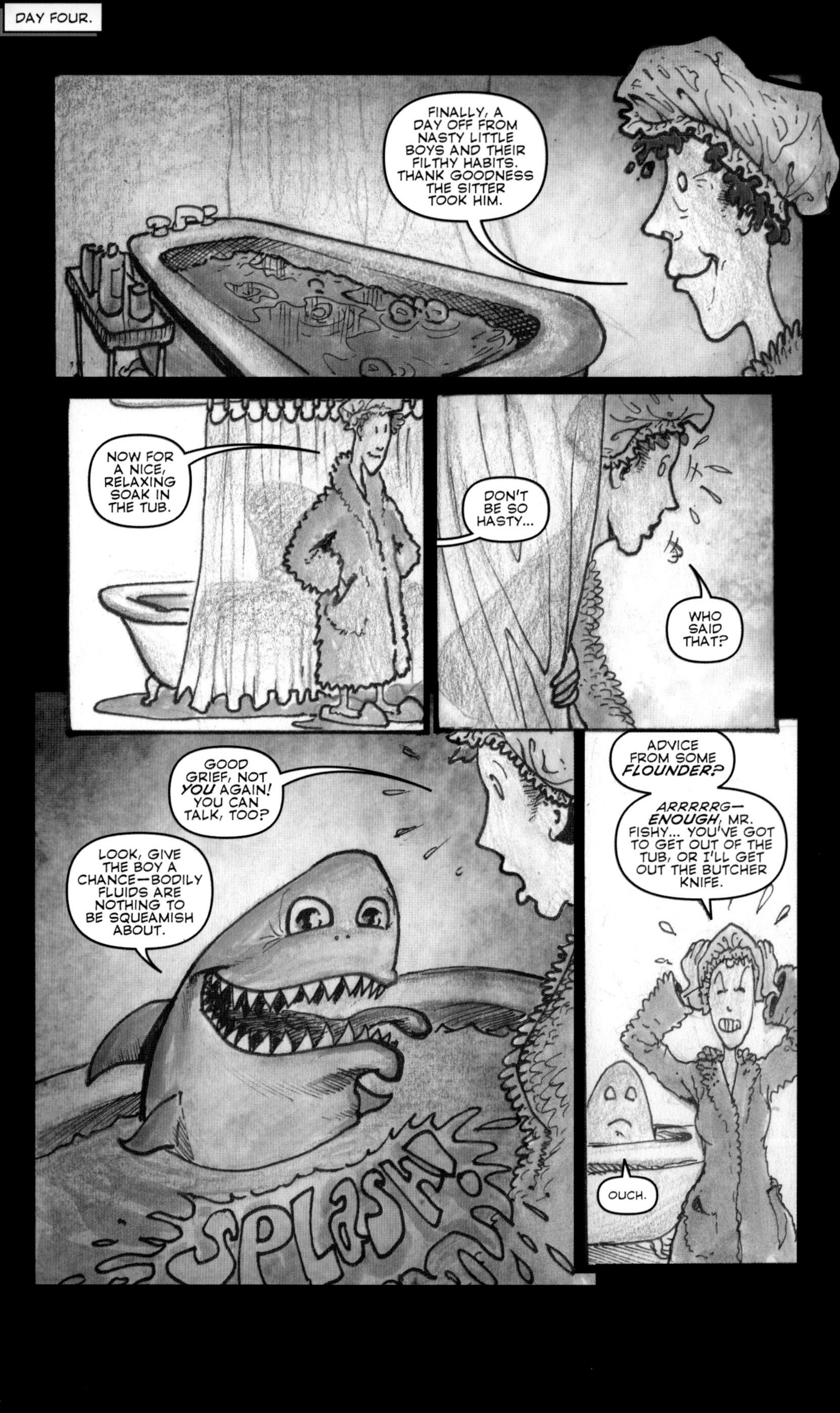
DAY FOUR.
FINALLY, A DAY OFF FROM NASTY LITTLE BOYS AND THEIR FILTHY HABITS. THANK GOODNESS THE SITTER TOOK HIM.
NOW FOR A NICE, RELAXING SOAK IN THE TUB.
DON'T BE SO HASTY...
WHO SAID THAT?
GOOD GRIEF, NOT *YOU* AGAIN! YOU CAN TALK, TOO?
LOOK, GIVE THE BOY A CHANCE—BODILY FLUIDS ARE NOTHING TO BE SQUEAMISH ABOUT.
SPLASH!
ADVICE FROM SOME ***FLOUNDER?***
ARRRRRG— ***ENOUGH***, MR. FISHY... YOU'VE GOT TO GET OUT OF THE TUB, OR I'LL GET OUT THE BUTCHER KNIFE.
OUCH.

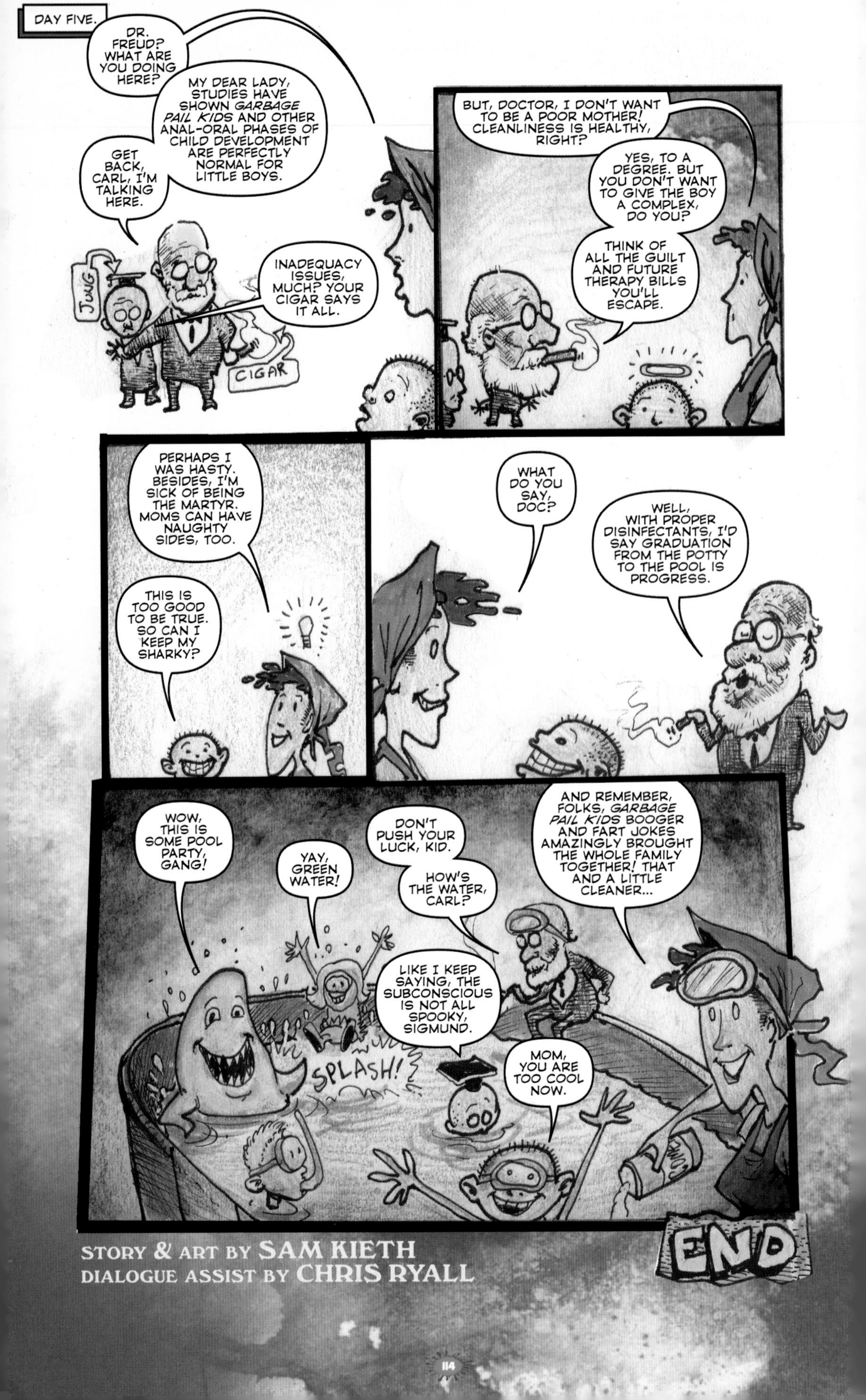
DAY FIVE.
DR. FREUD? WHAT ARE YOU DOING HERE?
MY DEAR LADY, STUDIES HAVE SHOWN *GARBAGE PAIL KIDS* AND OTHER ANAL-ORAL PHASES OF CHILD DEVELOPMENT ARE PERFECTLY NORMAL FOR LITTLE BOYS.
GET BACK, CARL, I'M TALKING HERE.
JUNG
INADEQUACY ISSUES, MUCH? YOUR CIGAR SAYS IT ALL.
CIGAR
BUT, DOCTOR, I DON'T WANT TO BE A POOR MOTHER! CLEANLINESS IS HEALTHY, RIGHT?
YES, TO A DEGREE. BUT YOU DON'T WANT TO GIVE THE BOY A COMPLEX, DO YOU?
THINK OF ALL THE GUILT AND FUTURE THERAPY BILLS YOU'LL ESCAPE.
PERHAPS I WAS HASTY. BESIDES, I'M SICK OF BEING THE MARTYR. MOMS CAN HAVE NAUGHTY SIDES, TOO.
THIS IS TOO GOOD TO BE TRUE. SO CAN I KEEP MY SHARKY?
WHAT DO YOU SAY, DOC?
WELL, WITH PROPER DISINFECTANTS, I'D SAY GRADUATION FROM THE POTTY TO THE POOL IS PROGRESS.
WOW, THIS IS SOME POOL PARTY, GANG!
YAY, GREEN WATER!
DON'T PUSH YOUR LUCK, KID.
HOW'S THE WATER, CARL?
AND REMEMBER, FOLKS, *GARBAGE PAIL KIDS* BOOGER AND FART JOKES AMAZINGLY BROUGHT THE WHOLE FAMILY TOGETHER! THAT AND A LITTLE CLEANER...
LIKE I KEEP SAYING, THE SUBCONSCIOUS IS NOT ALL SPOOKY, SIGMUND.
SPLASH!
MOM, YOU ARE TOO COOL NOW.

END

STORY & ART BY **SAM KIETH**
DIALOGUE ASSIST BY **CHRIS RYALL**

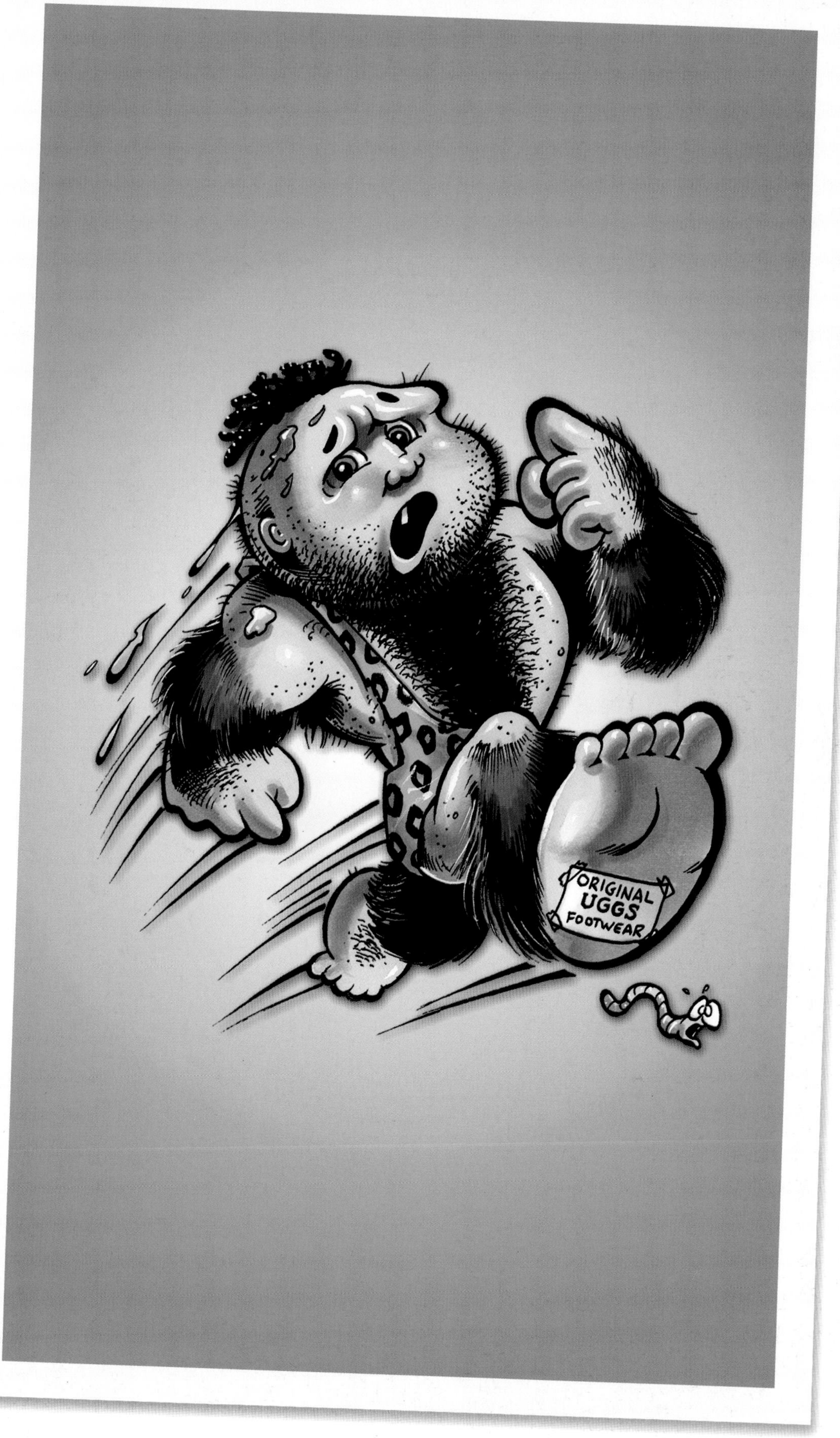
ORIGINAL
UGGS
FOOTWEAR

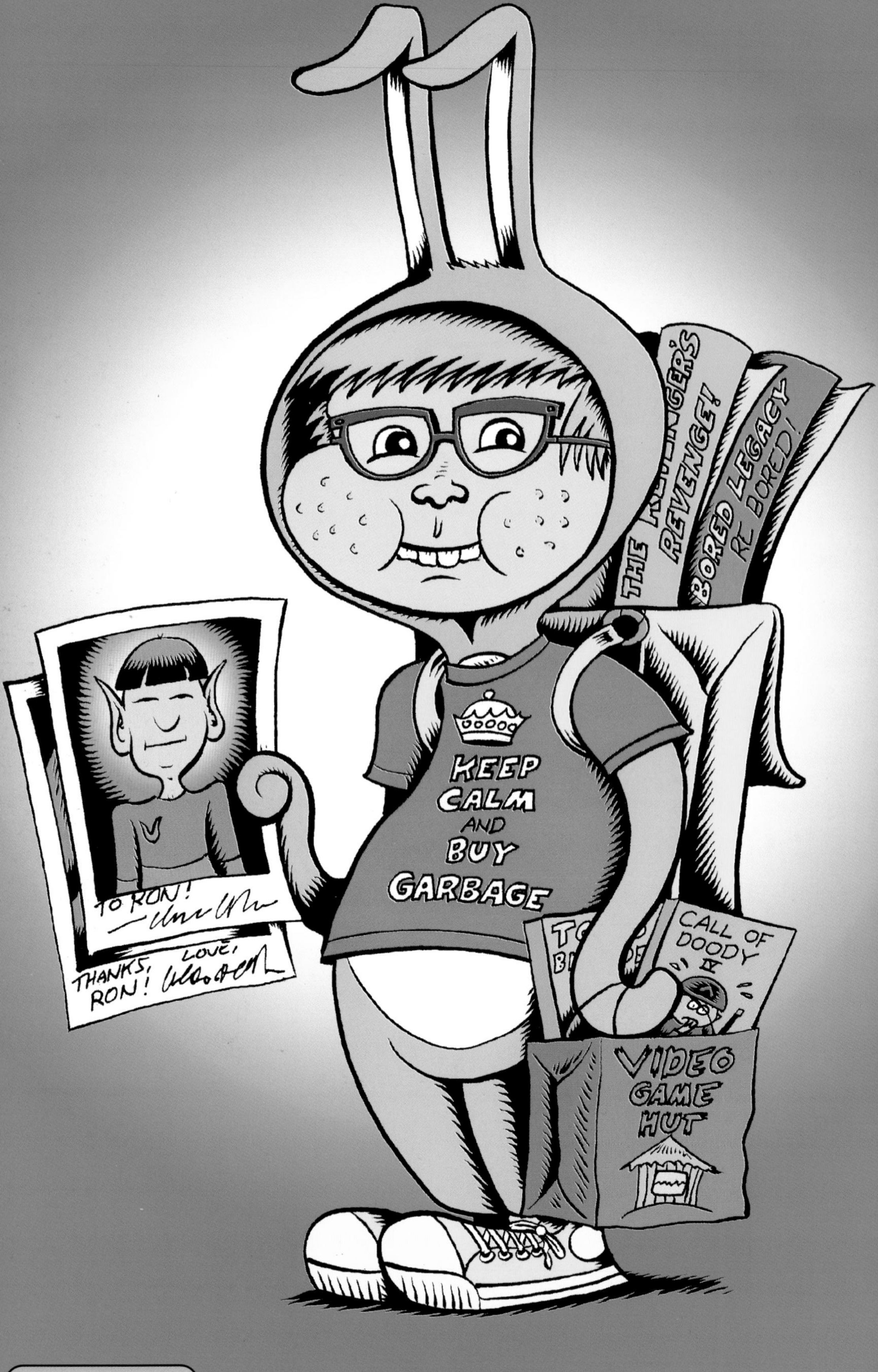
THE
REVENGE!
BORED LEGACY
RL BORED!
TO RON!
THANKS, RON! LOVE,
KEEP CALM AND BUY GARBAGE
CALL OF DOODY IV
VIDEO GAME HUT

art by **PETER BAGGE**

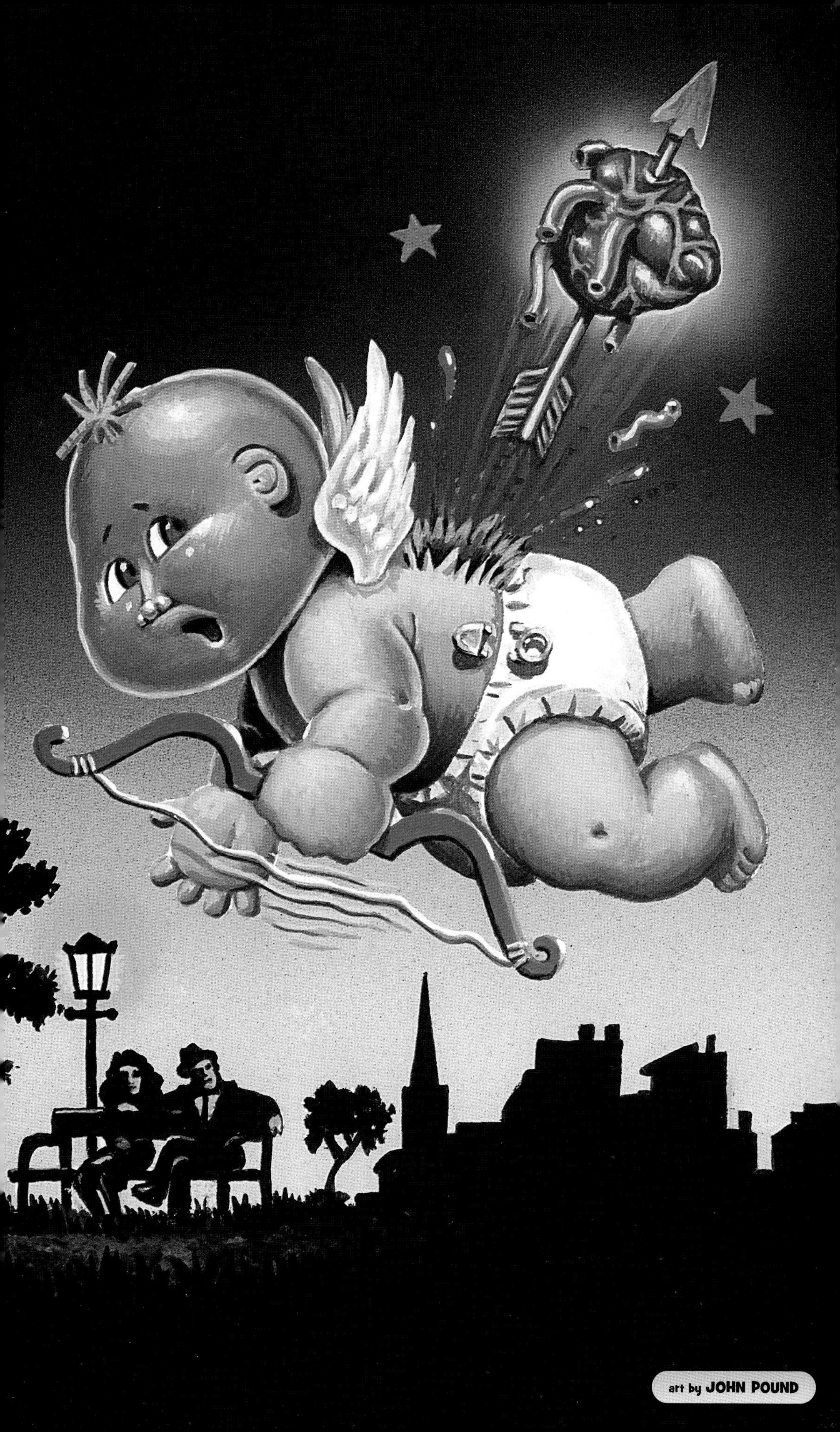

art by JOHN POUND

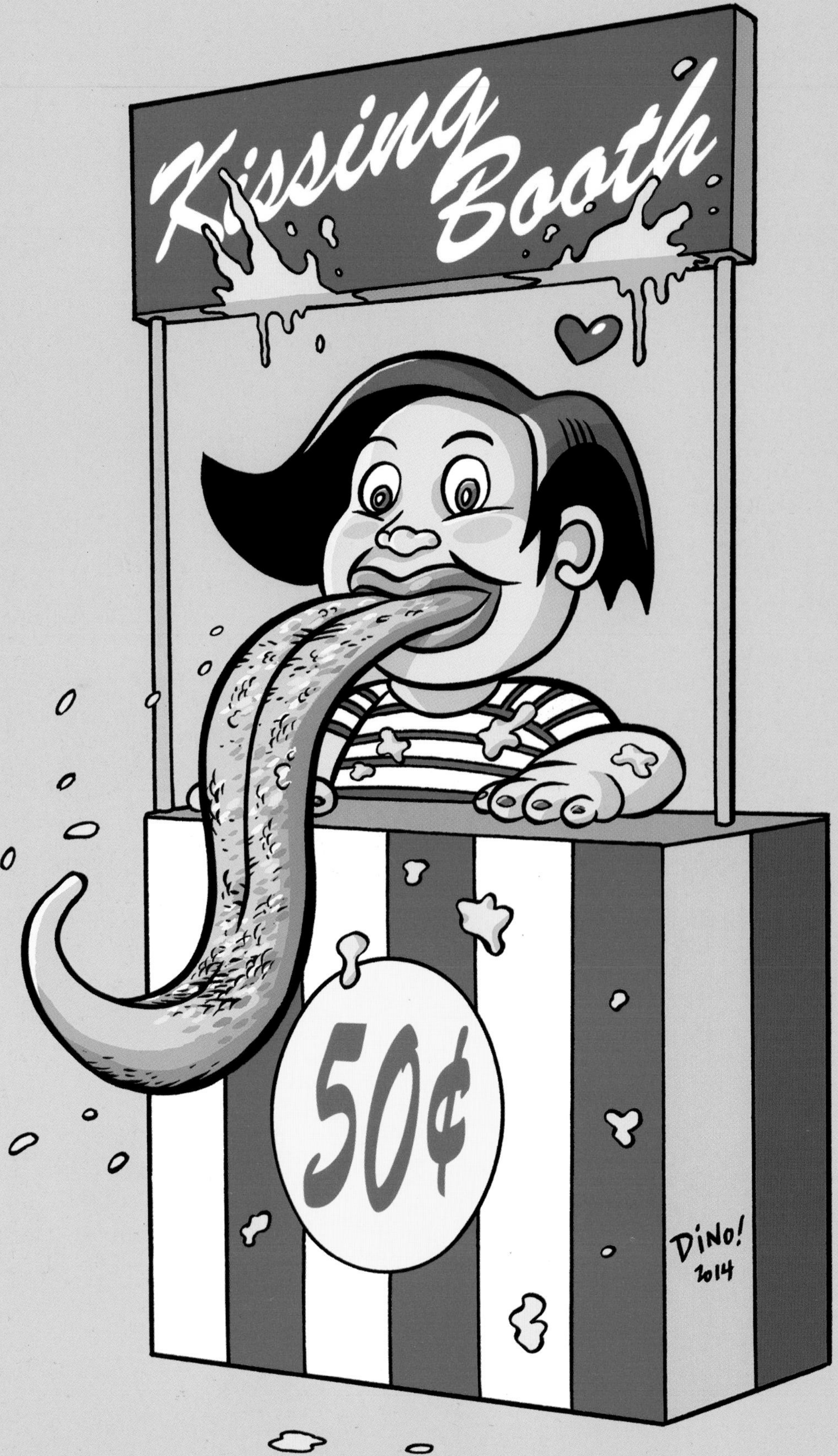
Kissing Booth
50¢
DINO!
2014

art by DEAN HASPIEL

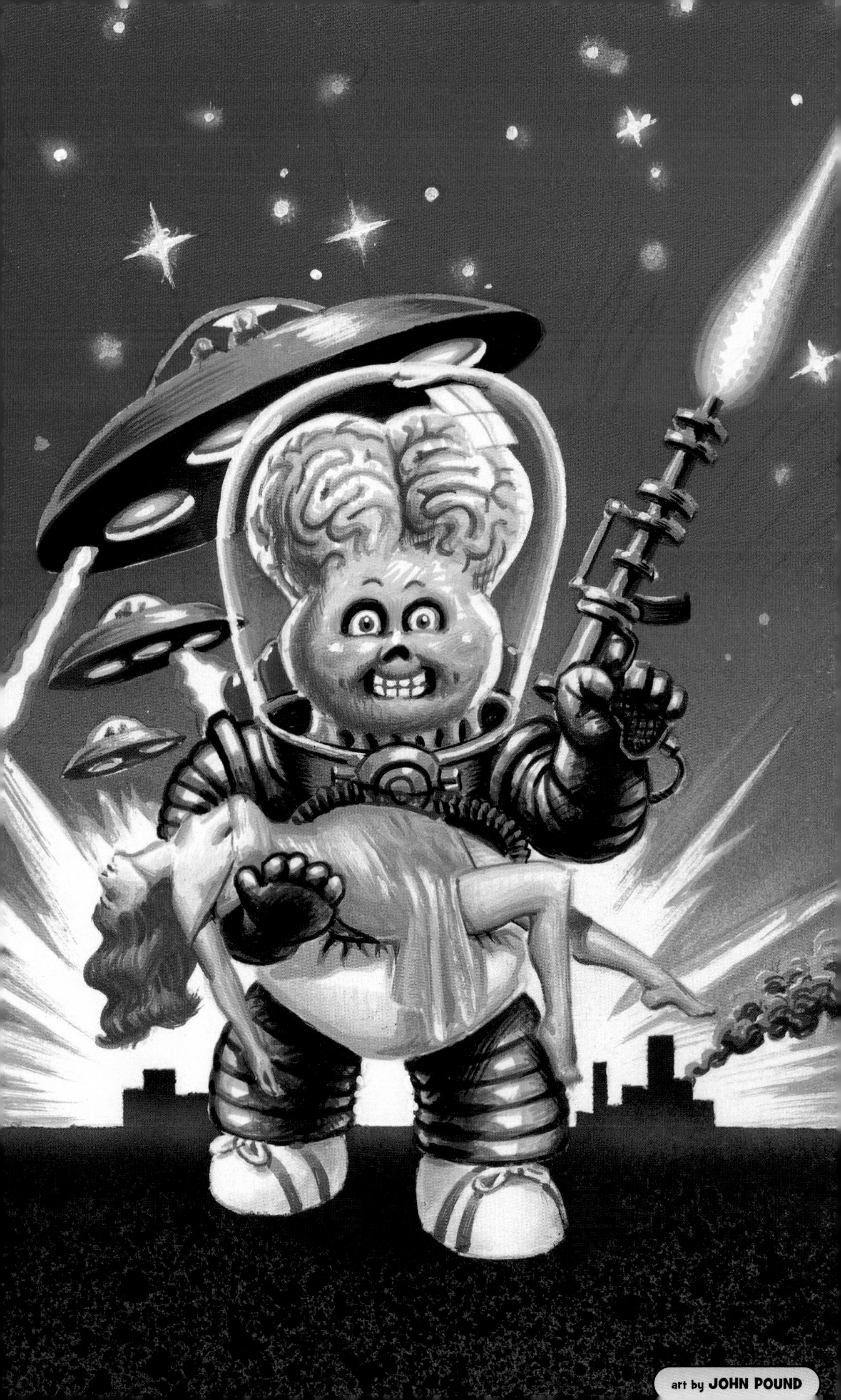

art by JOHN POUND

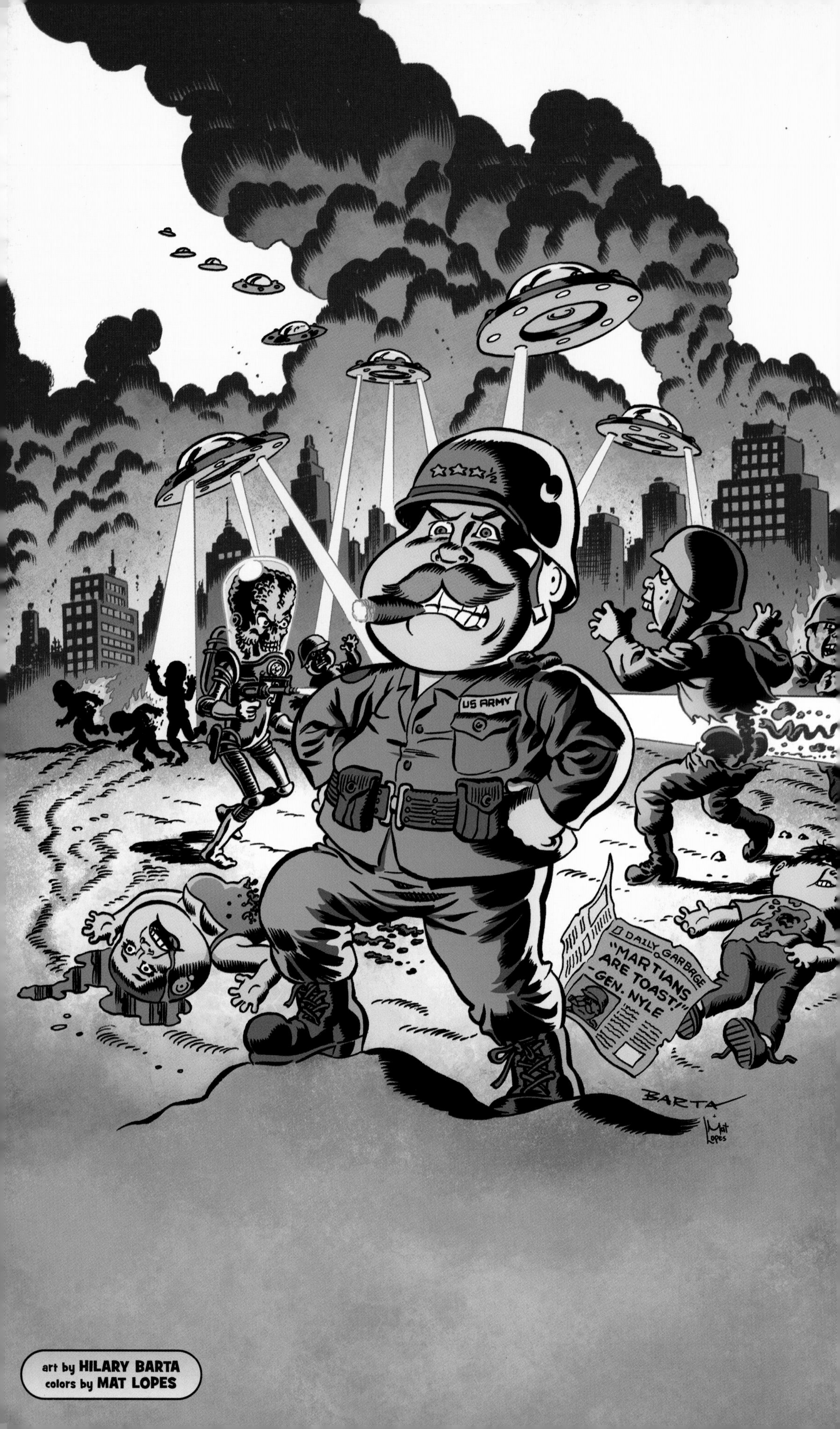
US ARMY
DAILY GARBAGE
"MARTIANS ARE TOAST!" -GEN. NYLE
BARTA
Mat Lopes

art by **HILARY BARTA**
colors by **MAT LOPES**

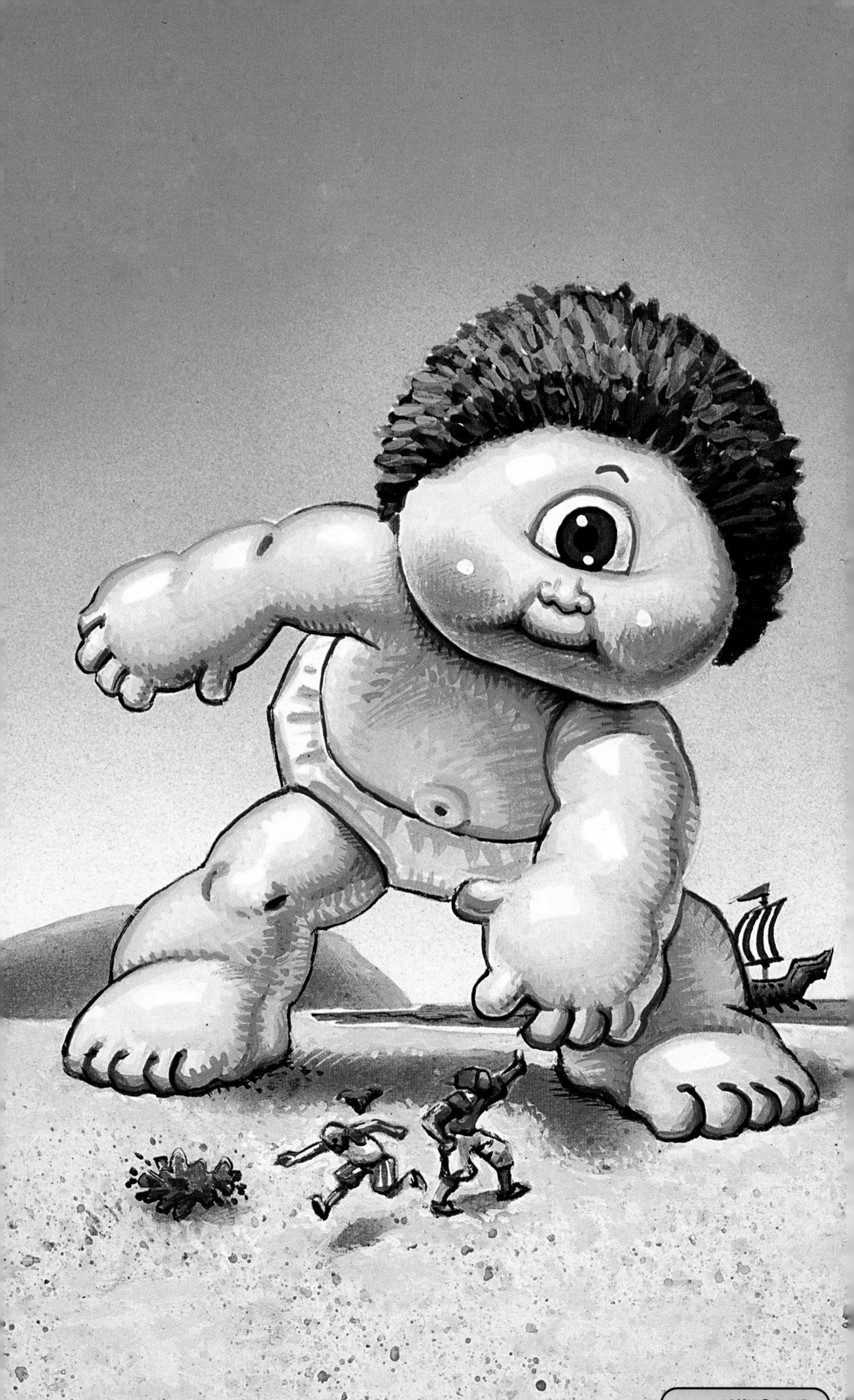

art by JOHN POUND

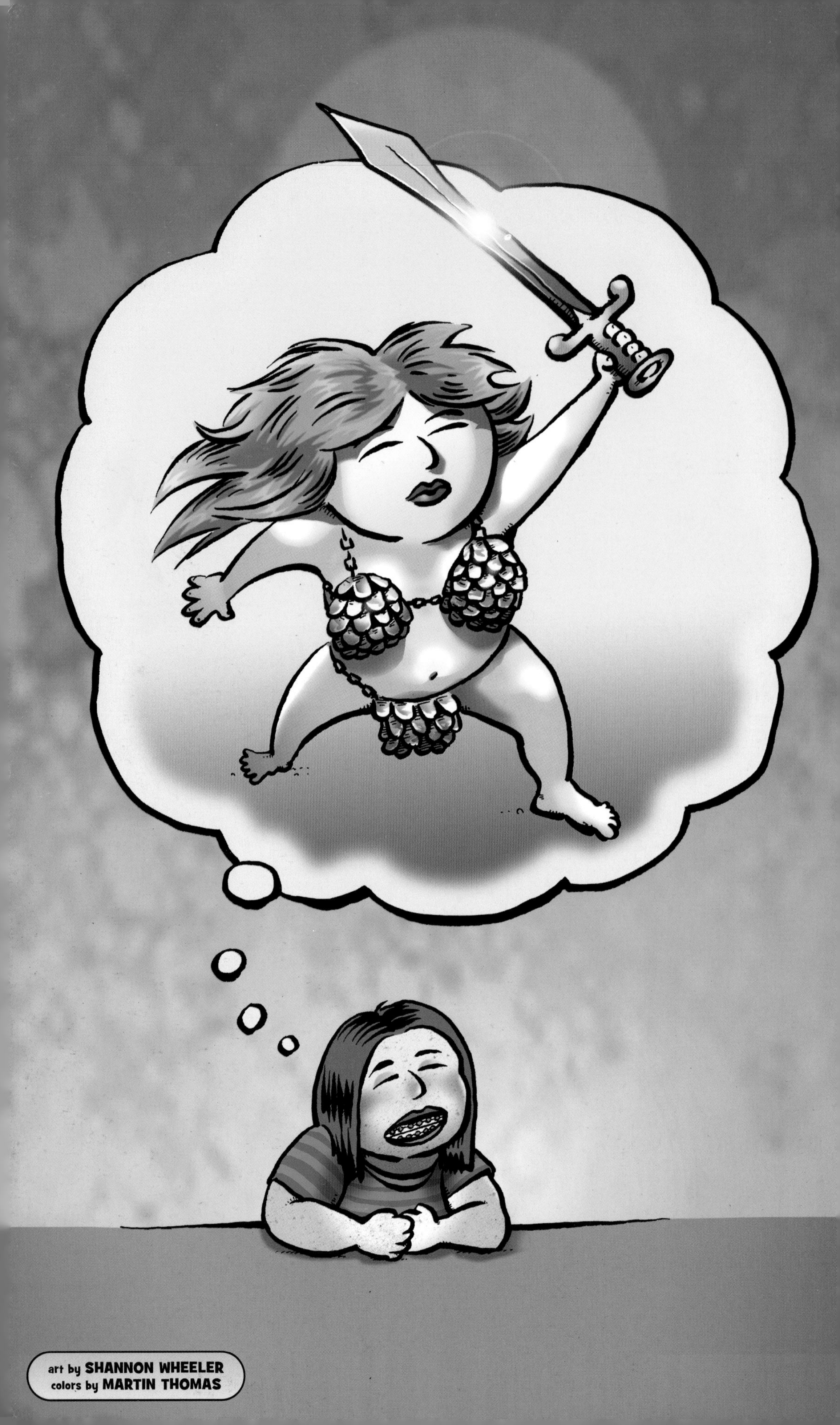

art by SHANNON WHEELER
colors by MARTIN THOMAS

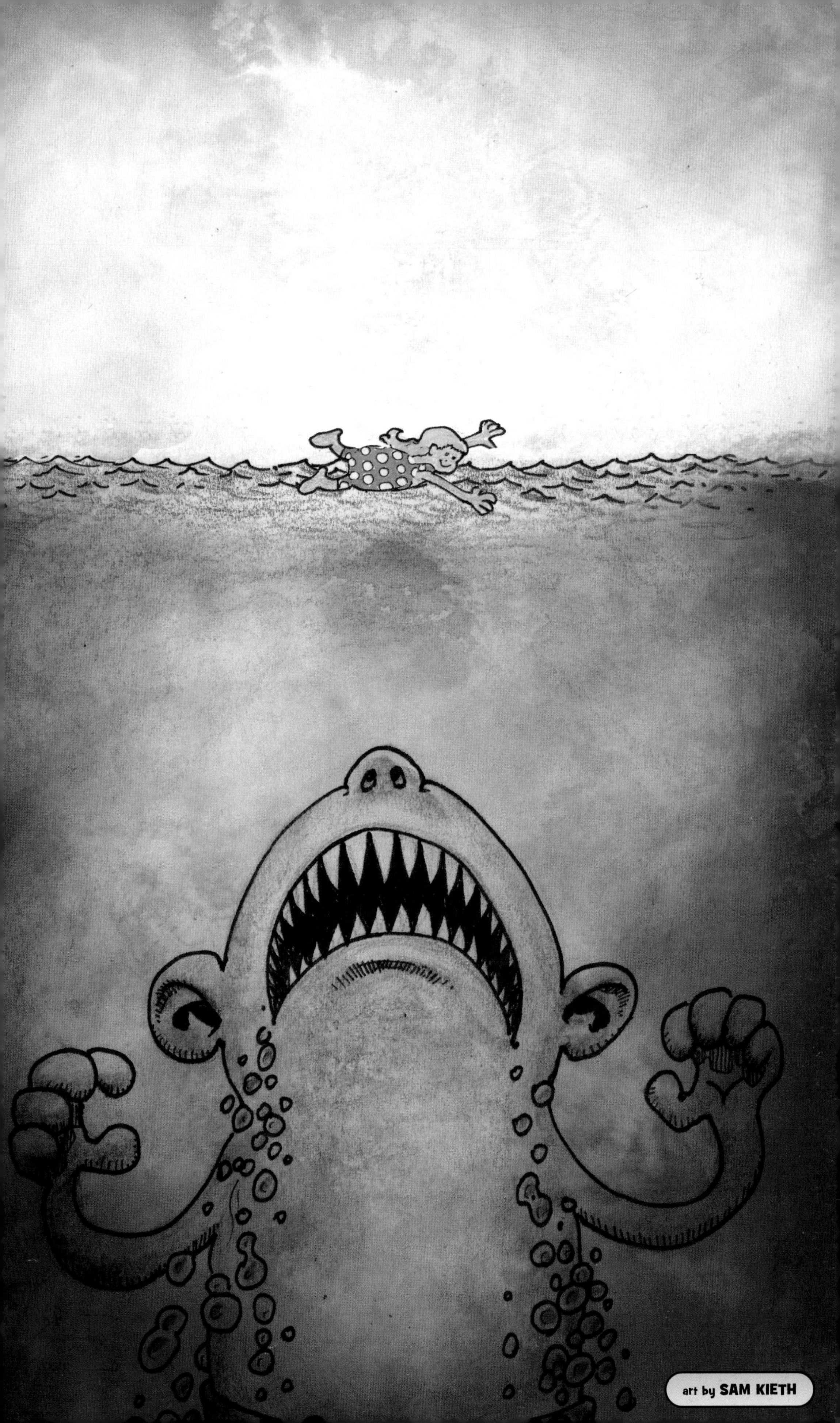

art by **SAM KIETH**

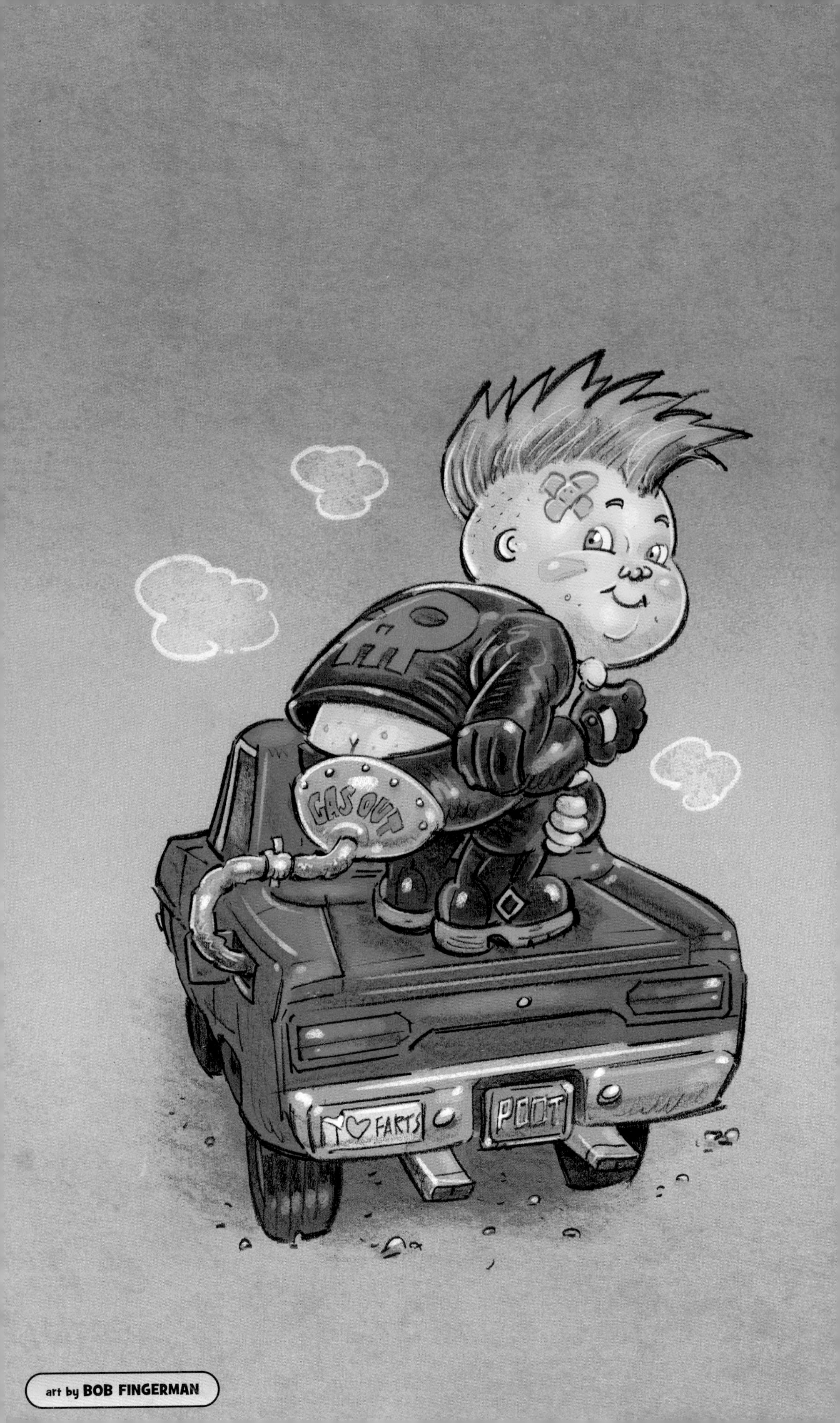
GAS OUT
I ♥ FARTS
POOT

art by **BOB FINGERMAN**